The Umma and the Dawla

The Umma and the Dawla

The Nation-State and the Arab Middle East

TAMIM AL-BARGHOUTI

Pluto  Press

LONDON • ANN ARBOR, MI

First published 2008 by Pluto Press
345 Archway Road, London N6 5AA
and 839 Greene Street, Ann Arbor, MI 48106

www.plutobooks.com

British Library Cataloguing in Publication Data
A catalogue record for this book is available from the British Library

Hardback ISBN   978 0 7453 2771 6
Paperback ISBN   978 0 7453 2770 9

Library of Congress Cataloging in Publication Data applied for

This book is printed on paper suitable for recycling and made from fully managed
and sustained forest sources. Logging, pulping and manufacturing processes are
expected to conform to the environmental regulations of the country of origin.

10   9   8   7   6   5   4   3   2   1

Designed and produced for Pluto Press by
Chase Publishing Services Ltd, Fortescue, Sidmouth, EX10 9QG, England
Typeset from disk by Stanford DTP Services
Printed and bound in the European Union by
CPI Antony Rowe, Chippenham and Eastbourne

Contents

Preface

In a lecture at Boston University, shortly after 11 September 2001, a prominent professor, previously a reporter for a leading American TV channel, stated that the causes of 9/11 were more cultural than political. Islam to him was a form of psychopathy that somehow increased people's tendency to kill others as well as themselves. Most of the perpetrators came from countries that had good ties with the United States and to whom the United States had been very kind, rich Saudi Arabia and friendly Egypt, for example. The United States hardly caused any real harm to the Taliban, it had helped liberate the country from the Soviets and had not taken any severe action against them since. In his view their harbouring of terrorists who had been attacking America since 1996 was therefore irrational. The Palestinians started their Intifada when Ehud Barak offered them 97 per cent of their land at Camp David. The lecturer thus suggested that American action should be taken, not only against political entities, but against the culture itself. He said that, besides Afghanistan, the United States should attack Iraq, Iran, Syria, the Palestinians, and even Saudi Arabia and Egypt.

The next speaker, a former US ambassador to a number of key states in the region, argued differently. He said that there were liberal forces in the Arab world worth supporting and that Islamism was the product of economic difficulties, domestic corruption and mismanagement. If a good strategy of alliance was applied, moderate, liberal voices in the Middle East could overcome their quasi-medieval rivals. The ambassador also noted that, counter-intuitively, governments in the Middle East were more liberal than much of their population, and as such, support for countries like Saudi Arabia and Egypt was necessary, their input regarding ways by which to fight their rogue neighbours such as Iraq and Afghanistan should be listened to. Finally the ambassador cautioned: 'I am not saying we should be less supportive of Israel, not in the least, all I'm saying is that supporting the liberal forces in the Middle East is best for Israel, for our interests in the region, and for the region itself.'

Both arguments are good examples of what I frequently used to hear about the Middle East when I was a graduate student in Boston from 2001 to 2004. One doctorate student of political philosophy once even told me that the reason for the demonstrations against the war in Afghanistan and Iraq raging from Morocco to Oman, the reason for political violence Muslims practised throughout the world, and the reason for 9/11 in particular was simply civilizational jealousy; that we, Arabs and Muslims, could not psychologically and mentally accept the fact that our civilization had failed. It failed to produce working forms of human organization that could allow us to meet the challenges of the time, including those of Zionism and imperialism. The student then challenged me: 'mention one useful idea that came out from your part of the world in the last five hundred years'.

I could not escape being exposed to such arguments, despite the genuine support, understanding and even sheer love I enjoyed from within the academic community. Friends were in my room, my office and my classroom. But Fox News was in the air, and so were the F16s.

Most of the people around me did not really have the knowledge to understand why a Saudi could be so angry about having American troops in his country, after all Germany and Japan still have them. They could not understand why Pakistanis could be so angry at America for what Israel does to the Palestinians, or why Moroccans could be so angry for what happens in Iraq. Undergraduate students of comparative politics could not understand the emotional unity that is expressed from time to time when there is nothing in the histories of these states to suggest a real drive towards unity and cooperation.

This book is an attempt to provide the answer to two questions; how Muslims think of themselves politically, and why they are uncomfortable with their current political situation. Two answers the reader will not find in this book are that it is because Muslims are irrational and that it is because Muslims are perfect victims.

By way of answering the first question, I present two concepts that have not, to the best of my knowledge, been satisfactorily dealt with in English; the concept of the Umma and that of the Dawla, 'Umma' has usually been translated into the English word 'nation' and 'Dawla' translated into 'state'. I argue in the book that they are very different from their English counterparts, and that this difference matters greatly in understanding patterns of Muslim political behaviour and public opinion.

The second question goes back to the issue of colonialism, nationalism and the establishment of states in the Middle East.

The main argument here is that independent Arab Muslim states are not much better off than the ones under occupation, and that nationalism in the region has been a continuation of, rather than an antithesis to colonialism.

This book is comprised of five chapters, of which the first two discuss the concepts of Umma and Dawla, the third sets a theoretical framework by which I deconstruct nationalisms in the region and the fourth tackles Egyptian nationalism. Two thirds of this fourth chapter are taken from my doctoral dissertation, modified to become a case study in a more general argument. The last chapter is on Arab nationalism.

I should mention that by deconstructing nationalism in this book I am not endorsing an Islamic alternative, I am just describing it. That is to say, I am only trying to direct the attention of the reader to a system of political organisation and allegiance that has been so far neglected and understudied. I am describing the sense of political identity as it appears in the texts that are considered by contemporary Muslims to be canonical, and that are used in the political discourses of both Islamists and their opponents. The fact that this sense of identity is being advocated by one side, rejected by another and negotiated by a third proves that it exists and that it merits some attention.

I would like to caution readers that the presentation made here of the Islamic Sunni and Shiite canons, and their historical development is intentionally simplified, a detailed account would require a multi-volume work whose focus would be more to record than to explain. I am not a jurist or a theologian. I am more trained in political science and classical Arabic literature and my knowledge is therefore of history and language. Nonetheless, I think I can provide a basic understanding of Islam which, despite being basic, is painfully absent from the political work done on the Middle East.

Tamim Al-Barghouti
18 June 2007

Introduction

The outcome of the last war in Lebanon, between Hezballah and Israel (12 July–14 August 2006), the ascendance of Hamas to power through democratic elections in Palestine amidst divisions within the ranks of its rivals in Fateh earlier the same year, the persistence of the various Iraqi armed groups in fighting coalition forces in almost all of Iraq, from Basra to Arbil since 2003, the survival of the Taliban, as an organization, after the American invasion and the installation of a new regime in Afghanistan in 2001, were not expected by many experts on the Middle East, and certainly not by most decision makers in Washington and London. Unlike cold war revolutionary organizations, the new armed Islamic ones do not attempt to seize control of the states in which they operate, they do not seem to recognize the borders of those states and they neither confine their activities to them, nor confine their cause to righting the wrongs of the peoples of such countries. Rather, they have a global outreach, composition, ideology and field of operation. What the Americans, the Israelis and their allies are facing in the Middle East, is an old form of human organization that holds similarities to, but is crucially different from, the modern nation state, or the classical national liberation movement. Palestinian, Iraqi, Lebanese, or Afghani nationalisms fall short of explaining the flow of Saudis, Egyptians, Syrians and Moroccans to countries of conflict or to the remote mountainous training camps. An imagined Islamic nationalism, falls short of explaining the fact that such organizations do not attempt to overthrow governments and unify Muslim states, but simply transcend them and work as if such states did not exist.

On the other hand, the Arab states are failing. For the colonial powers that created them, and the neo-colonial powers that support their existence, they failed to keep peace and stability in the region, especially in preventing their own citizens from acts of dissent that disturb neo-colonial interests. For their own peoples they failed to meet the challenge of Zionism, create some sort of Arab or Islamic unity, and achieve development and social justice. The consequences of this failure are quite visible, but not well understood in today's turbulent Middle East. The doctrine and behaviour of Islamic non-state organizations are seen as random consequences of this failure of the state. This book, however, argues that such organizations draw upon a long history of political theory and practice, based on a pre-colonial Islamic sense of identity. These organizations are Dawlas, non-territorial, temporary political arrangements whose allegiance lies with the whole Umma, the whole community of Muslims regardless of borders and nationalities. The book also argues that the current conflict has been going on for the last 200 years since the first colonial contacts between Arab Muslims and European colonial powers. In this conflict, colonially created nationalisms and nation states in the region were designed to mediate between the local sense of identity, that of belonging to the Islamic Umma, along with the forms of political organization that stem from it such as the Dawla on the one hand, and the colonial interests in keeping the region in a state of economic dependency, military vulnerability and political subordination on the other. Thus, the book has two objectives: first, to establish an understanding in English for the concepts of Umma and Dawla, which is lacking despite the abundance of literature on political Islam, and second, to make the argument that nation-states, and the nationalisms woven around them, failed because they were bound to fail. The colonial process of redefining the colonized, which includes colonial nation building, suffers from an irreconcilable structural contradiction, for the colonially created nation is required to be both legitimate and subordinate, that is, to be a happy slave.

The first objective of the book is to provide a sketch of the positions of various Islamic sects on the issue of political leadership. That being done, the concepts of Umma and Dawla are examined in the texts considered by contemporary Muslims to be canonical. The argument is made that there exists a non-colonial political culture in the Middle East by which most people perceive of themselves as belonging to an Umma and of the political bodies that govern them as Dawlas. The Umma is a group of people who might not necessarily desire to be ruled by one government, but would rather expect any government ruling over any portion of them to be accountable to the whole group not only to the portion under its authority. The Dawla is a non-sovereign, non- territorial, temporary political arrangement that is accountable to and responsible for the whole Umma, not only to that portion of the Umma under its jurisdiction.

The implications of the existence of this culture cannot be neglected. According to such a doctrine, the Egyptian government is expected to be as accountable to the peoples of Iraq and Palestine as it is to the people of Egypt, yet a desire to unite Egypt, Iraq and

Palestine into one state does not have to necessarily follow from such an expectation. This might help explain why Hezballah is more popular in Lebanon than the Lebanese government, even among non-Shiites, why the argument that Hezballah's attack on Israel could have been an act of relief both to the Palestinians engaging the Israeli forces in Gaza or to the Iranians facing political pressure regarding their nuclear program as an asset rather than a liability when it comes to Hezballah's popularity inside and outside of Lebanon. It might help explain why the decision of Saudi Arabia to invite foreign troops to defend it against a perceived Iraqi threat in 1990–91 was so unpopular that it was capitalized on by Islamists to create an armed movement against the Saudi government and its allies. Had Saudi Arabia been perceived as a sovereign nation-state whose main responsibility was the safety of the Saudis, the decision to forge an alliance with the United States could have been expected to be less unpopular. It might explain why, in his speech declaring his decision to support the American war in Afghanistan, General Pervez Musharraf of Pakistan was extremely apologetic, citing verses from the Quran and excerpts from the tradition of the Prophet to explain how his action was in the best interest of all Muslims, with very little reference to Pakistani nationalism. It might explain why Egyptian President Hosni Mubarak, facing popular pressure to cancel the Peace Treaty between Egypt and Israel, usually argues that the treaty is in the best interests of the Palestinians, rather than making the case that it is in Egypt's interest.

The second objective of the book is to study how weak and contradictory the territorial nationalisms are that have been manufactured around the colonially created states in the Middle East. Using concepts from post-colonial studies, I argue that the creation of nations and nationalisms in the Middle East was part of the colonial process of redefining and renaming the native to fit into a frame of reference familiar and useful to the colonial master. The nation-states created by Britain and France in the Middle East were created to provide raw materials, cheap labour, markets and, above all, security of international trade routes. Security could not be achieved by deploying colonial troops since that would have caused armies to be used as police forces in populous Middle Eastern cities, a task not unlike that of the coalition forces in Iraq today. Local police forces, Ministries of Interior and governments with monopolies on the use of force had thus to be created. Such governments of occupation by proxy had to have some legitimacy in order to be expedient. Therefore the creation of nationalisms, and the quest for the independence of these governments, took place in fulfilment of, rather than in opposition to, the colonial process.

The confrontations between colonial powers and national liberation movements that accepted the colonial definition of the self, in the late nineteenth and early twentieth centuries, were competitive in nature. National elites and colonial officers competed to perform mainly the same tasks to secure colonial interests. National liberation movements attempted to disrupt security at times in, for example, the 1919 revolt in Egypt. These attempts were made to show the colonial powers that the native elites would be more effective in securing colonial interests in the country than foreign military occupation.

When the colonial powers were strained during the two world wars, their Middle Eastern colonies got their formal independence and, because of the way they were structured and the elites that governed them, continued to behave as colonies. During the cold war, the competition between the heirs to the British and French colonies in the Middle East, the United States and the Soviet Union, allowed those nation-states to act with more freedom, and assert the legitimacy of their nationalisms vis-a-vis the native Islamic culture as a form of natural progress and modernity. Nonetheless, elements of the native political culture still infiltrated the discourses of the Middle Eastern nationalist regimes in that period. Advocates of Arab nationalism, the official ideology of many Arab states during the cold war, while asserting modernity and secularism on the one hand, stressed the supremacy of the Umma over the territorial colonially created states like Egypt, Syria, Iraq, Lebanon or Jordan on the other. The failure of these nationalisms to meet the challenge of Zionism, especially after the Six Day War, dealt a considerable blow to those fragile states. With the fall of the Soviet Union and the swift American military advance into the Middle East in 1990–91, the whole state system created by Britain and France began to totter. Fewer and fewer people believed in the possibility of compromise between the modern nation-state and the native political culture where the interests of all Muslims were seen as one, and governments were expected to protect the interests of all Muslims, not only those of their citizens. Non-territorial, non-sovereign forms of organization started to appear, ones that exercised authority over the lives of their subjects much more than the formal nation-states in which such subjects were citizens. The fall of Iraq in 2003, the practical destruction of the Palestinian Authority between 2002 and 2005 and finally the ability of Hezballah to defend Lebanon against an Israeli invasion – a task three Arab armies including that of Egypt could not fulfil in 1967 – made it quite clear that the compromise Arab elites tried to achieve, by leading colonially created nation-states, had failed. Their promises to secure colonial interests on the one hand, and gain the legitimacy and acceptance from their populations on the other, had come to nothing. Nation-states, constrained by economic dependency, military vulnerability and international law could not achieve the demands of their populations. Egypt, Jordan, Lebanon, Saudi Arabia and pre-2003 Iraq, just like the Palestinian Authority and post-2003 Iraq, were themselves expressions of a compromise between colonial and neo-colonial powers on the one hand, and the people of the region with their native political culture on the other. This book shows why such a compromise failed, and moreover, how it was bound to fail from the very moment Napoleon invaded Cairo to the moment Bush invaded Baghdad.

1

The Formation of the Canon

INTRODUCTION: ON ESSENTIALISM

The study of political concepts in the context of a tradition that stretches over 15 centuries is almost impossible. Ideas are continuously being produced, changed and reproduced across time and space. It could easily be argued that assuming a definite or authentic meaning for a term or idea, like the Umma or the Dawla, that has been in usage for so long, would be a reflexive imposition of the present on the past. One occasionally comes across talk-shows on Arabic satellite channels in which a caller asks a jurist: 'What is the view of Islam on such and such an issue?' Whatever the answer, it is not the view of Islam, rather it is one of the views of the school of thought and jurisprudence to which the said jurist belongs. Nonetheless, it is worth noting that the caller chooses to phrase the question in such a manner, and that the jurist usually does have an answer that the caller accepts as the view of Islam.

At any given point in time and among any given group of people, there prevails an understanding of their culture that they see as the most authentic, essential and therefore eternal. This understanding changes from one era to another, yet in every era it is seen as unchangeable. This is not only true of Islam, even for the staunchest historicists, be they modernizing liberals or modernizing Marxists, the idea that history has its own logic, is considered 'scientific', 'natural' and therefore a timeless truth in and by itself. This illusion of truth or timelessness is necessary to legitimize institutions and practices. The practice of science itself is no exception. Even the most sceptical scientist acts on certain assumptions. The scientist might strive to change these, but only to substitute them with other assumptions that would be accepted as truths until they were challenged again. In other words, communities live in the shadow of truths that are temporarily believed to be eternal. I am not making the argument that the understanding of the concepts of Umma and Dawla presented in this book formed the essence of Islamic culture for the last 15 centuries. Rather, I am making the argument that the two concepts were believed to be essential to that culture by the majority of Muslims living in the Middle East in the nineteenth and twentieth centuries. Thus I deal with the concepts in the texts that have been regarded as canonical by modern-day Muslims, (since the canon has changed more than once throughout history). This chapter, as well as the next, dealing with the origins of the concepts of Umma and Dawla in the canonical Islamic texts is necessary to clarify the concepts to the English reader, so that he or she can make sense of the discourse analysis that follows in the rest of the book. It is also necessary because it shows why and how many forces in the modern Middle East could root their modern understandings of such concepts in those ancient texts and thus consider them authentic, essential and eternal.

The history of the canon is part of the canon. That is, an image of the history of Muslims is an essential part of any understanding of the religion. This is especially important because, unlike the differences between Christian sects, which revolved around metaphysical questions such as the human and divine nature of Christ, the main differences between Islamic sects revolved around purely political questions concerning the form of government, the rights, responsibilities and powers of the ruler and the ruled.

Since the study of the concepts of Umma and Dawla will involve recurrent references to the different sects of Islam: Sunnis, Shiites and Kharijites as well as to the various schools of thought within each one of the three major sects leading up to what constitutes the Islamic Canons today, a brief account of the context in which those sects emerged is necessary for comprehending the rest of the chapter. It is worth noting here again, that what is going to be presented below is but the current understanding of Islamic history. For example, the naming of Sunnis, Shiites and Kharijites as the three major sects in Islam, the third of which is much less influential than the other two, is a modern construct. For a good part of the Umayyad and Abbasid periods, the Sunni-Kharijite conflict was the one occupying the centre stage of Islamic history. Later on, in the second Abbasid period, the Ismailite Sevenist version of Shiism, now confined to tiny communities in Iran and Pakistan, was the version posing the most serious military and ideological threat to Sunnism and Kharijism, as well as to the Jafarite Twelvist version which has now become synonymous with mainstream Shiism.

THE POWER OF POETRY

A note on the tribal culture of Arabs before Islam (before 610 AD) might be necessary to understand the context of the following account of Islamic history. The mobile nature of the tribes in the Arabian Desert, moving from one place to another in search of water and grazing lands, deprived them from establishing the kinds of social bonds prevalent in settled societies. People did not associate on the basis of neighbourhood, economic specialization, or commercial and agricultural interdependence. The most basic of links, that of blood, was the basis of solidarity in most of the Arabian Peninsula. Thus the tribe became the predominant form of political association in ancient Arabia. Again, because of the nomadic nature of the society, it was quite impossible to establish great cities with temples, colossal statues, town halls or stadiums. The creation of symbols, which is essential for fostering and strengthening the ties between the individual and the collective, was therefore confined, in most cases, to language.[1] Poems were texts in which the activities of tribes were recreated. The history of the tribe, its seasonal grazing lands, its ancestors and its friendly or hostile relations to other tribes would be recorded in poetry. Most tribesmen knew those poems by heart, and through them, identified with the tribe, or with the image of the tribe created therein. A tribe's poet was the tribe's spokesman. There were professional poets whose main function was to praise the leaders of the tribe, and sarcastically and bitterly attack their enemies. But members of the political and military elite in any tribe were expected to be able to compose poetry by which to record their historical decisions, wars, alliances and, sometimes, express their personal feelings. The word for 'poet' in Arabic, 'sha'ir', also means 'the knower', he who knows or senses or feels. Lines of poetry were used as proverbs and moral references. The more a line of poetry was beautiful, the more it was used as a proverb, and therefore as a moral authority. Such poems, or bits of poems, had yet another political function that depended totally on their aesthetic

1. Temples, palaces, senates and town halls were signs of political power and communal solidarity in settled communities. Such constructions were abundant in the settled Arab communities in Iraq, southern Syria and Yemen, but for most of the Arabs living in the Arabian heartlands, construction works were quite limited. The relatively small house of worship in the city of Mecca, the Ka'ba, was one of the very rare pre-Islamic exceptions, and it caused the host city to become the site of one of the rare gatherings of almost all Arab tribes, the annual pilgrimage and commercial festival known as the Market of *Okaz*.

value; the better crafted a line of poetry was, the more likely it was to break the boundaries of the tribe and become current among all Arabs, thus boosting the status of the poet, and the poet's tribe, as a producer of art, and also, because of this proverbial tendency in Arabic poetry, as a supra-tribal moral authority.[2] In other words, the more people liked a line of poetry, the more they believed in its truth and judgment.[3] This link between beauty and truth, is important in understanding the Islamic argument that the literary beauty of the Quran, is the evidence for its divine origin, and therefore its truth. This epistemological axiom was then passed on to rule the debates between the various Islamic sects.

These roles related to the creation of identity in texts taken over by the Quran. A highly metaphoric and mostly rhyming text, whose literary and aesthetic value was unmatched by any other text in Arabic, whether in verse or prose, the Quran was set above poetry and therefore above the tribes. Instead of talking about the ancestors of individual clans, it spoke of the ancestry of Humanity, and of all Arabs, through the stories of Adam, Noah Abraham and Ishmael. Instead of attacking the enemies of a certain tribe, it attacked all evil, and evil's followers, the enemies of God and humanity, and, in less abstract terms, the political and military enemies of the Prophet's followers. Just like poetry, its beauty was the evidence of it being true and the condition for it performing its function as a textual

2. Inversely, the tendency of a line of poetry to become a proverb eventually became a criterion by which to measure the line's beauty and merit. It is not a coincidence that the most famous and most revered Arab poet by most accounts, Ahmad Ibn Al-Hussein Al-Mutanabbi (915–965 AD) was the one who contributed most to the reservoir of Arabic proverbs. It is also not a coincidence that his belief in the power of his poetry led him to claim to be a prophet and lead a military revolt in his youth. Despite the fact that he soon gave up his claim, his title 'Al-Mutanabbi' by which he became mostly known, meant 'he who pretended or wanted to become a prophet'.

3. In the third century after Hijra, the great poet and anthologist Habib Ibn Aws (*ca.* 805–845 AD), referred to this moral authority of proverbial poetry and to the link between liking a line and believing it. In one of his poems he wrote: 'It [poetry] is considered wisdom even when it is farce, and people follow its judgement even when it is unfair.' Habib, best known as Abu Tammam, was the most famous poet of his time. He introduced a new technique in poetic writing based on playing with antonyms and synonyms, and he also compiled a voluminous anthology of Arabic poetry produced before and after Islam, which he called *Diwan Al-Hamasa*: the book of valour.

expression of collective identity and source of political power. As shall be discussed below, the Quran created the Muslims. It produced a narrative of human history that culminated in a political community, an Umma, defined by moral and spiritual codes, common language and rituals, common enemies and allies, common history and future. It is worth pointing out here that the Arabic word for 'poem', '*qaseeda*', and the word for 'political community', 'Umma', come from synonymous roots. We shall return to this point later when discussing the etymology of the term 'Umma'.

Just as lines of Arabic poetry were used as proverbs from which moral judgments were derived, the literary beauty of the Quranic expression was the evidence for its divine nature and thus for its authority as a source of moral judgment. And just like poetry, the Quran, or parts of it, was to be known by heart by the members of the community it described/created, as a sign of their membership.

Finally, since it was a current belief among Arabs that poetry was revealed to poets by friendly demons, *jin*, the argument that the Quran was revealed by God to His Prophet through an Angel sealed the superiority of the Quranic text over all other literary texts in source, recipient, medium, form, content and therefore authority.

Of course, despite, and because, of all these resemblances, it had to be asserted, by the words of the Quran itself, that the Divine text was not a poem, nor was the Prophet a poet. For classifying the Quran as poetry would have confined it back into the Arabian tribal context it was meant to surpass and transform. An authentic and revolutionary discourse, the Muslim Holy Text's entrenchment in the culture of its audience was, and has been, the vehicle by which to change and transform it.

The fact that the Quran was highly metaphorical had implications for the political community it created. Though the Umma was not a nation, and the Quran not a poem, the political effect of the metaphorical nature of the Quran could best be understood if one imagined a modern day nation with a poem as its constitution. In such a case, the whole political, legal, and social system would rely on the interpretation of the metaphorical text. Thus, in the following account of Islamic history, training in law, politics and literary interpretation were seen as inseparable. Every interpretation resulted in creating a distinct political, legal and social system based on the Quran. The Islamic sects whose history I shall briefly discuss below were therefore as much works in metaphysics and ethics as they were works in politics and literature.

A BRIEF ACCOUNT OF THE EMERGENCE OF ISLAMIC SECTS

The two main sects of Islam today are Sunnism and Shiism. The majority of the world's 1.5 billion Muslims are Sunnis, the largest minority is Shiite, and a relatively tiny minority belongs to various sects. Of those smaller sects, one has been considerably more influential in challenging and therefore shaping the two major ones, that is Kharijism. Zaidi and Ismailite Shiites played important roles at various points in Islamic history as well, but they were subsequently overshadowed by the mainstream Jafarite Twelvist Shiism, and were not as influential in shaping their rivals' theories during the formative years of the first Abbasid era.[4] The sects discussed below will therefore be Sunnism, Twelvist Shiism and Kharijism.[5] Of Sunnism I shall discuss three sub-sects; Murji'ite, Mu'tazilite and Ash'arite Sunnism. Only the latter one of the three officially represents Sunni Islam today, and Kharijism is confined to only one Muslim state, the Sultanate of Oman in southeast Arabia. Yet the polemics between political actors

4. The history of the Abbasid empire 749–1517 is conventionally divided into three eras; the first era is characterized by the absolute power of the Arab Caliphs 749–861, the second by the influence of the Turkish military casts 861–1258 and the third begins with the fall of Baghdad to the Moguls, and moving the seat of the Caliphate to Cairo, under the protection of the Mamlouk Sultans from 1258 till the Ottoman conquest of Egypt in 1517, after which the Arab Abbasid Caliphate ended, and Turkish Ottoman Sultans declared themselves to be the Caliphs of all Muslims.
5. Two offshoots of Shiism are still active in modern Middle Eastern politics, the Druz in Lebanon and the Alavids in Syria, the conflict between the Druz and the Maronite Christians in Mount Lebanon dominated the history of the small Ottoman province, and later the state, of Lebanon, for most of the nineteenth and early twentieth centuries. During the most recent civil war in Lebanon 1975–90 the Druz became a secondary ally to Sunni and Shiite Muslims in the fight over the country. The Alavids, though very few in numbers, took control of the higher ranks of the ruling Baath party in Syria and of the Syrian armed forces. Former President Hafez Al-Asad and his son the current President Bashar are Alavids. Political tension between the secular Baath regime in Syria and the Sunni movement of the Muslim Brothers sometimes led to sectarian political discourses. Nonetheless, neither the Druz nor the Alavids ever proselytized their beliefs and they never participated in the great debates between the major sects, which rendered their contribution to the evolution of Islamic political thought minimal.

in the Middle East would be incomprehensible without discussing all three sects and three sub-sects. For example, in the discourse of violent Islamic organizations Arab governments are referred to as Murji'ite heretics, while those governments call violent Islamists Kharijites. Muslim quasi-liberal reformists call themselves, and are sometimes called by their opponents, Mu'tazilites. These labels are quite effective in legitimizing and delegitimizing political actors, despite the fact that all three parties; governments, reformists and Islamic violent groups, formally belong to the Ash'arite sub-sect of Sunni Islam.

The following lines should give a brief sketch of the context within which these sects and sub-sects emerged. This narrative, as will be shown, charts the movement of two formative forces in Islamic and pre-Islamic Arab culture; one is the authority based on words and metaphors, discussed above, and the other is the authority based on blood ties. It is strictly based on what contemporary Muslims regard as canonical sources, such as the histories of Mohammad Ibn Jarir Al-Tabari (838–922 AD), Ahmad Ibn Mohammad Ibn Abd Rabboh (*d.* 940 AD), Izz Al-Din Ali ibn Mohammad known as Ibn Al-Athir (1160–1233 AD), and the Prophet's biography by Abdel Malik Ibn Hisham (*d.* 833 AD) have been studied and taught by both Sunni and Shiite scholars from Cairo to Najaf.[6]

The Hashemites and the Umayyads

It was mentioned above that the tribe was almost the only political unit in the Arabian Desert before Islam, with the exception of the settled Arab kingdoms in western Iraq, southern Syria and Yemen. Tribal alliances did occur, however they used to break down at the first disagreement over water or grazing lands. Tribes worshipped their own ancestors and a variety of deities, while in many cases believing them to be of a lesser rank than the One Creator. Each tribe had its own customs and practices that were linked to such ancestral beliefs. The monotheistic message of Islam thus had a political content. Believing that there was no other god but God entailed subjecting

6. The history in the following sections is based on the works of these historians. The medieval style of writing history consists of recording a number of oral and written versions of each event, and citing the passages where the said historians mention the events discussed here would therefore make the text unreadable. The above account also follows the points over which there is a historical consensus. When there are significant differences say, between Shiite and Sunni versions of an event, it shall be noted.

oneself to one law, and therefore subjecting the various tribes to one worldly authority that represented that law. Hence the first metaphysical '*shahada*' (testimony) one has to make to embrace Islam literally goes: 'I bear witness that there is no god but God', and this directly leads to the political second '*shahada*': 'and I bear witness that Mohammad is God's messenger', acknowledging the worldly authority of the Prophet and the Texts he delivered.

The Prophet was a member of Quraysh, a tribe of merchants residing in the commercial crossroads-city of Mecca, trading seasonally with Syria and Yemen. It also hosted one of the few commercial and cultural festivals held in the peninsula, *Okaz* Market. Most importantly, the city of Mecca hosted the Ka'ba, a building believed by Arabs to have been built by their ancestor Abraham, and a place of pilgrimage to most Arab tribes before Islam. The Ka'ba hosted more than 360 idols representing the various mini-gods of the visiting tribes. Paganism was therefore a central source of income to the tribe of Quraysh; the pilgrimage season usually resulted in an upsurge in commercial activity and flow of wealth. Of that tribe, there were two strong houses competing for the control of the city; the house of Hashem to which the Prophet belonged, and their rivals, the rich merchants of the house of Umayya. When Mohammad started calling for Islam in Mecca, the Umayyads seized on the opportunity to consolidate their grip on power against their rivals. The Hashemites were besieged, boycotted and eventually pushed out of their homes to the outskirts of the city. Weaker followers of the Prophet were systematically tortured and some were killed. Eventually this led to the Hijra (622 AD), the emigration of the Prophet and his followers form Mecca to Medina, a rival city to the north of Mecca. In Medina there were two tribes fighting for dominance, as well as a number of Jewish clans, allying themselves with either one of them. The Prophet's arrival seemed to provide the fighting tribes in Medina with an arbiter and a law for settling disputes. He was on the same footing with both warring sides, and his teachings were not yet rejected by the city's Jewish community. A series of wars followed between Medina under Mohammad's leadership, and Mecca under the Umayyads. The eight-year war ended with Mohammad's complete victory, conquest of Mecca (630 AD), and the subjugation of the leader of the Umayyads and all Meccans, Abu Sufian, who eventually embraced Islam.

The Question of Succession

On the death of the Prophet (632 AD) the question of succession became the main issue over which Muslims disagreed. It was quite clear that if succession was given to a relative of the Prophet, a Hashemite, or to an Umayyad, the strength of the tribal base of the successor might lead to the establishment of a hereditary dynasty. While Ali, the Prophet's cousin, son-in-law and father of the Prophet's only male descendants, Hassan and Hussein, was busy preparing for the burial, the other Companions met and chose one of the Prophet's older friends, Abu Bakr, a member of the tribe of Quraysh, but who was neither an Umayyad nor a Hashemite, to succeed him. Ali and his wife, the Prophet's daughter Fatima, were late in acknowledging Abu Bakr's authority as the Prophet's first successor. That delay was to have dire repercussions on the formation of the different sects in Islam. Two years later, on his death, Abu Bakr appointed Omar, another Companion of the Prophet, who was neither an Umayyad nor a Hashemite, as his successor. Omar chose six of the Prophet's Companions on his death, all of whom the Prophet had promised paradise, and asked them to choose one from their midst to become the third successor. This choice of the number six is the basis for some theories on the validity of electing successors that we shall discuss later. Of the six, there were only two real candidates, Ali the Hashemite and Othman the Umayyad. The accounts, both Sunni and Shiite, seem to suggest that the reason the Umayyad was chosen was that he made an unconditional promise to follow the path of the previous two successors, especially in not favouring his clan over other Muslims, that is, not to establish them as a ruling dynasty.[7] Nonetheless, Othman's policies were controversial; he ended up keeping the other Companions of the Prophet at bay, and appointing young Umayyads governors to the newly conquered provinces in Iraq, Persia, Syria and Egypt. Upheavals followed, and in the year 35 after Hijra (655 AD), crowds of angry Muslims objecting to the appointment of an Umayyad governor of Egypt, among other grievances, succeeded in killing Othman. Ali was elected successor by the surviving Companions who were still in Medina. Some of the Companions, however, were not present. Mu'awiya, the Umayyad young man whom Othman had appointed governor of Syria, and son of Abu Sufian, the Umayyad leader of the Meccans in their wars against the Prophet, refused to recognize Ali's authority, and claimed

---

7. See Tabari 2: 750–55 and Ibn Abd Rabbu 5: 26–36.

that he was complicit in the killing of Othman, or at least not strict enough with the rebels who killed him. Civil war ensued.

Al-Fitna and the Early Formation of the Sects (The Rule of the Umayyads)

Al-Fitna Al-Kubra or the Great Upheaval as it came to be known in Islamic history went on for five years, during which the main three sects of Islam were formed. The theological, metaphysical and juridical propositions of each one of the three major sects were expressed in more elaborate and sophisticated forms much later. But even then, continuous reference was made to the events of *Al-Fitna* in search for authenticity and legitimacy. The events of *Al-Fitna* are mentioned in vivid detail in all classic accounts of Islamic history and it would be redundant to mention them here; nonetheless, one of the most formative details should be mentioned for it triggered the declaration, if not the formation of the first of the three sects.

In the final battle of Siffin (657 AD) between Ali, the fourth successor of the Prophet, and Mu'awiya, the governor of Syria who did not recognize his authority, the former was on the brink of victory when Mu'awiya suggested peace talks. Based on an interpretation of the Quran, an arbiter from Mu'awiya's side and an arbiter from Ali's side were to meet for a year and negotiate a solution to the civil war. According to the most authoritative accounts, Mu'awiya's arbiter tricked Ali's arbiter by proposing the impeachment of both leaders and electing a third candidate. However, after Ali's arbiter declared the decision, and complied by stating that he was impeaching Ali, Mu'awiya's arbiter declined, and maintained that he still held Mu'awiya as the legitimate successor of the Prophet and ruler of Muslims. War was therefore resumed. However, the direst consequence of this arbitration incident was the dissidence of a considerable number of Ali's followers, to form the first of the three sects, the Kharijites, or the rebels. Ali supposedly based his legitimacy on an interpretation of the Quran and a number of sayings by the Prophet that would indicate his right to succeed him and his right to be obeyed by all Muslims once he did. By accepting the arbitration, the Kharijites argued, Ali had made a mistake, allowing two fallible men to alter and twist the meaning of the Quran. The fact that each arbiter came up with a different decision strengthened their argument that neither of the two had the right interpretation. To the Kharijites, the Quran could be interpreted by all men and women who understood Arabic. Delegating the right to interpret the Quran to two men was a sin. Had Ali been sure of his interpretation of the Quran, and had that interpretation been right, he should not have allowed the two arbiters to negotiate it. If, on the other hand, he was unsure of the right interpretation of the Quran, then he should not have been allowed to rule over Muslims and take them to war on the basis of an uncertain interpretation. The Kharijites thus impeached both Ali and Mu'awiya, and stated that their leader and guide was no other but the Quran, as they, collectively, interpreted it, hence their motto: '*la hukma illa lillah*', which could be roughly translated as 'no rule but God's' or 'all power to God'.

Ali fought and decimated the Kharijite forces. He was preparing for another round against Mu'awiya when he was assassinated, while praying in his mosque in Kufa, by a Kharijite survivor.[8] His supporters then elected his eldest son Hassan to succeed him. However, fearing for the collapse of the whole Islamic entity if the civil war continued any longer, Hassan, accepted Mu'awiya's authority on the condition that on Mu'awiya's death, new elections would be held, and that Mu'awiya would not name a successor. Nonetheless, Hassan died before Mu'awiya, and according to some accounts, he was poisoned. Mu'awiya did not honour his promise and named his son, the notorious Yazid, as his successor, thus establishing the first hereditary dynasty in Islamic history, the Umayyads, with their capital in Damascus.

The Kharijites having distinguished themselves, those who stayed with Ali after the arbitration were called *Shi'at Ali*, the Partisans of Ali, or just the Partisans (*Shi'a*/Shiites) while those who supported Mu'awiya and those who were non-aligned were not given a name until much later. That name was the Followers of the Tradition (of the Prophet) and the Consensus (of the Community of Muslims- the Umma), the word for 'tradition' in Arabic is '*Sunna*', hence the name 'Sunnis'.[9]

We shall return to the arguments of the three sects in detail regarding the concepts of Umma, 'the community of Muslims', and

8.   Kharijites had decided to end the five-year long civil war by killing Ali, Mu'awiya and Mu'awiya's tricky arbiter Amr. Three men were sent to kill the three leaders while they were praying. Ali was killed, Mu'awiya was injured, and the cunning arbiter Amr, sensing the tension in the air, had sent someone else to pray in his stead; his double was mistaken for him and killed in his place, while he escaped injury.

9.   Of course, the believers of each sect claim that it existed since the time of the Prophet. In fact it is essential for any sect to gain legitimacy to maintain that the Prophet himself was its arch model. Also there are

the Imam, 'the guide/leader/ruler'. However, a general review of their arguments is useful at this point.

THE SHIITES

According to the Shiite interpretation of the Holy Texts and the historical accounts, Ali had been designated by God, in the Quran, and by the Prophet, through his sayings, to become the Prophet's successor.[10] Since Ali was chosen by God and His prophet, he was infallible. And any man Ali chose to succeed him must therefore be infallible as well. The act of arbitration, though apparently a mistake, was interpreted by Shiite historians as being the mistake of Ali's followers not of Ali. Ali himself was against the arbitration, while his followers forced him to accept it under the threat that they would not continue the fight against Mu'awiya. This fact is consolidated by most Sunni accounts as well. Ali's followers who forced him to accept the arbitration were the very same ones who rebelled against him on the basis that the arbitration was a mistake and that he was therefore not infallible. According to this narrative, the incident of arbitration becomes a demonstration of the fallibility of the rebellious followers of Ali, and the inconsistency of the Umma, or the collective, thus establishing a theory of the divine duty and right of the chosen successor of the Prophet and his descendants to rule and guide the community of Muslims, independent of that community's consensus.

---

different accounts of the exact point in time at which any sect was declared. This becomes especially difficult regarding the moment when Shiites and Sunnis were separated, mainly because the Sunnis did not formulate a viable theory for government till much later. Nonetheless, there is consensus that the event of the arbitration played a major role in distinguishing the Kharijites from the Shiites, and that Shiites and Sunnis were separate before that date, even if their differences were not yet codified in their final form.

10. The following 15 verses in the Quran are interpreted by Shiites to refer to Ali: Quran 3: 61, Q 26: 214, Q 33: 33, Q 42: 23, Q 20: 29, Q 5: 55, Q 53 1–2, Q 2: 207, Q 39: 33–5, Q 2: 37, Q 13: 7, Q 37: 24 Q 56: 10–11. Q 78: 1–2 and 98: 7. Ali's name is not mentioned in any of these verses. However, Shiites deduce that they refer to Ali from the circumstances in which they were revealed. Sunnis disagree either on the historical accuracy of the events during which the verses were revealed or about the method of deduction and interpretation. For a compilation of quotations by the Prophet that refer to the Imamate of Ali and his descendants see Al-Kulaini 1: 286–92. For a summary of the arguments of Sunnis and Shiites over the said verses see Sobhi 1964: 175–208.

This was the basis of the Shiite doctrine of the fallibility of the Umma and the infallibility of the Imam that we shall discuss in detail in the next chapter.

To the Shiites, only the Prophet, Ali, Ali's descendants, and those of the Prophet's Companions who supported Ali and his descendants, were to be considered models of moral authority, whose sayings and doings had the strength of law. The other three successors of the prophet, Abu Bakr, Omar and Othman, are excluded. All Caliphs and rulers from Mu'awiya on are illegitimate.

THE KHARIJITES

According to the Kharijites, whose name came from the verb *kharaj* (to rebel or dissent) the incident demonstrated that no man, except the Prophet, was infallible, including Ali and the descendants of the Prophet. Infallibility lay in the text, which did not need interpretation. Majority, minority and consensus politics were irrelevant since they were no more than techniques to twist the clear meanings of the Quran to suit the devious desires of men, regardless of how many or few they were. A leader who did not abide by the universal, clear and unmediated teachings of the Quran was therefore impeachable. Compliance with a bad leader was tantamount to treason and infidelity and impeaching a wrong doing leader, even if this led to civil war, was not only a right, but a duty. Kharijites disagreed on the punishment non-rebels should receive. One sub-sect argued that all the subjects of a tyrant were complacent unless they took up arms against him, that their complacency was equivalent to apostasy, and that they were therefore not immune to military attacks by the righteous rebels. Followers of this sub-sect of Kharijism, called the Azraqites, thus declared war on the whole of society. Though this sub-sect is formally extinct today, we can compare their arguments with the ideas of the Sunni-Islamist thinker of the Egyptian Muslim Brothers, Sayyed Qutb, on the apostasy of modern Muslim Societies, and the redundancy or malice of the interpretation of the Quran. Other more lenient sub-sects gave more leeway to societies under the rule of tyrants, seeing them more as weak victims rather than complacent collaborators. Nonetheless, all Kharijite sub-sects maintained the right and duty of rebellion against illegitimate rulers whenever possible and by all means necessary.

To the Kharijites, the Prophet, Abu Bakr and Omar are models and figures of authority, while Othman, Ali and Mu'awiya are not revered and are awarded different degrees of blame.

THE EARLY SUNNIS (THE MURJI'ITES AND THE MU'TAZILITES)

Finally the Sunnis argued that infallibility lay in consensus. The leader chosen by the whole community was to become the legitimate successor of the Prophet. In case there were two candidates, the first of the two to be elected was the rightful successor; the second was treated as a dissident and therefore a transgressor. This meant Sunni recognition of Ali's authority, since he was elected before Mu'awiya, up until his death, the arbitration notwithstanding. It also meant Sunni recognition of Mu'awiya's authority afterwards, when Hassan, Ali's son and successor, decided to end the civil war by accepting Mu'awiya's rule, thus achieving consensus. Sunnis equally revered all four successors of the Prophet as figures of authority; Abu Bakr, Omar, Othman and Ali.

It is worth reiterating, though, that this Sunni view was not formulated as such until much later. The seeds of Sunnism that were sown by non-Shiite and non-Kharijite scholars, who were complicit with the Umayyad rule, were quite different from its fruits mentioned in the above paragraph. The formal ideology of the Umayyads was very hostile to Ali, and did not recognize his authority at all. It therefore encountered a dire dilemma. It could neither base the legitimacy of the Umayyads on elections or consensus, because of the Umayyad intention to establish a hereditary dynasty, nor could it base their legitimacy on a theory of divine right of a noble bloodline, since Ali and his descendants were of a more honourable line, being linked directly to the Prophet rather than to his ancient enemies, the pagan merchants of Mecca.

The dilemma was solved by developing the ideology of 'Irjaa' or postponement, whose supporters were called the postponers or 'Murji'ites'. The main argument here was that nothing could happen in God's realm that was against His will. If everything was predestined, it would be folly to oppose God's wisdom. Since the Umayyads could in fact control the community, then God must have predestined it, and therefore their rule must be accepted as an expression of His will. If the Umayyads trespassed, judging them should be left to God, not to the Muslims, and thus judgment should be postponed to the Day of Judgment, hence the term 'postponement'.[11]

---

11. Though this ideology was quite beneficial to the Umayyad rulers in fighting their political rivals like the Shiites and the Kharijites, it was not created by them nor was it initially encouraged. One of the leading jurists who established the school, Jahm ibn Safwan (*d.* 128 AH, 745 AD),

We shall discuss the arguments of this sub-sect in more detail when dealing with the concept of the Umma and the Imam. For the time being it is sufficient to say that the Umayyad Murji'ite discourse provoked various intellectual responses from within the non-Shiite non-Kharijite community that later called itself Sunni. The most important of those responses was 'I'tizal', or rejection, whose supporters, the rejectionists, were called 'Mu'tazilites'. I'tizal is the most sophisticated and philosophical of the various Islamic sects. The school was established by the end of the Umayyad rule and the beginning of the Abbasid rebellion (749 AD), it became the official state ideology of the Abbasids for some time. The main argument was that the interpretation of the Quran was necessary to discern its meanings, and that reason had superiority over the text. Ali was a better ruler than Mu'awiya; he did honour his promises and was fairer in dealing with his subjects. Therefore Mu'tazilites preferred him to his rivals, yet they did not argue that he was infallible or divinely chosen. Preferring him was thus an act of rational judgment rather than a matter of divine designation. A ruler could be a wrongdoer and his subjects had the obligation to disobey him in such cases, but they didn't have the right to take up arms against him. The Mu'tazilites argued that a wrongdoing ruler was neither a good Muslim whose judgment should be left to God, as the Murji'ite

---

was in fact an oppositionist. Massive conversion of Persian peasants to Islam resulted in the decrease of the state's revenues from the poll tax paid by non-Muslims. The Umayyads decided that those who did not speak Arabic and therefore could not understand the Quran should not be considered Muslims, and therefore should continue to pay the poll tax. The early Murji'ites in eastern Iran then made the argument that embracing Islam guaranteed the receipt of God's mercy regardless of how well the religion was practised, and it was not up to mortals to judge how correct the belief of others was. Jahm Ibn Safwan involved himself in a local quarrel between two competing governors of the Umayyad provinces in eastern Iran and was, ironically, killed in rebellion (see Tabari 4: 1488). However the political corollary to his theory was then taken up by the Umayyad rulers, as it prevented their subjects from judging their policies. As long as they were Muslims, the Umayyads were worthy of God's mercy no matter how much they transgressed. This relieved rulers from any moral or constitutional constraints. A variety of Murji'ite schools developed, most of which were substantially different from the early Jahmite version, yet the main arguments regarding the negation of human free choice, and the postponement of judgment till the Day of Judgment stayed the same (for more on the different versions of Murji'ite schools see Shahrustani: 137–43).

postponers argued, nor was he an infidel against whom rebellion was a duty as the Kharijites believed. The debate between the Murji'ite postponers, the Mu'tazilite rejectionists among the Sunnis, as well as the debate between them on the one hand and the Kharijites and the Shiites on the other formed the crux of Islamic political philosophy and philosophical theology throughout the first Abbasid age (749–861 AD).

The question of governance entailed making arguments on the nature of the Quran: whether it was eternal or historical, literal or metaphoric; and on the manner by which it was to be interpreted. For, if the Quran was historical and metaphoric in nature, its meaning would definitely need interpretation, reason being given priority over the literal meaning of the text. If, on the other hand, the Quran was eternal and literal, interpretation would be an attempt to twist the originally clear meaning of the text. If that apparent meaning did not conform with reason, it would be because of the inadequacy of the human mind, just as miracles seem unreasonable, but are true nonetheless. The debates were also concerned with the important issue of the attributes of God and the free choice of human beings.

As mentioned above, these debates started around the end of the Umayyad period, though they only gained momentum after the fall of the Umayyad dynasty and the establishment of the Abbasid state in the Iraqi city of Kufa then in the newly built city of Baghdad.

The 90 years of Umayyad rule (661–749 AD) were ridden by upheavals and civil wars. After the death of Hassan and the election of Yazid son of Mu'awiya, Hassan's brother, Hussein son of Ali, rebelled and was killed by Yazid's army in Karbala-Iraq (680 AD). His death became the most emotional instance in Islamic history, and established a cult of martyrdom among Shiites. The Lord of Martyrs as he was called was opposing the illegitimate succession of Yazid, against the explicit agreement his father had with Hassan. Hussein's death, it can be argued, was the most influential single historical event in consolidating the Shiite belief. It was also the event that shook the very basis of the Umayyad claim to be following the implicit consensus of Muslims. For it was definitely without the consensus of Muslims that Yazid killed Hussein. In some accounts Yazid himself had to claim that he had not ordered the massacre. Nonetheless, Yazid's sudden death, and the death of his only son three months later, ending his bloodline forever, looked like Divine punishment, and could thus be manipulated, for some time, by other

Umayyads and their Murji'ite apologists to strengthen their argument about leaving judgment and punishment to God.

THE HASHEMITE ABBASID RULE

After the martyrdom of Hussein, a series of rebellions by Kharijites, Shiites and other Sunni competitors destabilized the Umayyad Empire, which eventually fell to the Sunni-led Shiite rebellion of the Abbasids. The main call of the revolutionaries was to appoint a member of the House of the Prophet as a successor, one about whom there would be real consensus, after the Umayyads' claim to legitimacy had been proven false by all measures. Throughout the Umayyad rule, Shiites had their 'shadow government', that is, they followed the teachings of the descendants of Ali and Hussein, who succeeded one another on the basis of the father choosing his successor from among his sons. Those Imams did not have the actual political power of the Umayyad rulers; rather, they had only the moral authority of being models to their followers. Like Ali, Shiites believed in their infallibility, and that they were chosen by God. The vague call of the Abbasids to appoint a ruler from the House of the Prophet, around whom there would be consensus, thus lured them into joining the rebellion. However, the Abbasids ended up appointing one of their own, a descendant of another cousin of the Prophet, other than Ali and his descendants, as a ruler of Muslims. The Abbasid rule was therefore opposed by the Shiites, but it was easier to defend than the Umayyads'. According to the Sunni tradition, the prophet had four uncles, two of whom embraced Islam and two of whom died before doing so.[12] Abu Talib, Ali's father, died an infidel, while Abbas, the ancestor of the Abbasids, died a Muslim, and therefore if political authority was to be inherited, Abbas should inherit it from the Prophet rather than Abu Talib. This argument allowed for a strong tribal base of Hashemite legitimacy, since authority was based on blood links to the Prophet, but without

12. Though according to the Shiite belief, Abu Talib, Mohammad's uncle and mentor, and Ali's father, had embraced Islam in secret, yet had to conceal his belief to be able to protect the Prophet during the first days of his call while still in Mecca. The fact that Mohammad had to leave Mecca after Abu Talib's death strengthens their claim that his protection was vital for the survival of the first Muslims in the city. For the official discourse of the Abbasids making their claim against the descendants of Ali based on this argument, see the mutual letters between the second Abbasid Caliph Al-Mansour and Hassan ibn Hassan Ali's grandson, in Ibn Abd Rabboh 5: 337–42.

having to endure the argument of the infallibility of the ruler because authority was not based on Divine designation of the person of the ruler in the Quran and through the sayings of the Prophet.

Moreover, through the Umayyad and Abbasid eras the Shiites disagreed on whom Ali, Hassan and Hussein delegated their power to. There were various lines of succession, and as many Shiite sub-sects, the most dominant of which was the Jafarite sect, with the longest line of succession. Whenever a line of succession ended, the last Imam in the line was considered the Messiah, the Mahdi, the leader who 'would return by the end of the time to fill the world with justice as it was filled with injustice'. The last of those Imams was Mohammad son of Hassan, the twelfth in the line of succession from Ali. He disappeared in the city of Samarra in Iraq in the year 940 AD, towards the end of the first Abbasid era. From that point on Twelvist Shiites adopted a theory of compliance with Abbasid rule; they were not to rebel until the advent of the awaited Imam, the saviour who would lead the rebellion against the unjust rulers of the world. This argument formed the crux of Shiite political theory up until 1979 when Khomeini developed the theory of the rule of the scholar, to which we will attend later.[13]

An Ismailite Shiite Caliphate was formed in North Africa then in Egypt, and an Umayyad survivor established a renewed Umayyad Caliphate in Spain. The rush to theorize and legitimize the rule of each dynasty catalysed the debates among the existing sects.

It was during the rule of the Abbasids that much of the Greek, Persian and Indian philosophies were translated into Arabic, and became available to scholars of theology, politics and literature. These philosophies posed great challenges to the Arab Muslim intelligentsia, who had to base their theories on grounds firmer than pre-Islamic tribalism and citations from the Quran, the sayings of the Prophet and the biographies of his Companions, Ali and his descendants. The Mu'tazilite argument of the historicity of the Quran, and the

---

13. Other Shiite sub-sects were formed around alternative bloodlines from Hussein down. While the Twelvist Shiites believed Hussein named his son Ali II who named his son Mohammad Al-Baqir, Zaidi Shiites believe that Ali II named his son Zaid. After Mohammad Al-Baqir, Twelvist Shiites believed the Imamate went to his son Jaafar Al-Sadiq, then to his son Moussa Al-Kazim, while Ismailites believed that Jaafar chose his other son, Ismail to be his successor. Ismailite Shiites led various rebellions against the Abbasids and succeeded in establishing their states, in North Africa and Egypt (the Fatimids) and in eastern Arabia (the Karmatians). Zaidi Shii-- had a long rule in Yemen that only ended in the twentieth

superiority of reason over text, and the necessity of interpretation to deduce political and social forms of organizations, seemed quite appealing. Also politically, their position that Ali was a better candidate for his own qualities and not because of a divine designation, were quite convenient, since they delegitimized the Umayyads yet gave no edge to the descendants of Ali over the Abbasids. Al-Ma'mun (reigned 813–833 AD) the seventh Abbasid Caliph, declared I'tizal to be the official ideology of the state; he was also the Caliph that established Dar-Al-Hikma, 'the House of Wisdom', which was an academy for the translation of Greek, Syriac, Persian and Indian texts. The imposition of this ideology, however, created a reaction among Arab scholars in Baghdad. The Ash'arite sub-sect of Sunni Islam was then formed in response to the Mu'tazilite domination. The debate between the Mu'tazilites and the Ash'arites over the historicity or eternity of the Quran, and the necessity or malice of interpretation took centre stage, more so than the Shiite-Sunni-Kharijite debate of the previous century.

THE ASH'ARITES

The Ash'arites argued that the Quran was eternal as opposed to historical, literal as opposed to metaphorical; interpretation was to be strictly limited. On the issue of the Imamate, Ash'arites maintained the Sunni argument about the infallibility of the Umma. If among two candidates the Umma chooses the less qualified to become a Caliph, then the Umma must have seen some good in that choice. The point should not be which of the two is better, but which is better for the Umma. Regarding the events of the Great Upheaval, Ash'arites maintained that all the Prophet's Companions were to be revered, despite the fact that they were at war with each other. The awkward position in which two diametrically opposed parties were to be equally revered was dealt with using the Murji'ite argument of leaving judgment to God. However, this time the arguments were more nuanced. The methodological rule was applied of giving priority to text over reason. Since the Prophet had promised paradise to Companions who, after his death, fought with each other, it was not for ordinary Muslims to judge them, no matter how unreasonable such a position might seem. It must be for an unknown Divine wisdom that such events transpired. Any political judgment would mean giving individual human reason priority over the Holy Text, in this case the saying of the Prophet promising paradise to the concerned Companions. On the issue of the Imamate, Muslims were to obey any ruler that was strong enough to impose his rule, for a bad ruler was better than anarchy. If rebellion took place, Muslims should stay unaligned and follow the victor, victory being the sign of consensus. Nonetheless the ruler was not infallible, nor was he immune to criticism. In fact it was the duty of the Umma to advise the ruler on every matter, and his duty to take that advice seriously, yet Ash'arites did not mention any worldly penalty the ruler might suffer if he did not do so. We shall return to their arguments on the Imamate in detail later.

The Ash'arite position gained ground throughout the Empire. It gave enough leeway to rulers and enough prestige to scholars. By the tenth century AD, the Abbasid Caliphs held but nominal power over their governors. Nonetheless, this nominal power was important since it was the sign of the legitimacy of the de-facto independent rulers of the provinces. There were two Shiite states in the Middle East: the Ismailite Shiites in Egypt and Palestine, with their own anti-Abbasid Fatimid Caliphate, and the Twelvist Shiite Buihids in Persia. The latter recognized the nominal authority of the Sunni Abbasid Caliph in Baghdad, as part of the policy of acquiescence adopted by Twelvist Shiites in the absence of the awaited Imam. By the next century, the Sunni Turkish Seljuk dynasty replaced the Shiite Persian Buihids in the east, and the Fatimid Empire was tottering towards its fall in the west, thus consolidating Sunni Islam over Shiism.[14]

ASHAB AL-HADITH (THE LATE SUNNIS)

Around that time the whole political, religious and social system faced existential threats. The attacks from Byzantium, and then from

14. Another school of thought that gained huge influence, especially under the Ottomans, was the Maturidi version of Sunnism. There are trivial differences between Ash'arite and Maturidi interpretations regarding the metaphysical attributes of God. Nonetheless, when it comes to the question of the Imamate and political matters, both interpretations are identical. Maturidism was established by Abu Mansour Al-Maturidi (*d.* 944 AD), named after his village Maturid, near Samarqand in what is today the republic of Uzbekistan. His theories were later adopted by the Ottoman Turks and were declared the formal creed of the state. Followers of the Maturidi version of Sunni Islam still exist in Pakistan, India, China, Central Asia, Turkey and Morocco, but the overwhelming majority of the Sunnis in the Arab Middle East are formally Ash'arites.

the Crusading Franks threatened the very heartland of Islam.[15] By the early thirteenth-century Mogul raids on the eastern borders of the Abbasid Empire were alarming. By the middle of the century Baghdad itself fell and the Caliph was executed by the invaders. The practice and science of theological debates was seen as a cause of political fragmentation because every one of the schools mentioned above, whether Kharijite, Shiite, Mu'tazilite or Ash'arite Sunni, ended up recommending certain forms of legal and political organization. There were as many political systems as there were interpretations of the Quran. To a community facing imminent military threats this was unaffordable. The most popular of the schools, Ash'arite Sunnism, presented itself as the most moderate. It avoided the Shiite arguments on the infallibility of the Imam, as well as the Kharijite allowance of civil war, while avoiding the heavy philosophical jargon of the Mu'tazilites. It also gave much needed 'constitutional' powers to Muslim princes at war with non-Muslim invaders. With the culture itself threatened by invasion, and with Muslims being ruled en masse for the first time by non-Muslim princes, the main obsession among the intelligentsia was to preserve rather than to innovate. The Mu'tazilite borrowing from other traditions was therefore almost abandoned in favour of Ash'arite authenticity. The Ash'arite sub-sect was renamed Mazhab Ashab Al-Hadith (the sect of the followers of the tradition [of the Prophet]). This standardized school of Sunni Islam preserved all the main arguments of the Ash'arite theology, yet it did not indulge in the deconstruction of the arguments of other sects. Other sects were heretical, and the very practice of debating with them was dangerous and not worthwhile. The main scholar establishing and representing this line of thought, especially when it came to matters of government, was Ibn Taymiyya.

THE CANON

From the thirteenth up to the eighteenth centuries, the two main sects of Islam were thus Ashab Al-Hadith, Ash'arite-based Sunnism, and the Jafarite Twelvist Shiism, acquiescing to the rule of Sunnis, in waiting for the advent of the Mahdi. Both schools gave much

15. The Crusades to the east are usually considered to have been started by Pope Urban II in Claremont, France, in 1095. However, by that time a state of intermittent war had prevailed between the Muslim princes of northern Syria and Byzantium for more than a century.

leeway to rulers and military prowess, thus reflecting the pressures and threats faced by the various Islamic empires. The other sects and sub-sects, however, still existed in the collective memory of Muslim scholars. The Shiite and Sunni canons, which stayed more or less the same from the fall of Baghdad till the end of the eighteenth century, were thus defined by continuous intellectual processes of contrast with the other non-canonical sects.

After the fall of Baghdad, a state recently established in Egypt by a caste of slave warriors, called the Mamlouks (sing. Mamlouk, literally, 'the one owned by another') re-established the Abbasid Caliphate in Cairo and considered their state to be the bastion of the Ashab Al-Hadith sub-sect of Sunni Islam. The Mamlouks were succeeded by the Ottoman Turks who resumed their ideological role after moving the Caliphate to Istanbul. The western Mogul Emperors in Persia and Iraq embraced Islam but were succeeded by several dynasties, the last of which were the Safavids, making Twelvist Shiism the official ideology of the Empire. Iraq moved several times from Safavid to Ottoman hands and back. By the advent of the first colonial wave to the Middle East, namely Napoleon's invasion of Egypt (1798 AD), the whole Middle East, including Iraq, was part of the Sunni Ottoman Empire. As mentioned in the footnote above, the Ottoman Empire adopted the Maturidi version of Sunni Islam as a state ideology, the political arguments of which were identical to those of the Ash'arites. In the Arab provinces of the Ottoman Empire, though, the Ash'arite-based sub-sect Ashab Al-Hadith came to dominate the ideological and theological scene. Some Sufi schools also came to prominence, but they were of comparatively minimal political significance in the region studied in this book.

WAHHABISM

Wahhabism, a puritan branch of Ashab Al-Hadith, appeared in the eighteenth century about the time of the first colonial encounters in the Middle East. Following tradition, the sect was named after its founder, a Sunni scholar by the name of Mohammad Ibn Abdel Wahhab (1703–91 AD) from Eastern Arabia. On the constitutional issues of the Imamate, the attributes of God and other metaphysical foundations of the religion, Abdel Wahhab strictly followed the proposition of Ashab Al-Hadith and on matters of everyday jurisprudence he belonged to the Hanbali school of law. Of the four Sunni schools of law, the Hanbali is reputed to be the strictest.[16]

Ibn Abdel Wahhab's arguments on the fundamental issues were purely Ash'arite. But there was one main difference. It was mentioned that the Ash'arites borrowed heavily from the Murji'ites in giving priority to text over reason, and leaning on consensus. One of the arguments of the Murji'ites was that all Muslims were worthy of God's mercy, non-Muslims however were not. The main condition for a ruler to be accepted by the community was to be a Muslim. The ruler could not be impeached for transgressing against his subjects, but if he was found to be an apostate or an infidel, he was to be resisted. In fact fighting against him would become a form of Jihad, a duty of all able Muslim men. Wahhabis argued that Muslims who revered saints or visited the shrines of holy men – a common practice among Shiites with regards to the shrines of the twelve Imams and among Sufi Sunnis – were in fact assuming that such figures had posthumous powers. Only God was immortal. Praying to those saints was another sin by which the community was attributing divinity to them. Muslims practising these rituals were practising, knowingly or not, some form of polytheism. According to Wahhabis they should be called back to Islam, and give up such practices. If they refused, they were to be fought against.

It is worth noting that Ibn Abdel Wahhab did not make the above argument by way of logical deduction or literary interpretation; rather, he followed the late Ashab Al-Hadith style of compiling textual citations from the Quran and the Sunna in support of his argument. Nonetheless, Despite his classic condemnation of *Ilm al-Kalam* (lit. 'the science of words'), which referred to the practice of theological debates among Islamic sects, Ibn Abdel Wahhab did resort to etymological and linguistic explanations of Quranic expressions.[17] For example, he discusses the meaning of 'Tawheed' (monotheism), 'Shirk' (polytheism) and 'Ibada', 'Sala' and 'Do'aa';

16.   Again it should be remembered that the schools of law are different from the constitutional schools. Hanbali, Maliki, Shafei and Hanafi schools all belong to the Ash'arite-based Ashab Al-Hadith sub-sect of Sunni Islam. These four schools deal with day to day legal matters such as marriage, divorce, penalties, taxes, and so on, while the constitutional schools such the Ash'arites and the Mu'tazilites deal with such constitutional matters as the attributes of God, the priority of text or reason, free choice, and political organization.
17.   For example, he cites the following Quranic verse describing a conversation between the Prophet and the polytheists in Mecca, who argued that they

(worship and prayers) in a manner supportive of his arguments.[18] As such Abdel Wahhab's version of Ashab Al-Hadith Sunni Islam remains but an interpretation of the Holy Text, even though it employed etymological, rather than contextual methods.

It is also worth noting here that in declaring the majority of the Umma wrong, Wahhabis slipped from the Sunni tradition that maintained the infallibility of the consensus of the Umma, to the Kharijite proposition of the infallibility of the text. And, like the Kharijites, they legitimized violence against such a community led astray. These resemblances led the Ottoman authorities to declare them as such, and it further played a role in the name-calling between modern Muslim governments and violent Islamic organizations with Wahhabi backgrounds.[19] Opponents of the Wahhabis argue that by calling the majority of the Umma polytheists, Wahhabis cut themselves off from the political identity common to all Muslims. This of course is not the case. Wahhabis themselves recognize that theirs is but one interpretation or understanding of the Holy Texts. Even if it was the most righteous, it was still one among many. They also recognize that before declaring Jihad they have to exhaust all manners by which to proselytize this understanding to the rest of

---

recognized God's powers, but nonetheless believed in lesser deities that bring them closer to Him:

> Say [Prophet], 'Who provides for you from the sky and the earth? who controls hearing and sight? Who brings forth the living from the dead and the dead from the living, and who governs everything?' they are sure to say, 'God'. Then say, 'So why do you not take heed of him? (Quran 10: 31,32)

Abdel Wahhab then draws a parallel between those polytheists against whom the Prophet waged war, and modern Muslims who, while recognizing God's existence and powers, attribute some of those powers to other beings such as saints. By condemning them to polytheism, Abdel Wahhab was virtually declaring war on them unless they changed their ways (see Abdel Wahhab, quoted in Azmeh 2000: 32).

18. See his arguments on this in his message 'on the Explanation of the Word *Tawheed*', in Azmeh 2000: 31–4. Also, see his rejection of interpretative theology and the grand debates in another message called 'Against the [Science of] Words]', in Azmeh 2000: 35–7.

19. Kharijites and Wahhabis differ on everything, except on the argument that the majority of the Umma could in fact be led astray and that unless they returned to the right path, they were to be fought. For a compilation of texts from Quran and the biography of the Prophet cited by Abdel Wahhab in support of this argument, see 'The Imperative to Fight the Polytheists of today' in Ibn Abdel Wahhab, *Kashf-Al-Shubuhat* (the Clarification of Ambiguities), 83, also quoted in Azmeh 2000: 91–2.

the Umma. This makes them no different from other Islamic sects in setting their point of reference in the whole Umma regardless of how many of the Umma believed in their point of view.[20]

Figures 1.1 and 1.2 sum up the above account, and the relations, as we see them, between the various Islamic sects.

The Revelation (beginning of the religion/ideology: in Arabic Din/Da'wa) 610–22

The Hijra (beginning of the Dawla in Medina) 622

The Prophet's Rule (in Medina) 622–31

The Four Companions (in Medina, except for Ali in Koufa-Iraq) 631–61

The Great Civil War (the Rule of Ali) 655–61	(formation of Shiism & Kharijism, non-aligned call themselves Sunna)
The Umayyads (in Damascus) 661–749	(Murji'ites & Mu'tazilites' response)
The Abbasids: 749–1517	
The First Abbasid period (in Baghdad) 749–861 (Umayyads continued in Cordoba-Spain)	(Ash'arite response to Mu'tazilites the beginnings of Ashab Al-Hadith)
The Second Abbasid Period (in Baghdad) 861–1258	(Fatimids in Egypt, Palestine and North Africa, the Crusades, the Mogul raids)
The Fall of Baghdad 1258	(dominance of Ashab Al-Hadith)

The Third Abbasid Period (in Cairo) 1261–1517

    The first Mamlouk State (the Mamlouks military rule – fighting the Moguls)
    The second Mamlouk State (The beginnings of the Ottoman Empire in Asia Minor, the Safavids in Iran and the Moguls, now Muslims, in India-Pakistan)

The Ottoman Empire in the Arab World 1517–1917

The Colonial Era 1798–present

First colonial wave 1798–1801	(Wahhabism)
Second colonial wave 1831–99	(Salafiyya and revivalism; Afghani
Third colonial wave 1917–48, continued by the existence of the state of Israel	and Abdu)
Fourth colonial wave: the Second Fall of Baghdad 2003	

Figure 1.1 Chronology

20. For this division between proselytizing and the declaration of Jihad in the thought of Abdel Wahhab see Delong-Bas 2004: 198–206.

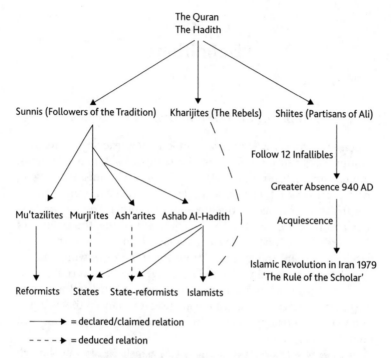

The Quran
The Hadith

Sunnis (Followers of the Tradition)   Kharijites (The Rebels)   Shiites (Partisans of Ali)

Follow 12 Infallibles

Greater Absence 940 AD

Acquiescence

Mu'tazilites   Murji'ites   Ash'arites   Ashab Al-Hadith

Islamic Revolution in Iran 1979
'The Rule of the Scholar'

Reformists   States   State-reformists   Islamists

⟶ = declared/claimed relation
- - - ⟶ = deduced relation

Figure 1.2   Islamic sects on the issue of the Imamate

Notes: This chart is substantially simplified; the Shiite line describes the development of the mainstream Twelvist (Ja'farite) version of Shiism; Sevenist (Ismailite) and Zaidi Shiism are not represented here in order to make the chart easier to follow. It is also worth noting that lines are drawn based on the sect's positions on the issue of the Imamate and political leadership. The chart would look quite different on other theological matters.

By the end of the eighteenth century the first major colonial encounter between Arab Muslim Middle Easterners and Europe came with the French invasion of Egypt. The encounter influenced almost all aspects of social life, from public administration to gender relations, and from academia to architecture. What concerns us most here, however, is the impact of the encounter between the two political ideologies giving legitimacy to political institutions, nationalism and Islam, the idea of the nation and the nation-state, versus that of the Umma and the Dawla.

In the following chapter, I shall briefly discuss the concepts of nation and state in modern European political thought in order to contrast them to the ideas of Umma and Dawla.

2

Definitions

When I was four, my Hungarian kindergarten teacher insisted that Tamim was the Arabic form of the Hungarian Tamash/Thomas. Thomas originates from the Hebrew *Toma*, which means the twin. In Arabic, the twin is *taw'am*, a *taw'am*, like a 'half' is an entity whose identity is determined by the presence of another. The incompleteness and need for 'another' to be complete is thus the essence of the words twin, *taw'am*, *toma*, Thomas or Tamash. On the other hand, Tamim, in Arabic, comes from the stem *tamm* which means completed; it is actually a formula of exaggeration, that is, it means the one who is very complete and self sufficient. Thus, in translating the name into her cultural sphere my teacher changed the meaning of my name to its opposite; fortunately such an interpretation had no political repercussions.

Domination is inherent in the act of translation in which both native and colonial powers indulge, for translation is a process of subduing the logic of one language to that of another. In translating non-European terms into European languages the conceptual richness and thus the true operative meaning and function of political ideas are distorted and muted. The translation of 'Umma' into 'nation' and 'Dawla' into 'state' holds such biases. Umma and Dawla are Arabic words whose meanings are different from those of nation and state, and the relation between which is almost the inverse of the relation of their European counterparts.

The political self-definitions of groups in the world of Islam like Umma and Dawla, are being dealt with in two basic manners; either Umma is seen as different from 'nation', and therefore the Umma is denied any political significance, or Umma is understood to mean nothing but the European sense of the nation, that is, the Umma must have a well defined people, territory and sense of togetherness expressed in a political tendency to have institutional unity and independence, and when no such tendency for institutional unity or well defined territory are found, observers come to the conclusion that the Umma as a political entity does not exist. Had it existed it would have had the political significance of a nation. Obviously, both ways of dealing with the concept lead to its 'quarantine' outside politics, and thus to the denial of any substantial political identity to native Middle Easterners in the pre-colonial era. This is the classical colonial rule; assimilation is the condition for equality, applied to abstract concepts as it has been applied to native peoples, applied to Arabic as it has been applied to Arabs. The concept of Dawla has almost always been translated into that of 'state', overlooking the difference, almost the contradiction, in the etymologies of the two concepts, and in their usage as political terms in Arab and Western traditions respectively. While the fields of meaning of Umma and 'nation' on the one hand, and the meanings of Dawla and 'state' on the other, could indeed intersect, occasionally allowing for an overlooking of differences, in the lines below, I argue that the relation between Umma and Dawla is almost the inverse of the relation between 'nation' and 'state', precisely because of these overlooked differences.

THE NATION AND THE STATE

The Nation

A detailed review of the debates about the definition of the nation and its relation to the state could not fit in this chapter. In such cases categorizing the main trends in the debate could offer a summary while avoiding simplification. The debate could in fact be conceived of as addressing two questions: what is the nation? And how did the nation come about? The first question is descriptive, the second is explanatory. The answers to the first question revolve around two main trends: the first sees nations as objective realities, and the other sees them as subjective imagined communities. The answers to the second question regarding the origin of nations could also be summarized as revolving around two axes that correspond to the two axes around which answers to the first question revolve: one sees nations as discoveries and the other as inventions. The first of these arguments asserts the natural existence of nations stretching back to pre-modern eras. Modernism in this view discovered the nation releasing always existing popular sentiments and translating them into political power. Nations are the products of nature, and the nation-states are then the products of nations. The second argument asserts that the nation is a product of a socio-economic process that is associated with the rise of capitalism in the modern age. The nation is thus a construct whose function is to legitimize a certain pattern of the social distribution of values, that is, that nations are the products of states and states are the products of the economy.

Most of the arguments on nations and nationalisms could be related to one of the above trends. However, there are some crucial commonalities among all these arguments on nations and nationalisms. Whether the nation is imagined or real, whether it is the state's creator or its creature, its function is to keep that nation-state in being. If the nation is an objective reality consisting of a group of people, having in common a number of traits such as language, ethnicity, memory and territory which all result in a sense of togetherness, then these elements are associated with a quest to express them politically by forming a nation-state where it did not exist, and by defending and endorsing such a state where it did. If, on the other hand, the nation was an abstraction invented and propagated through government discourse, its function as an invention is still to legitimize such a state, defend it and increase its power among other states by expansion or otherwise. In both cases the state is the purpose, end and aim of the nation. This is exactly the inverse of the relation between Umma and Dawla. For, at least in theory, the quest for an all encompassing Dawla is not necessary for a group of people to become an Umma.

This relation between nation and state also resulted in the centrality of the issue of territory. While the centrality of territory to the definition of the nation is debated, it is not debated regarding the definition of the state. If the nation is an objective reality, a territory is necessary for any political expression of such a reality in terms of a nation-state; if the nation is an abstraction created by a pre-existing state, an imagined territory is also necessary to legitimize the state's existence. Such an imagined territory is either congruent with that of the existing state, or else it differs in a way that expresses its ambitions of expansion.

Therefore in providing a definition for the nation, the *International Encyclopedia of the Social Sciences* chooses John Stuart Mill's definition that is ambiguous regarding the subjective or objective nature of the nation, yet it is clear on the link between the nation and self-government:

In prevailing usage in English and other languages, a nation is either synonymous with a state or its inhabitants or else it denotes a human group bound together by common solidarity: a group whose members place loyalty to the group as a whole over any conflicting loyalties. This latter definition was first proposed by John Stuart Mill, except that he called the concept 'nationality'. 'A portion of mankind may be said to constitute a nationality', Mill wrote, 'if they were united among themselves by common sympathies – which do not exist between them and any others – which make them co-operate with each other more willingly than with other people, *desire to be under the same government*, and desire that it should be government by themselves or a portion of themselves, exclusively' (1861, chapter 16). (*International Encyclopedia of Social Sciences* 1968, 11: 8, emphasis mine)

The common sympathies mentioned above could be generated by objective reasons such as *ethnie* or territory as Anthony D. Smith would argue, or by imagination as Benedict Anderson would argue, yet one thing common to Mill, Smith and Anderson, and for that matter even Hegel and Marx, is that the assertion that there is a nation implies a desire for a nation-state ruling over it. This relation of the state being the end, purpose and aim of the nation, whether real or imagined, is also clear in most definitions of nationalism. In *Nationalism: Five Roads to Modernity*, Greenfeld (1992) describes five routes to nationhood, all of which are related either to sovereignty or territory. Kedourie defines it as: 'a doctrine [that] pretends to supply a criterion for the determination of the *unit of population proper to enjoy a government exclusively its own, for the legitimate exercise of power in the state*' (Kedourie 1966: 9, emphasis mine); and Guibernau as: 'an ideology closely related to the rise of the nation state and bound up with ideas *of popular sovereignty* and democracy brought about by the French and American revolutions' (Guibernau 1996: 3, emphasis mine).[1] Again the definition in the *Encyclopedia* emphasizes this common factor regarding the relation between nation and state:

Nationalism is a political creed that underlies the cohesion of modern societies and legitimizes their claim to authority. Nationalism centers the supreme loyalty

---

1. Guibernau argues that there are two fundamental attributes of nationalism, political and cultural: the first is attached to the state, the second is attached to territory: 'The fragmentary nature of current approaches to nationalism originates from their inability to merge its two fundamental attributes: the political character of nationalism as an ideology defending the nation that state and nation should be congruent; and its capacity to be a provider of identity for individuals conscious of forming a group based upon a common culture, past project for the future and attachment to a concrete territory' (Guibernau 1996: 3). As shall be shown below, this attachment to state and territory sets nationalism apart from the sense of belonging to the Umma.

of the overwhelming majority of the people *in the nation state, either existing or desired*. The nation-state is regarded not only as the ideal, 'natural' or 'normal' form of political organization, but also, is the indispensable framework for all social, cultural and economic activities. (*The International Encyclopedia of Social Sciences* 1968, 11: 63, emphasis mine)

Etymologically the word nation has a racial resonance to it in addition to its linkage to state and territory. The term stems from the Latin *nasci* which means 'to be born'. Nation is defined as:

An extensive aggregate of persons so closely associated with each other by common descent, language, or history, as to form a distinct race of people, usually organized as a separate political state and occupying a definite territory. … In early examples the racial idea is usually stronger than the political, in recent use the notion of political unity and independence is more prominent. (*Oxford English Dictionary* 1989, 10: 231)

This racial resonance, the fact that the state is the end, aim and purpose of the nation and the relation that the nation has with territory which is a product of its relation to the state, are the main differences between the concept of nation and that of the Umma. While the common belief or ideology is not a major criterion in determining the nation, it is a primary criterion in defining the Umma, and the Umma is non-territorial and non-racial.

Yet the contrast between nation and Umma cannot be understood without investigating and contrasting the concepts of state and Dawla.

The State

The debate about the state is more concerned with the state's relation to society and/or different forms of states rather than the meaning of the word itself. Such debate ranges from giving up the concept of the state as an analytical tool to substitute it with the more inclusive 'political system', to re-establishing the state as a leading independent actor in politics that is distinct and autonomous vis-a-vis the society, and finally to the argument that the boundaries between state and society are permeable by definition, and that the organization of the society by measures of supervision and control creates the effect that there is an independent entity called the state, and that the state's nature as an effect allows it to interact with the society on the one hand and to control it without being dissolved in it on the other. Yet these debates are mainly concerned, as mentioned above, with the state's interaction with the society, not with the abstract meaning of the concept of the state itself. Most definitions of the state include territory, sovereignty, civil organization, and monopoly on legitimate violence. The elements of territoriality and sovereignty are emphasized in the works of Hegel, Marx and Weber (how the state is used and what it represents is another matter since it falls into the scope of the interaction between state and society).

Etymologically, the word state is derived from the Latin stem *stare* which means to stand, most of the word's meanings revolve around the notion of fixity (*Oxford English Dictionary* 1989: 550). It is a 'condition, manner of existing...a dispensation or system of divine government during a particular era. Also, *state of things*...30-A body of people occupying a defined territory and organized under a sovereign government...31-the territory or one of the territories ruled by a particular sovereign' (ibid.: 553–4). The above ties the state more and more with territory and brings it closer to the meaning of estate.

This 'static state of the state' is one of the principal differences between it and the concept of the Dawla, which revolves mainly around the notions of temporality, change and rotation. It is also a feature that corresponds with its relation to the nation as its end and purpose. It is a fixed order in which a nation aspires to organize itself (if the nation predated the state) or a fixed order of things in which the nation should aspire to organize itself (if the state predated the nation).

THE UMMA AND THE DAWLA

The Umma

Unlike the nation, the Umma has no racial or territorial connotations. According to *Lisan al-Arab*,[2] Umma comes from the stem *Amm* which, as a verb, means to head for, to quest, to lead, to guide, or to mean and to intend. As a noun it means destination, purpose, pursuit, aim, goal and end.

The Umma also means the way, the main road, or the law, tradition and religion. The words for law, 'Sharia' and 'Sunna', also mean the 'way' or the 'main road' and the word for religion, '*din*', also means tradition. In a sense, Umma means the way, 'Tareeqa', the intended way or the ideal way of doing things, the quest, and, of course,

2. The most authoritative dictionary in the standard Arabic language, written by Mohammad Ibn Makram Ibn Manzhour Al-Ansari (1233–1311 AD).

the number of people who commit the act of *Amm* (*Lisan al-Arab*, 5: 22–3).

While the Umma is the body that follows, the entity that is followed is the 'Imam'. Etymologically as well as theoretically and historically the Imam means a book, a guide, one that is followed by a group of people: 'and the Quran is the Imam of the Muslims...and God said [referring to the Day of Judgment] *Yawma nad'ou kulla unasin be'Imamihim* (The Day we'll call upon every people by their Book)' (*Lisan al-Arab*, 5: 25).[3] The Imam also means the person followed: 'The Messenger of God is the Imam of his Umma and they all have to follow [the verb used here is *etimam* which is a participle of *Amm*] his way [*Sunna*]'; the Imam means the ideal, 'the Imam is every ideal to be followed'; the Imam is the rope or piece of wood by which the equilibrium of any building is measured; 'the Imam [like the Umma] is the way or the road (*al-Imamu al-Tareeq*)'; finally and most importantly: 'the Imam is the Umma' (*Lisan al-Arab*, 5: 24–6).

The Umma of Muslims, then, are the people who follow the Imam, and the Imam is the guide of the Muslims, be that the ideal book-guide: the Quran, or their ideal human-guide: the Prophet. The Prophet died leaving a number of texts as his biography; everything he said or did which was then reported in text form is called his *Sunna* (his way). In this sense the following of the Quran and the Sunna is what defines the Muslim Umma, that is, the text of the Quran and the Sunna is the Imam (the guide or the entity to be followed) by the Umma. The Quran and the Sunna are texts; they are systems of symbols by definition expressing ideas and ideals. Saying that these are the guide, that is Imam of the Muslims means that Muslims are defined by following ideas and images. Who the Muslims are, then, depends on what these ideas and images are. These texts then offer a definition of the Umma; a definition is an abstract image of a reality.[4] This means that in following the Quran and the Sunna the Muslims are following their image, their ideal image. To put it in clearer terms, a Muslim's image about who the Muslim is depends on a number of texts from the Quran and the Sunna. But these texts do not exactly define who that individual person is, rather they define who that person should be, they define an *ideal* self that this individual Muslim

3. Unless otherwise noted, all translations from Arabic references are mine.
4. Refer to the previous chapter on the power of poetry to compare the function of the Holy Texts to that of the poem in creating identity. The word for poem, *qaseeda*, means the 'one aimed at', the destination persued. The word stems from the verb *qasad*, which is a synonym of *Amm*.

should *pursue* (again the verb *Amm* means to pursue). Just like the pre-Islamic poem created an image of the tribe and the tribesman to be followed and pursued by the individual tribesman. The collective, then, is defined by the very action of pursuing. The action of pursuing which is the action of being a Muslim is an act of doing things in certain *ways*, certain ways of worship, inheritance, taxation, war and peace.

The above is imbedded in the very meaning of Umma. Since, in a poetic sense of equating the journey with the destination, the word Umma, which means the followers, also means the Imam which is the ideal and the entity to be followed. This is backed by other meanings of Umma 'everything to which other things belong and converge is their *Umm*; the main road is the *Umm* of the small alleys leading to it...and the Umma is the *Umm*' (*Lisan al-Arab*, 5: 32).[5]

Thus, the Umma follows itself, follows an image of itself, yet it and its image are, at least etymologically, one. Each Muslim follows all Muslims, that is, *a physical existence of individuals is called an Umma when these individuals have an image of themselves as a collective, and when this image is guiding them to do things in certain ways distinct from others.*

It should be noted that the number of the individuals considered in the above definition could be only one. The Umma could be only one person, if that person had a creed by which he defined himself and that was expressed in his actions, even if no one followed him in his quest. Ibrahim (Abraham) was thus described in the Quran as an Umma by himself: 'Surely Ibrahim was an Umma obedient unto God a man of pure faith and no idolater' (*Quran*, 16: 120, see also *Lisan al-Arab*, 5: 27).

According to the above definition, *Al-Umma Al-Islamiyya* (the Islamic Umma) predated any political arrangement, since, on the first day of revelation, the Umma consisted of only one man: the Prophet himself, then the Umma became the Prophet, his wife, his young cousin Ali, and his closest friend Abu Bakr. This fact will be touched upon again when discussing the concept of Dawla.

But, given the above definition of the Umma, what is there about it that is political? The answer to that question is twofold. First, it is the politics imbedded in the definition of Muslims in the Quran and Sunna, especially the verses of the Quran and the texts of the Hadith that order all Muslims to fight whoever drives them out of their

5. The most common meaning of the word Umm is simply 'mother'.

homes, not to forge alliances with infidels against fellow Muslims; the verses on taxation, as well as other verses regarding different social interactions including peace, war, marriage, inheritance, execution of laws, the acceptance of testimonies, and so on. Yet this is not the main aspect that makes the Umma a political entity; rather, it is its relation to institutions of authority that determine its political significance. Here we should go back to investigate the relation between Umma and Imam, which also means the leader, the teacher, leader of prayers, head, and 'every caretaker of an entity is its Imam' (*Lisan al-Arab*, 5: 24–5). This investigation would also have to show how the etymological meanings of Umma and Imam correspond to their usage in political theory so as for the above arguments to have any significance.

It has been established above that the Imam is part of the definition of the Umma, and that the Umma could not exist without an Imam, because the Umma and the Imam are, in a sense, one. It has also been argued that the Imam is the system of symbols presented by the text of the Quran, the figure of the Prophet and the ideal image of the collective constructed by such symbols. Yet, as mentioned above, Imam also means a teacher, a leader and ruler, all of which are connected to authority and power. Is the Imam as a unifying ruler for the Umma necessary for its existence? This question is crucial, because if that was the case, the relation between the Umma and the institutional authority would be the same as that of nation and state, that is, the existence of the Umma stays doubtful or incomplete until an Imam is appointed just as the existence of a nation stays doubtful and incomplete till it is expressed in a nation-state. In the lines below I am going to argue, referring to the most authoritative pre-colonial thinkers on the issue of the Imamate, who are considered part of modern day Islamic canon, that the Umma as an imagined community stayed independent from, yet extremely influential on, the institutional authority represented in the numerous Imams in history, and that the Umma was the legitimizing entity, both physical and imagined, for any executive authority from the Imam down.

The Umma and the Imam: The Imam as a Teacher

Here we should discuss the capacity of the Imam as a teacher as well as a ruler. As a teacher, the Imam is seen as the interpreter of the symbols of the Quran and the Sunna. This capacity, however, is not confined to one person, nor does it necessarily go with any political authority. As mentioned above, the three sects that constitute the overwhelming majority of Muslims today are the Sunnis, 'The

Followers of the Prophet's Tradition', the Shiites, 'The Partisans of Ali', and the Kharijites, 'The Rebels'.[6]

For the Sunnis and Kharijites the right of interpreting and understanding the religious texts belongs to everyone. Shiites confined this capacity to their twelve consecutive Imams. After the disappearance of the last Imam, however, the interpretations as well as the independent biographies of the twelve infallible guides became themselves texts to be interpreted by any scholar. From that point on, in all three main sects, the authority of an interpreter depended mainly on the public acceptance of his ideas. It is in this sense that the scholars who established the four Sunni schools of law, *'mazhahib'*, were called Imams.[7] Due to the authority of the texts, this power to

6. After the death of the Prophet Muslims disagreed about the best form of government, and Islam's three main sects were formed around this issue. The Shiites believed that some verses of the Quran referred to Ali, the Prophet's cousin, son-in-law and the father of his only male descendants as the righteous heir to the Prophet's political authority. They also believed that Ali was infallible and therefore whomever Ali assigned as his successor would be the righteous guide, hence their name Shi'at Ali, or the Partisans of Ali. The Kharijites believed that no human was infallible, and that, accordingly, no hereditary rule was to be allowed in Islam. Rulers were normal men elected for life; however, they were impeachable by the Muslim population if they violated the teachings of the Quran. To the Kharijites, rebelling against a hereditary ruler or an elected ruler who has betrayed his mandate is not only a right but a duty, hence the meaning of their name: the rebels. The Sunnis were the last sect to be given a formal name, and it consisted of the majority of the non-aligned Muslims. The main doctrine of the Sunna is the infallibility of the collective; whatever form of government accepted by the community of Muslims, hereditary or not, would be the righteous form. They chose the most uncontroversial of names: *Ahl Al-Sunna wal-Jama'a*, followers of the tradition of the Prophet and the consensus (of Muslims), referring to the Prophet's saying that the Community of Muslims as a whole would never be misguided. The problem with the Sunni doctrine, however, is that the mechanism by which to reach and express the consensus of the community of Muslims was left ambiguous. At different stages in Islamic history it meant the acceptance of the majority, universal consensus, the acceptances of the learned few or the de-facto acquiescence in dealing with the victorious faction in a civil war. Refer to the chronological section above on the establishment of the Muslim sects.

7. The four schools of law in Sunni Islam, the Hanbali, the Hanafi, the Shafi'i and the Maliki, should not be confused with the sub-sects mentioned in the above sections, the Murji'ites, the Mu'tazilites and the Ash'arites. While the latter three deal with constitutional matters, usually referred to in Islamic thought as *Al-Osoul*, 'the roots', like the attributes of God, the definition of the Umma, and the issue of the Imamate, the former four schools deal with legal matters such as inheritance, rituals, commercial dealings, and so on, which are referred to as *Al-forou*, 'the branches'. All four Sunni Schools of law follow the Ash'arite constitutional school.

interpret from the Quran and the Hadith was thus a power to legislate. Accordingly, the legislative power of the Umma does not lie in the ruler, but in the scholar. The ruler can offer interpretations: however, this he does in his capacity as a scholar not as a ruler. The fact that the Imams interpret the original texts of the Quran and Hadith make them followers as much as they are leaders, for they can only interpret those legal and constitutional texts, but they can't make up texts or rules of their own. It is this fact that resulted in calling their followers, groups 'firaq', parties 'ahzab', sects 'mazhahib', but never Ummas. In a sense, they all claim to be seeking, pursuing and aiming at the real meaning of the same texts; they are all followers of the same entity. An important consequence of this fact (the unity of the text and the variety of interpretations) is that each scholar, claiming to be interpreting the Quran and the Hadith, must necessarily be addressing the whole Umma. *The whole community of Muslims then becomes the arena for legislation regardless of the territorial boundaries of kingdoms and princedoms or any other executive authority.*

We can conclude from the above that the existence of various Imams in this scholarly-legislative capacity is a logical consequence of the existence of the Umma (as an image) rather than a necessary precondition for its existence.

The Imam as a Ruler

As for the Imam as an executive ruler, all Islamic parties and sects agreed that there must be an Imam, except for one sub-sect of the Kharijites (the *Najdat),* who argued that if people obeyed the rules of the Quran and the Hadith, that is, the textual guides, there would be no need for a human guide, or for any kind of authority (Shahrustani, n.d.: 119, Afghani 2002, 4: 83, Imara, 1977: 12). Yet the rest of the Kharijites as well as the Shiites and the Sunnis agreed that there must be an authority; that having a human Imam to protect and execute the rules of the Quran and the Hadith is absolutely necessary. However, they disagreed whether this was necessary because of reason (*wajibun 'aqlan),* that is, because of worldly needs or because of divine order (*wajibun Shar'an),* they also disagreed on the right to rebel (*al-khorouj)* and on how many Imams there could be at a given moment in time as well as on the functions of the Imam; a symbol whose presence is necessary for the welfare and protection of the Umma but whose absence would not necessarily lead to its non-existence, or an executive officer liable to scrutiny and mutiny and whose person is the core of political life in Islam. Below I shall argue that according to the authoritative writings considered to be canonical in the major

Sunni and Shiite teaching centres in Egypt and Iraq, during the past two centuries; a non-textual, human Imam whether a symbol or an executive officer is required for the welfare of the Umma not for its existence. In all cases the Imam has no legitimacy if he does not follow the rules of the Quran and the Hadith, the meanings of which are interpreted by scholars. This means that the Umma is independent of the human ruler Imam while he is totally dependent on the Umma.

While the Shiites asserted that belief in the Imam is part of Islam itself and therefore it is part of the definition of the Umma, they differentiated between the Imam (guide) and the Caliph (successor of the Prophet/king/supreme executive). Except for Ali who was both an Imam and a Caliph, that is, a legislator and an executive officer respectively, the rest of the twelve Imams were only legislators. The Imam had to have a direct hereditary claim to Ali the son of Abu-Talib and to his wife Fatima the daughter of the Prophet (Shahrustani, n.d.: 163). The Caliphs on the other hand were executive officers, they could be good or bad; the belief in the Caliphs was not part of Islam unless such a belief was ordered by an Imam (for the full theory of the Imamate and the Caliphate see Al-Kulaini 1968, 1: 168–96; 1: 286–329 on divine choice of the Twelve Imams including the last hidden Imam). By the disappearance of the twelfth Imam, this duality ended. Since then the Imam became a figure who was alive but hidden and who would return at the end of time 'to fill the Earth with justice just as it was filled with oppression'. The Imam turned into a figure expressed in texts. Accordingly, the unity of the Umma under one executive leader (whom the Sunnis would call an Imam while the Shiites would just call a Caliph) might or might not be necessary for the welfare of the Umma but is definitely not necessary for its existence. The definition of the Umma still lay in texts interpreted by scholars and followed by the people; the legitimacy of any ruler, the Caliph included, would lie in his following of such texts. Since 940 AD, the year of the disappearance of the twelfth infallible Imam,[8] and

8. According to the Shiite beliefs the twelfth Imam was born in the year 255 AH (869 AD); he was hidden in an underground Tunnel is Samarra, north of Baghdad, from birth. Nonetheless, he assumed his Imamate when he was five years old, and gave his guidance to Shiites through four consecutive spokesmen, who stayed in direct contact with him for 70 years. This is called the period of the 'Lesser Absence'. Since 940 AD, no one assumed the position of being the Imam's personal spokesmen. However, all scholars and religious references are considered to be the heirs of those four spokesmen. They are to guide the community through studying and interpreting the

up until his return, the supreme ruler to the Shiites is a follower rather than a leader, a successor rather than a head.[9] It should be mentioned however, that to the Shiites, the belief in the infallible Imam, and the desire for him to rule over all Muslims, was part of the definition of the Umma. In other words a good Muslim was not considered a member of the Umma unless he harbored that desire for the infallible Imam to rule. One could see similarities between this sense of belonging to the Umma and nationalism, since both involve the desire to establish some form of ideal political authority that encompasses the whole community. However, this was only true up until 940 AD. After the disappearance of the twelfth Imam, his Imamate turned into text, and the Shiites no longer had candidates for worldly political power. Thus the desire to establish a state vanished. It is true Shiites still consider the belief in the hidden Imam to be part of the belief in the correct interpretation of the Quran. But not believing in this interpretation does not exclude one from the Umma. That is, a Sunni Muslim who does not believe in the hidden Imam is still a Muslim, only a misguided one according to the Shiite doctrine.

Moreover, Sunni scholars, whether Murji'ite, Mu'tazilite or Ash'arite, repeatedly made the argument in their debates against the Shiites that the functions of the Imam were the normal functions of the political authority, protecting the community against external threats and keeping law and order internally. Since the absent Imam was unable, while hiding, to perform such functions, it would make no difference to believe or not to believe in him. The Shiite response to this proposition further clarifies the point made here. The Shiite argument is that the presence of the Imam is like the revelation of the Quran or the divine sending of the Prophet as a messenger; it is not God's will to force human beings to obey, but it is rather His scheme to leave that to their free choice. The whole point of an Imam

---

biographies of the hidden Imam, his eleven predecessors as well as the Prophet's biography and the Quran. Shiites believe that the Imam is still alive and in hiding, waiting for the time of his reappearance. This period of time between the death of the Imam's last spokesman and his final reappearance is called the 'Greater Absence'.

9. One should not confuse the official titles of Shiite Islamic scholars of authority like Imam Khomeini or Imam Khaminai in modern day Iran with the infallible Imams. These titles only refer to the capacity of those men as teachers and leaders of prayers, and to an extent, as worldly role models. There is nothing in modern day Twelvist Shiism to suggest their infallibility. In fact any such assumption would amount to heresy according to the Shiite canon, for the hidden Imam is the only infallible alive.

being a Guide is that people should be free to obey or disobey him. His powerlessness thus becomes essential in his function as a guide rather than a benevolent enforcer (for the theory of the Imamate and the debate with Sunni scholars over the functions of the Imam, see Sobhi 1964: 69–79). This argument also entailed that the Shiites adopted positions similar to those of the Mu'tazilites on human free will, the absence of predestination, and the vitality of interpretation (for the more on the Twelvist Shiite position on these matters, see Al-Mufid 4: 34–45, 112–14).[10] The call for the Shiite hidden Imam was then, since 940, a desire to proselytize a certain version of the religion, with little political impact, and with gradual abandonment of exclusionist discourses.

The desire to proselytize the most authentic interpretation is common to all Islamic sects and sub-sects. Claiming that followers of other sects are led astray is also common. It is not common, however, that the believers of other sects are considered infidels. The Shiite doctrine changed drastically in 1979 with the establishment of the Islamic Republic in Iran. The main argument presented in Ayatollah Ruholla Khomeini's work *Al-Hukumat ul-Islamiyya* (The Islamic Government, Arabic edition, 1979) was that in the absence of the Imam, the scholars, the best qualified interpreters of the text, and therefore the traditional legislators of the Umma, should also inherit his executive powers, that they should supervise the execution of the laws they extract by interpreting the Holy Texts. In doing so, Khomeini brought Shiism and Sunnism one step closer to each other, as the 'Sunni' consensus of the Umma, and the now 'Shiite' rule of the scholars, practically amount to the same thing. According to both theories, a political system is established based

10. Al-Mufid (*d.* 1022 AD) is one of the greatest authorities in Shiite theology. Another two major references on Twelvist Shiite doctrine were his students. The first was Ali ibn Hussein, known as Al-Sharif Al-Murtada (*d.* 1044 AD), author of *Al-Shafi fi Al Imama* (the Remedy: on the Imamate) the Shiite principal work in refuting the metaphysical, methodological and political arguments of other sects including Mu'tazilite and Ash'arite Sunnism. The other student of Al-Mufid was Mohammad Ibn Hassan Al-Tusi (*d.* 1068 AD). Of the four most authoritative works of Shiite jurisprudence, two are authored by Tusi, *Tahzhib Al-Ahkam* (the Perfection of Rulings) and *Al-Istibsar* (The Insight). Together with Mohammd ibn Yaqoub Al-Kulaini (*d.* 941), who lived during the time of the 'Lesser Absence', and who is the author of *Al-Kafi* (the Sufficient), the above scholars are the most authoritative references on Shiite theology, epistemology and jurisprudence.

on the interpretation most popular among the scholars of the Umma. Like all other sects, since Khomeini's arguments were based on an interpretation of the Quran, the Islamic Republic, at least theoretically, sets as its point of reference the whole community of Muslims, not only the people of Iran. Also like other sects, the belief of the community in this particular interpretation of the Quran is not a condition for their inclusion in the Umma. According to the Twelvist Shiite doctrine, whether in its pre- or post-Khomeini versions, the point of reference of political authority must be the whole Umma for that authority to be legitimate, while it is not necessary for a group of people's inclusion in the Umma that they recognize such an authority.

As for the Kharijites, it was mentioned above that their distinctive slogan was 'al-Hukmu li-Allah' (no rule but God's), meaning that the human-leader Imam is not even part of the symbolism of the Umma; there is no sacred Imam. The Imam is only an executive officer, who should observe the holy infallible clear and self-explanatory texts, the Quran and the Sunna, and in the event that he does not, he is not to be obeyed. A Kharijite Imam is necessary for the protection and welfare of the Umma, yet he is not necessary to its existence. The Imam to the Kharijites, like the Caliph to the Shiites, lacked any symbolic capacity, his executive capacity made him subject to scrutiny and mutiny and thus he was not part of the definition of the Umma. The legitimacy of the ruler is dependent on his following the rules of the Quran and Sunna. While the Shiites disagreed about the right to rebel, some of them granting it against the unfair Caliph and others confining it to the second coming of the twelfth Imam, the right to rebel against the spoiled Imam/Caliph (al-Imam al-fasid) was central to the Kharijites.[11] The Kharijites, as well as some late Sunni sects, went as far as excluding Muslims who did not accept their interpretation of the Quran from the Umma, thus treating them as infidels. There were three main Kharijite sub-sects: the Azraqites mentioned above, who were the strictest of the three, declaring the whole society to be in a state of apostasy until Kharijite rule was established; the Baihasids, who called for taking up arms against illegitimate Caliphs but excused those who could not do so; and the Ibadis, the only surviving sub-sect, who called for armed mutiny,

11. For more on the Kharijites see *Al-Milal wa-al-Nihal* (Religions and Creeds), Shahrustani n.d.: 106–11.

but excused those who could not and those who would not do so too, thus being the most tolerant of the three sub-sects (see on the sub-sects of the Kharijites, Mubarrad 2: 220, also see for their main arguments the speeches of Abu Hamza Al Mukhtar ibn Awf Al-Khariji to the people of Medina commenting on the ascension of Yazid ibn Abdul Malik in *Diwan Al-Khawarij* 1983: 283).

The Sunnis are the most confused of the three sects on this issue. For while the Shiites lived with a symbolic, textual Imam since the disappearance of the twelfth Imam, Mohammad al-Muntazhar (Mohammad the Awaited), and while the Kharijites lived with an executive Imam who had no religious claim, the Sunnis lived with Caliphs who were executive officers and who backed their claims by texts from the Quran.

There are many trends in Sunni political thought; however, as mentioned above the principal arguments revolve around the two axes of the Ash'arites and the Mu'tazilites. Despite differences on divinities and metaphysics, Ash'arites borrowed much of their position on the Imamate from the Murji'ites. It should be remembered that advocates of the latter school argued that there was no right to revolt against the ruler and that his power was a gift from God; he should not be judged according to his deeds but rather by his creed as a Muslim. A bad Muslim ruler was better than any good non-Muslim ruler. This school was used by the Umayyads to legitimize their otherwise extremely illegitimate hold on power during the times of expansion and conquest. However, most of the other Muslim sects and schools of thought came to being as an intellectual and political response to the Murji'ites. During the Abbasid period, with the relaxation of expansionary wars, Murji'ites gave way to the Mu'tazilites and the Shiites. However, by the end of that period, during the Crusades and Mogul raids, the Ash'arites, an intellectual response to the Mu'tazilites, resurrected the Murji'ite argument that a Muslim ruler's hold on power was unquestionable even if he committed vice, as long as he stayed a Muslim. This was further consolidated by the teachings of Ibn Taymiyya and the school of Ashab Al-Hadith. Ibn Taymiyya offers the theoretical background for a considerable portion of modern Sunni Islamic political thought. The Ashab Al-Hadith concept of Islam, accepting the texts as the only origin for legislation, adopting the doctrine of military-type obedience to the Muslim ruler and rejecting any mutiny against him due to the fact that he was dealing with a foreign non-Muslim threat, was adopted by the Mamlouks, and later by the Ottoman Empire till the advent of colonialism.[12]

Mawardi (972–1052) is the most prominent Sunni Islamic theoretician on the issue of the Imamate. He asserts that the Umma should have an Imam, meaning a supreme executive officer. He then goes on to state the criteria according to which the Imam should be chosen, and lists the powers of the Imam, which include the appointment of ministers, local governors, judges and supreme judges, the declaration of Jihad and the collection of taxes. Mawardi discusses the case in which two Imams coexist, which is crucial to the argument made here. Mawardi argues that the Umma should have only one Imam, and that in case any other person claimed the Imamate, the existing Imam should fight him. Like all other Muslim scholars, he supports his argument by citing the Quranic verse:

If two groups of the believers fight, you [believers] should try to reconcile them; if one of them is [clearly] oppressing the other, fight the oppressors until they submit to God's command, then make a just and even handed reconciliation between the two of them; God loves those who are even handed. The Believers are brothers, so make peace between your two brothers and be mindful of God, so that you may be given mercy. (Quran 49: 9, 10)

12. Ashab Al-Hadith also holds the doctrine that only the literal understanding of the Holy Texts is allowed as opposed to dealing with the texts as metaphoric, thus allowing for interpretation. Due to the strict relation between textual interpretations and claims to power, intellectual freedom of interpretation meant more political fragmentation under the pressing threat of the Moguls and the Crusaders. Ashab Al-Hadith gave the highest priority to fighting the infidels; political fragmentation was thus seen as an act of treason and a factor of internal weakness. Forbidding mutiny was necessary especially when Muslim princes needed to impose illegal taxes, that is, taxes that were not sanctioned by the Quran and the Sunna, in order to fend off the invaders. The right of mutiny against a Muslim ruler was forbidden just as acquiescence under a non-Muslim ruler was forbidden. Thus Ibn Taymiyya's famous argument that a ruler who kills or taxes unjustly could be forgiven if that was for the better of the Muslims, yet if he did not pray five times a day, which means he stopped being a Muslim, he is to be killed. The difference between this school and the original *Irja* is that Ashab Al-Hadith were much less lenient on issues of worship and rituals than *Irja*. The Muslim ruler had to show and prove his Islam by all possible means and at all times and there could be no forgiveness of a Muslim ruler who broke the rules of religion or allied himself with infidels against Muslims. For more on Ibn Taymiyya's political theory see his *As-Siayyassa al-Shar'iyya, fi Salah al Rai wa al-Ra'iyya* (the Legal [could also be translated as legitimate or religious] Policy for the Good of the Ruler and the Ruled): 271–84.

The word here translated as oppression in Arabic is 'baghy' which also means excess, transgression, or taking more than one's fair share. Mawardi makes the argument that rebellion against the legitimate Imam is to be classified as 'baghy', an act that does not amount to apostasy, meaning that Muslim rebels are still Muslims. Yet Mawardi details the military measures that should be taken in fighting them which he maintains are drastically different from the measures to be used with non-Muslims:

fighting them [the transgressors, or the people of baghy] is different from fighting infidels and apostates, in eight ways: first that the purpose of fighting them is to deter rather than destroy them ... they should only be fought if they were attacking, not while retreating ..., their wounded are not to be attacked ..., those of them who are captured are not to be killed, whoever commits himself not to return to fighting [against the righteous Imam] is to be released, while those who do not make such commitment are only kept in captivity till the war is the over, after that they are to be released, ... their property and their women are not to be taken as spoils of war ... and sixth that no polytheist, who might have a treaty [with the righteous Imam], is to be summoned to fight against them [i.e. against the rebels/transgressors], seventh, he [the righteous Imam] cannot impose a truce on the them by which he is to receive regular tributes [a measure only applied to non-Muslims...], and eighth, that he cannot use catapults against them, nor burn their houses, nor burn their trees and palms, for they are still in the abode of Islam, and it [the abode of Islam] protects those who belong to it even if they transgressed. (Mawardi, 80–2)

Moreover, Mawardi maintains that Islamic funerary rituals should be performed with regards to those killed in battle, regardless of which side they were on (Mawardi, 82) Clearly Mawardi here maintains that both sides are Muslims, that is both of them are still part of the Umma despite the fact that they do not agree on a common Imam. Thus two Imams can be fighting each other, each claiming to be the rightful one, while the Umma still exists. Moreover, this abstract existence of the Umma is still functioning despite the conflict, since special military measures are taken in accordance with such an existence.

When Mawardi talks about the post of *Wazir al-Tafweed* (the minister of delegation), he states that the minister of delegation can have everything that the Imam has except the title (that is, except his symbolic capacity). In such a case there could not be two ministers having the same powers at the same place, yet there could be two ministers having the same powers in two distinct places, that is, two supreme executive powers that are actually independent from one another and only symbolically linked to the overarching Imam. To have two legitimate leaders, according to Mawardi, both should have one supreme reference to symbolize their appeal to the whole Umma, that is, to symbolize their legitimacy according to the Quran, Sunna and the image of the community of Muslims expressed therein (see Mawardi 1989: 30–9). The existence of such a king to act as a unifying symbol, according to Mawardi, is necessary for the interests of the Umma, yet it is not a condition for its existence. Moreover, such a symbol need not have any direct executive authority, that is, the Imam need not be a state.

Other more orthodox Ash'arite writers like the man who established the sub-sect Abu Al-Hassan Al-Ash'ari (873–944 AD) and the school's most prominent spokesman, Abu Bakr al Baqillani (d. 1012 AD), present arguments on the Imamate that did not differ much from those of Mawardi. For example, Baqillani writes a whole chapter of his book Al-Tamhid in explaining the Ash'arite theory of the Imamate. He calls the chapter 'Bab ul-Kalam fi Hukmi l-Ikhtiyar', 'A Chapter on the Legitimacy of Choice' (Baqillani, 178). He makes the argument that the texts of the Quran said by Shiites to imply the appointment of Ali as the legitimate successor of the Prophet, do not mention his name; that the interpretations presented by Shiites depend on the circumstances during which such verses were revealed to the Prophet or on assuming that the Prophet made statements by which to clarify the meanings of the verses. Baqillani argues that, had the Prophet made those statements in public, then it could not have come to pass that the majority of his Companions did not know about them, or knew but kept them secret. He also states that Ali himself did not refer to such statements as part of his known political discourse (ibid.: 164–6). Having stated that neither the Quran nor the Sunna included any divine selection among the Muslims, the choice of the Imam becomes a matter wholly left to the Umma. If there was no Divine selection, human election, by default, becomes the only way by which to form a government and appoint a supreme leader. It should be mentioned here, though, that while Baqillani makes the argument that the Umma is free to choose its leader, he still adheres to the Sunni position that the Umma cannot refrain from making that choice and thus stay without an Imam (ibid.: 178), nor can the Umma choose two Imams at the same time, without one being right and the other wrong. He writes:

If they said: what do you say if different groups of the people of power (ahl ul-halli wal 'aqd) elected different Imams in different countries, and they were all fit for the Imamate, and they were all elected in the absence of an Imam or a legitimate heir of an Imam [to their knowledge], what is your judgment of them, who would be more deserving of the Imamate among them? It is to be said to them: if such a thing happens ... we look at who was elected first, and he is to be given the Imamate, and the others are to be asked to concede ... if they don't they are to be fought as they will be in mutiny against the legitimate Imam. And if it cannot be known who was elected first, all elections are to be canceled and only one is to be chosen, be he one of the said candidates or another. (Baqillani, 180)

Baqillani makes the same argument in the case of all elections taking place at the same time. The sequence of election of candidates for the Imamate, rather than the merits of the individual Imams, thus determines their legitimacy.[13] Moreover, he argues that in case there were two candidates, one of whom was more qualified than the other, it is still legitimate to choose the less qualified if the choice of the best Imam was expected to cause civil war. He writes:

The evidence that proves the legitimacy of electing a candidate whose virtues are outweighed by those of another, leaving out the best of the two, for fear of upheaval and civil war, is that the Imam is elected for no other reason but to deter the enemy (of the Umma), protect the heartland (of the religion), right the wrongs, execute the laws and retrieve the rights. So, if electing the best was feared to cause upheaval, corruption, the rule of force, disobedience, the crossing of swords ... and raised the hopes of the enemies of Muslims to oppress and weaken them, it would be a clear excuse for not electing him. It [also] stands as evidence for [this argument] that Omar, may God be pleased with him, the rest of the companions and the [whole] Umma knew that some were better than others among the six [the six candidates to whom Omar delegated the power of choosing his successor from among themselves] yet he made it clear that it was possible that any one of them be elected, if that was for their best interest, and if they could achieve consensus about it, and no one objected to that at the time. (Baqillani, 184)[14]

13. This is a difference between the Ash'arites on the one hand and the Shiites and the Sunni Mu'tazilites on the other.
14. Two of the six to whom Baqillani refers in this passage were the Umayyad Othman and the Hashemite Ali. The choice of Othman is classically referenced by Shiites as an example of the fatal choice of the less qualified Imam over the most qualified.

It is clear from the above that an Imam is elected for certain worldly functions, and that the qualities required for the post, are not necessarily the qualities by which a Muslim would be considered 'best' or 'better' by the common ethical code of the Umma. Such qualities are directly linked to the political functions of keeping internal order and deterring external enemies, the ability to achieve consensus is thus essential in this regard.

The problem, however, with Baqillani's theory, as with all Ash'arite political thought, is that it is quite contradictory when it comes to the definition of consensus and the ways by which to reach it. For Baqillani, the reason why an ethically questionable Imam can be elected is to avoid civil war, but he recommends civil war as a means by which to elect an Imam in case more than one candidate claimed the title (see Baqillani, 181). This can be attributed to the technical impossibility to conduct elections in vast medieval empires. Nonetheless, that contradiction remained a weakness in the Ash'arite theory, for no reference to such practical obstacles was made by Baqillani or any other Ash'arite jurist. The acceptance of civil war as a means by which to choose the Imam resonates of the Murji'ite arguments, where victory of a certain candidate is an expression of the consensus, and therefore an expression of God's will. The textual and moral criteria of the Kharijites, the Shiites and the Mu'tazilites seemed more consistent and appealing for rebels throughout Islamic history. A Machiavellian theory of state ethics as opposed to private or social ethics could have solved the Ash'arite contradiction; it could have legitimized power politics as a means by which choose a government. However, such a theory would have entailed the separation of government and ethics, that is state and religion, which was impossible to the Ash'arites.

On the impeachment of the Imam, Baqillani makes the argument that will later become the main argument of Ashab Al-Hadith, that the Imam was not to be impeached if he breached any of the moral or ethical codes that were to be deduced from the teachings of the religion. Yet he was definitely to be impeached if he committed apostasy, or refrained from performing the essential rituals of the religion and called people to follow his example at that.

If someone said: what is it that makes it imperative to impeach the Imam according to you [to Ash'arites]: it is to be said to him: more than one reason; apostasy [to stop being Muslim], not performing his prayers and calling on people not to perform them. And to many people, his aggression, and oppression by usurping people's properties, inflicting injury, killing [illegally], the loss of [peoples'] rights and the non-execution of the laws [would make it imperative to impeach him]. Most of the people of knowledge and those who know the Hadith say [however] that he is not to be impeached because of such things, but he is to be preached and threatened and disobeyed in some of what he calls for in disobedience of God. (Baqillani, 186)

It should be mentioned that Baqillani refers to the people of knowledge and those who know the Hadith, while commenting on what is 'to many people' a reason to impeach the Imam. The reasons mentioned before the phrase 'to many people' are understood to be a matter of consensus. He then mentions a number of sayings by the prophet that support the latter position, that impeachment should happen only in case of apostasy.

The Imam has to be a Muslim, and it would be better if he was an Ash'arite. This emphasis on identity, rather than on practice, became more popular by the time of Ibn Taymiyya as more and more Muslims were under the threat of being ruled by non Muslims. It is an argument similar to the traditional third world nationalist preference, that to any given group of people a bad government of their own would be better than a good government of others. It should be underlined though, that the line is drawn on the basis of religion, on belonging to Islam in general not to any particular sect. Even when Baqillani makes the argument for supporting the Sunni Imam in case of a conflict between several Imams each following a different interpretation of Islam, he still recognizes the event as a case of civil war. He still calls the other groups members of the Umma. His adherence to the Ash'arite position of approving Ali's Imamate, while asserting that the Companions of the Prophet who fought against him were also Muslims, as well as his approval of the Caliphate of his rival Mu'awiya, reveals his assumptions about the existence of the Umma as a functioning political entity during civil war (see Baqillani, 232–3, on the events of the great upheaval). Moreover, he mentions the same special measures taken during civil war that Mawardi recommends, but he cites them as Ali's instructions to his forces before the Battle of the Camel in the first years of the Upheaval (Baqillani, 236).

Two centuries later, the threats faced by the world of Islam were much more immanent. The defence of cultural identity became much more pressing a task for the politico-cultural community than its development. The same arguments on consolidating the internal front made by Ash'arites like Baqillani were made again by scholars of the Ashab Al-Hadith School, like Ibn Taymiyya. Only this time the school was less lenient with regards to interpretations that can twist the 'authentic meaning of the Quran', and more willing to declare war and impeach Imams who do not publicly adhere to such an 'orthodox' version of the religion, thus acquiring some features of the Kharijite rebel spirit, in giving the text superiority, over both human interpretation and political power.[15]

As mentioned earlier in note 12, Ibn Taymiyya (1263–1328) promoted the doctrine that only the literal understanding of the Holy Texts is allowed as opposed to dealing with the texts as metaphoric, thus allowing for interpretation. Due to the strict relation between textual interpretations and claims to power, intellectual freedom of interpretation meant more political fragmentation under the pressing threat of the Moguls and the Crusaders. Ashab Al-Hadith gave the highest priority to fighting the infidels; political fragmentation was thus seen as an act of treason and a factor of internal weakness. Forbidding mutiny was necessary especially when Muslim princes needed to impose illegal taxes, that is, taxes that were not sanctioned by the Quran and the Sunna, in order to fend off the invaders. The right of mutiny against a Muslim ruler was forbidden just as acquiescence under a non-Muslim ruler was forbidden. Thus Ibn Taymiyya's famous argument that a ruler who kills or taxes unjustly could be forgiven if that was for the better of the Muslims, yet if he did not pray five times a day, which means he stopped being a Muslim, he is to be killed (see Ibn Taymiyya and the citations from the sayings of the Prophet to this effect, *Al-Muntaqa*, 32, 66–7). The difference between this school and the original Murji'ite School is that Ashab Al-Hadith were much less lenient on issues of worship and rituals than the Murji'ites. The Muslim ruler had to show and prove his Islamism by all possible means and at all times and there could be no forgiveness of a Muslim ruler who broke the rules of religion or allied himself with infidels against Muslims.

Nonetheless, even in cases where Imams are impeached, Ibn Taymiyya adheres to the common Sunni position that the Umma

15. It should be remembered that the Murji'ites gave political leaders the benefit of the doubt and did not allow for rebellion against them in case they twisted the meaning of the religion, as long as they stayed declaredly Muslims. The Ash'arites followed suit, though Baqillani stated that in the case of civil war, Sunni scholars should support the Sunni candidate. To Ibn Taymiyya and later to the Wahhabis, acquiescence to heretical Imams was much less tolerated.

stays in existence, and that special measures are taken to differentiate civil war from war with non-Muslims (Ibn Tyamiyyah, *Al-Muntaqa*, 64). He also unhesitating falls into the same contradiction seen in Baqillani, when he lists civil war as a means by which consensus can be achieved (ibid., 62).

Accordingly, in all three major sects of Islam, the absence of the Imam, or having two Imams, whether in their executive or symbolic capacities, does not mean the absence of the Umma or the creation of another Umma. However, the legitimacy of the Imam depends on his following of the Quran and the Sunna. In all sects the authority of the Imam has to be based on some interpretation of the Quran, and since the Quran is common to all Muslims, any Imam will have to address, as his constituency, all of the Muslim community, not only those under his actual jurisdiction. It also follows that it would be the right of any Muslim scholar, under or outside that Imam's jurisdiction, to revise the interpretation on which the Imam has based his legitimacy, and thus potentially delegitimize him. A scholar from Baghdad, for example, could issue a religious edict that delegitimizes an Imam in Cairo or Cordova. Whether the conflict between him and his rivals is dormant or active, the Imam's political discourse is one that has to appeal to the whole Umma and it is according to that discourse that he is judged. Throughout Islamic history, there were many Caliphates and Imamates, while the Abbasids in Baghdad accepted, de-facto, the existence of the Umayyads in Spain and the Fatimids in Egypt, the Imams of each dynasty held the claim and title to be the princes of all believers[16] world-wide including the believers under the jurisdiction of their rivals. In other words, while each Imam had to have a claim to the whole Umma to become an Imam, the Umma did not have to have a unanimous acceptance of one Imam to become an Umma.

While the Murji'ites, the Ash'arites as well as Ashab Al-Hadith almost relieved the Imam from all internal opposition, they still established his legitimacy on him being a Muslim. Mu'tazilites added that, for the Imam to be legitimate, all the other moral criteria that

16. *Amir al-Mu'meneen* (The Prince [or commander] of Believers) is the official title for the supreme ruler of Muslims, it is with this title rather than the other two, Imam and Caliph, that he was to be addressed. The title is telling regarding the ruler's terms of reference. Moreover, using 'believers' rather than 'Muslims' in the title was intended to include non-Muslim believers who decided to be part of the Umma through contractual alliances, as will be shown below.

are to be deduced through reason from the self defining texts of the Quran and the Sunna. Both Murji'ites and Mu'tazilites, as well as the rest of the sects after the disappearance of the twelfth Shiite infallible, see the supreme worldly ruler as a tool for the welfare of the Umma, the whole Umma, regardless of the territorial boundaries of that supreme ruler's jurisdiction. The legitimacy of that Caliph/supreme ruler/Imam is thus derived from his following the Quran and Sunna and from his appeal to all Muslims. The legitimacy of any other ruler, who has a territorial jurisdiction, is derived from his following the Quran and the Sunna, as well as his following of an Imam, through which such a ruler would symbolize his appeal to the whole Umma.

This one-sided dependence of the political entity, the Imam, on the Umma (Quran, Sunna, the collective image of all Muslims, as interpreted by scholars in and outside the Imam's jurisdiction) is a crucial difference between the concepts of Umma and nation. It is also a crucial difference between the concept of Umma and Christendom as it gives executive political power to the Imam that the Pope did not have over the princes of Europe, and gives legislative power to Muslim interpreters, since interpreting the Quran was a natural right for any Muslim, which laymen in Europe did not have before the reform. Unlike the Pope, The Imam could not make rules of his own. As mentioned above he could only interpret the Holy Texts, and this he did in his capacity as a scholar and not as a ruler. Theoretically his interpretation held no more authority than any other.[17]

The Umma and the Dawla

The above section on the relation between the Umma and the Imam was necessary despite its length, in order to clarify the relation between Umma and Dawla. Etymologically Dawla means term, turn and shift. It stems from the verb *dal* which morphologically, as well as semantically, falls between the verb *dar* (to rotate) and verb *zal* (to go away, or fall). Temporality and succession are thus essential connotations for the meaning of Dawla. Anything that is circulated from one hand to another is a Dawla, the verb of circulating currency

17. It should be noted that the above-mentioned books, especially Mawardi, Baqillani and Ibn Taymiyya, on the Sunni side, and Kulaini and Al-Mufid on the Shiite side, as well as the historical narratives of Ibn Hisham, Tabari and Ibn Al-Athir, were and still are the classical references in the main centres of Islamic learning in the Arab world, mainly in the Sunni Azhar of Cairo and the Shiite Hawza of Najaf in Iraq.

is derived from the same stem (*Lisan al-Arab*, 5: 252–3). Dawla also means the condition of well-being, for one person or a group of persons, since such condition will sooner or later end, by the death of the people who are enjoying it, if not by any other means, and hence the poetic proverb *li-kulli zamanin dawlatun wa rijalu* (for every time its Dawla and its men). Unlike the European concept of the state, whose fixity is its determining feature, the temporality and lack of fixity are the main determining features of the Arabic concept of Dawla.

As a political concept, Dawla refers to any authoritative political arrangement. It is temporary, not territorially fixed and usually associated with the ruling elite. thus the Imam in his executive capacity together with the executive officers he assigns form a Dawla, the term could also be used to describe the authority of a vizier or an emir in the presence of an overarching Sultan, Imam or Caliph. This means that the Dawla is not necessarily associated with supreme power or sovereignty. This also refers to the fact that the Imam is not sovereign, that is, he cannot legislate at will, nor make and break rules of Sharia. That, as has been discussed above, he does together with others who interpret the texts of the Quran and Sunna, and among whom he has no advantage. It is the scholar rather than the ruler that is sovereign. Yet the sovereignty of that scholar is checked by all other Muslim scholars as well as by the boundaries of the texts he, as well as they, have to interpret. It should also be mentioned that the authority of a scholar depends solely on how convincing his interpretation of the Quran is to his audience, and that any Muslim can become a scholar and an interpreter of the texts since there is no church or any other institution to monopolize the right of interpretation in the Islamic tradition.[18] The concept that refers simultaneously to the texts and to those who interpret them is the concept of Umma discussed above.

Accordingly, the sovereignty lied in the Umma not in the Dawla; whether that Dawla ruled over all Muslims and thus was headed by a Caliph (Imam as an executive officer) or it was a smaller entity ruling over only a part of the Muslim community. Because the Dawla referred to any authoritative arrangement, it was used to refer to different levels of political authority, some of which had legal priority over others but none of which were sovereign. During the longer part of Islamic history there were many Dawlas within one Dawla. For example, the

---

18. This, of course, is truer in theory than in reality. Caliphs and Sultans in the Middle Ages, as well as modern state-sponsored religious institutions, have more power than individual scholars.

Abbasid and Ottoman Empires were referred to respectively as *al-Dawla al-Abbasiyya* and *al-Dawla al-Uthmaniyya*, both of which were headed by an Imam who claimed to be the successor of the Prophet (only in his executive capacity) and therefore the representative and guide of the Umma. Within these empires different levels of political arrangements were referred to as Dawlas, such as the Hamdanite, Buwaihid, Ekhsheedi, Ayyubid and Mamlouki Dawlas within *al-Dawla al-Abbasiyya*, and Dawlat Mohammad Ali and Dawlat Ali Bey al Kabir within *al-Dawla al-Uthmaniyya*, to name just a few.

As mentioned above, the heads of the imperial Dawlas who claimed to represent the whole Umma, had to derive their legitimacy directly from it, that is from the texts of the Quran and the Sunna and the interpretations held by a body of scholars which are addressed to all Muslims. The heads of the smaller Dawlas within the virtual or nominal authority of the imperial Dawla still had to derive their legitimacy from the whole Umma; however, they did that indirectly by claiming to be following the Imam, head of the encompassing imperial Dawla. For example, the Abbasid Dawla derived its legitimacy directly from the Umma, that is, from a certain interpretation of some of the inheritance verses in the Quran, as well as on a set of sayings by the Prophet showing the virtues of their ancestor al-Abbas, the Prophet's uncle.[19] Their claim was thus addressed to the whole Umma.[20] The other five Dawlas mentioned above derived their legitimacy from the Umma indirectly through the Abbasids by claiming to be delegated by the Abbasid Caliph in Baghdad to rule their respective domains in Syria, Egypt and Iran. In all those cases, the Umma rather than the Dawla was the ultimate focus of loyalty, the arena of legislation and the source of legitimacy even if

19. This is the discourse used by Abbasid Caliphs in the first Abbasid era. Later on the Ash'arite argument about consensus became the basis of Abbasid legitimacy. It should be noted, however, that even that Ash'arite argument was based on an understanding of the Quran, and thus was addressed to all Muslims inside or outside the borders of the Abbasid Empire.
20. The fact that every Imam had to claim to refer to the whole Umma to be an Imam, while the Umma did not have to accept one Imam to become an Umma, guaranteed balanced elements of fixity and change in the Islamic political existence. However, the failure of finding a peaceful mechanism with which two Imams can compete for ruling the whole Umma resulted in a series of civil wars that started from the time of the Prophet's third successor Othman. One reason for the absence of such peaceful mechanisms might have been technical, like the impossibility of holding general elections in vast medieval empires without modern means of transportation.

the Dawla was headed by an Imam. The Umma is a symbol, whether this symbol was personified by a living Imam, or it stayed textual and un-personified yet equally present (for example, like for that sub-sect of the Kharijites who refused the symbolism of the human guide/Imam, stating that there was enough guidance in the texts and that the Quran was the only Imam, or in cases of civil war or truce between two competing Imams). Those systems of symbols have the power to legitimize or delegitimize any political authority, any Dawla, including that of the Imam/Caliph himself.

The Dawla could thus rule over all Muslims or over a portion of them, but in all cases it should derive its legitimacy from all Muslims not only from those under its jurisdiction. It should be remembered that this system is a natural outcome of an epistemology based on metaphor and poetic texts. Since the Umma was created by and in the Quran, which is a metaphorical text, how the Umma should express itself politically was a matter of interpretation of that metaphorical image. Roughly speaking, since the nation was seen as a product of nature and therefore 'a fact', the state was seen as a product of science. On the other hand, since the Umma was a metaphor, the Dawla was the product of interpretation, giving it a much larger structural flexibility and tolerance. A State inside a state is an unacceptable condition in a world of nation-states; a Dawla inside a Dawla was quite usual and more or less the norm throughout the best part of Islamic history.

It has been mentioned above that all Islamic sects, ranging from the Murji'ites and Ashab Al-Hadith whose scholars gave absolute power to the Imam, to the Kharijites whose whole political existence depended on the right and duty to rebel against an unjust Imam, agree that the Imam is a tool for the welfare of the Umma. The Murji'ites and Ashab Al-Hadith base their argument of accepting whatever the Imam does on the assumption that anarchy is worse for the Umma than a tyrant, rather than any theory of divine right. It is quite similar to the Hobbesian version of the theory of social contract.[21] The same

21. The main difference however between the creation of a Dawla to guarantee the welfare of the Umma on the one hand and social contract theories on the other, is that the creation of the Dawla does not come as an alternative to a state of nature, for the creation of the Umma precedes that of the Dawla, that is, Muslims would accept the principles and laws of communal life expressed in the Quran before creating a political institution to protect such laws. Moreover, their political identity does not stem from creating such a political institution, or even their desire to create one. As discussed above, this is basically the main difference between the concepts Dawla and state and Umma and nation.

is true for the Dawla; it is a temporary political arrangement whose function is to guarantee the protection and welfare of the Umma, regardless of its local boundaries.

This utilitarian nature of the Dawla as a tool could be traced back to the origin of the first Dawla in Islam. In the first political document signed in Islam between the Prophet and the people of Medina, the first Dawla was founded. Some modernist scholars consider the document an establishment of the Islamic Umma rather than the Islamic Dawla (for example, see Wendell, 42). However, as mentioned above, given the definition of the Umma, it predated the existence of any political arrangement. The Muslim Umma, theoretically, came to existence the day the Prophet perceived of himself as following a unique quest, and defined himself by pursuing it. By the time the Hijra to Medina took place, there was already a Muslim Umma following an ideal (Imam) embodied in the texts of the Quran and the person of the Prophet. The document signed in Medina established an institutionalized political arrangement that would guarantee the protection, expansion and welfare of the nascent immigrating Umma.

In The name of God the all Mighty the All Merciful:

This is the writing of Mohammad the Prophet, between the Believers and Muslims from Quraysh and [those from] Yathrib, and whoever followed them, joined them and fought along their side,

That of all people they are one Umma.[22] (*Ummatun Wahidatun min duni'l-nas*)

The pious believers are against whoever commits a crime amongst them, or seeks to do injustice, sin, aggression, or corruption among believers, even if he was one of their sons.

No believer is to kill another believer in revenge for an infidel, and no believer should help an infidel against a believer,

and that the trust of God is one....

22. The phrase *Ummatun Wahidatun min duni'l-nas*, here translated as 'of all people they are one Umma', has been translated by W. Montgomery Watt as 'one community distinct from (other) people' (Watt, W. Montgomery. *Islam and the Integration of Society*. London: Routledge and Kegan Paul, 1961: 221), and by A. Guillaume as: 'one community to the exclusion of all men' (Ibn Ishaq. *The Life of Muhammad*. Trans. Alfred Guillaume. London: Oxford University Press, 1955: 232), both also quoted in Wendell, 1972: 35, notes 29 and 30.

Believers are one another's allies vis-à-vis the rest of the world, and whoever
follows us of the Jews would be helped and supported and they are not to be
oppressed.

The peace of the believers is one; no believer is to make peace without the
consent of other believers when at war, unless they agree on that fairly.

And believers should take revenge for one another for their blood shed in
the way of God.

And whoever kills a believer and is proven to have done so in purpose and
in aggression should be killed in return unless the victim's relatives agree to a
settlement....

No believer, of who have accepted what is in this document and who believed
in God and in the Last Day, can help a criminal nor protect him, and whoever
does that will endure God's curse and wrath in the Day of Resurrection....

And whatever you disagree upon, you refer it to God the almighty [the Quran]
and to Mohammad....

And the Jews of *Bani 'awf* are an Umma with the believers [could also be
translated as form an Umma along side the believers], Jews have their *din*
[religion-tradition] and to the Muslims their *din* ... except for those who commit
an aggression or a sin, for they should not endanger but themselves and their
households ... and to the Jews of *Bani Najjar* the same rights of the Jews of
Bani 'awf....

And the friends and allies of the Jews are like the Jews regarding rights, and
that no one of them is to leave without the permission of Mohammad, and
whoever cheats or deceives, would only endanger himself and his family, except
in case of aggression [in case of all out war between the Jews and the Prophet]...
and that Jews and Muslims are allies against whoever fights against the people
of this document, and that they will defend Yathrib [Medina],

And that Mohammad is the Messenger of God.

(Ibn Hisham, 2: 109–12, emphasis mine)

The document shows how the Dawla was designed to be a tool for
the service of the Umma. It is an institutional imposer of threats and
provider of incentives for non-Muslims either to join or to be allies
of the community of Muslims. Nevertheless, it *does not define Islam.*
The first article in this document, I expect, was the one for which
some western scholars came up with the understanding that the
document established the Islamic Umma. In defining the believers
from Quraysh (the Prophet's tribe) and those from Yathrib (Medina)
as an Umma, the document was establishing an already existing
fact rather than creating a new entity. In the rest of the document,
the political implications for joining the Umma, forging an alliance

with it, or fighting against it, were set. This political arrangement that functions to protect and expand the community of Muslims is the Dawla.

For example, including 'whoever follows them [the believers] and joins them and fights along their side' in the definition of the Umma, opens the door for people, accepting the authority of Mohammad or his followers, to be part of the Umma, and enjoy its political and military protection, without having necessarily to change their traditions or manners of worship. This is another difference between Umma and Christendom, where a non-Muslim, provided he offers full political allegiance in times of peace and war to Muslims, is considered part of the Umma. This is emphasized by the article on the Jews of *Bani 'awf* and the other tribes listed in the document.

The ambiguity of the expression 'they form an Umma with [or alongside] the believers' referring to the Jews, indicates the position of the Scripturaries (People of the Scripture; Christians and Jews), where they are not considered infidels, nor are they considered, in terms of worship, Muslims. If they fight alongside the Muslims, and join them, they are considered part of the Umma, if they do not, they are not.

The article that no infidel should be made an ally against a believer and that no believer should be killed in revenge for an infidel was an offer of security for other tribes either embracing Islam or joining the Umma by allying themselves with Muslims yet not necessarily embracing the faith. This article had been a tribal law, where a member of a given tribe A cannot ally himself with tribe B against his own tribe. This is the ethic of *Assabiyya* on which Ibn Khaldoun[23] built his whole thesis about Bedouin forms of power. Unlike the pre-Islamic Arab tribes, however, one could join this new tribe of Muslims. If an Arab from the tribe of Taghlib, for example, was under a constant threat from the tribe of Bakr he cannot become a member of Bakr

23. Abdul Rahman Ibn Khaldoun, a fourteenth-century historian and sociologist, was born in Seville in Arab Spain, and died in Cairo under Mamlouk Rule. He is best known for his theory on 'Assabiyya' tribal solidarity. He argued that such an ethic developed because of the nomadic forms of production and social organization, and that it enabled nomads to invade settled societies, at which point they gradually turn into settled communities themselves, allowing tribal bonds to loosen, forming a specialized economy, where defense is delegated to mercenary forces, thus making them vulnerable to fresh nomadic invasions.

to avoid that threat. The only way to avoid it is for the whole tribe of Taghlib to forge an alliance with the tribe of Bakr. Such alliances would usually fall at the first quarrel over the control of oases or grazing lands.[24] If the same Arab from Taghlib was under a threat of the Muslim Dawla, he could join a confederation of Muslim tribes and thus be secure and protected as far as they were concerned. Moreover, he could do this on an individual basis without having to bring his whole tribe to the alliance as was the case in traditional, fragile tribal confederations. The Dawla thus offered an opportunity of security to all who joined it, as an incentive to embrace Islam. The Dawla was to create an offer of protection for whoever decided to join the Umma rather than to create a threat to those who decided not to, since the threat to those who decided not to join was there before the Dawla. The threat posed to non-Muslim tribes by non-Muslim Khazraj, Aws and Quraysh,[25] (the three major tribes that became the first Muslims) was greater than that posed to them by the same tribes once they became Muslim. Because, before Islam, none of those subject to the threat could become a Khazraji, an Awsi or a Qurayshi in order to avoid the threat. After the establishment of the Dawla, however, people could in fact avoid it by either embracing Islam or declaring their alliance with Muslims on individual basis.

The above meant the creation of new forms of tribes in the Arabian Peninsula, yet one whose raids would now have moral legitimacy, and other tribes would have the choice either to ally themselves with the Muslims, and thus fall under the category of 'those who followed them and fought along their side', or to embrace Islam, thus falling under the category of 'believers'. The first meant the increase in the number of their allies and the second meant the increase in the numbers of Muslims; the first step meant protection and the second

24. The cousin tribes of Taghlib and Bakr are known in Arabic Literature and Pre-Islamic History for the epic 40 years' war they fought against one another. The war is said to have been caused by a camel owned by the tribe of Bakr grazing in an oasis owned by the King of Taghlib without permission. The King killed the camel; a man from the tribe of Bakr killed the king for the insult, signaling the beginning of the war. While the story belongs more to the literary tradition than to actual history, the tribal confederacies and alliances, usually forged between related tribes, frequently fell apart over grazing lands; the story of the unfortunate camel is a literary equivalent of the recurring historical phenomenon.

25. Aws and Khazraj were the two tribes ruling Medina and among the first Arabs to embrace Islam; Quraysh is the Prophet's tribe.

expansion. In a sense, the Dawla was created to protect and enlarge the Umma, not the other way around.

However, the document itself became one of the defining aspects of the Umma. It is part of the life of the Prophet and the document is thus part of the Hadith and Sunna (the sayings of the Prophet and his way in life). The above design of the Dawla became part of the textual definition of the Umma; an ideal which should be followed by Muslims as part of their identity. Any Dawla that the Umma produces later will have to conform to the principles of this Dawla led by the Prophet. Here, just like the Prophet himself, and the twelve Shiite Imams, a living existence became a text, a system of symbols with a power to legitimize and delegitimize other existences. The Dawla in Medina was just that, a Dawla. Its boundaries, its laws, its form of military and civil government vanished. In the final analysis it was just a Dawla defined by its temporality and lack of fixity. However, this existence turned into an ideal which, like any ideal, is to be followed but never attained. A later Dawla is not expected by Muslims to be identical to that of the Prophet but it is expected to hold it as an ideal to follow, and is judged accordingly. This provides an element of fixity and identity among all Islamic Dawlas. On the other hand, since this Dawla of the Prophet has turned into text, it is subject to different interpretations, which is the task of the different Muslim scholars. This provides an element of diversity and plurality. Political Islamic history could be seen as a result of the interaction of these two factors, where Dawlas come and go, fight and make peace and differ greatly from one another, yet they have to maintain the claim of pursuing the same ideal example.

The Implications of the Difference

In a sentence, while the nation-state is the end and full expression of the nation, the Umma is the end and purpose of the Dawla. While a state can make a nation, a Dawla, by definition, cannot make an Umma.

It is not necessary for a group of people to be called an Umma to desire living under the authority of one government. Rather, a group of people are to be called an Umma if they demanded each government ruling over any portion of them to be accountable to the whole group, not only to that portion of the group under its jurisdiction. The Dawla is a temporary authority structure whose reference is the whole Umma rather than the people under its jurisdiction. A fixed territory and sovereignty are not necessary conditions for any power structure to be called a Dawla.

For example, while the state of the Taliban fell in 2001, their Dawla did not; while state power in Lebanon has always been in doubt, Hezballah's political existence in southern Lebanon can easily be called a powerful legitimate Dawla according to the above medieval definitions. Of course, stating that such organizations regard the whole Islamic Umma to be their point of reference does not necessarily mean that the Umma considers them to be its exclusive representatives. But, as mentioned above, the Umma does not have to recognize the authority of any given Imam (supreme head of a Dawla) to become an Umma, while any given Imam has to claim that he appeals to the whole Umma to become an Imam. This applies to all Dawlas; the above mentioned organizations must claim the whole Umma to be their reference, in order to gain any degree of legitimacy.[26]

The Dawla is the term, the shift, it is the state of well being, which is defined by its temporality, if only because of the death of those who are enjoying it. In Arabic usage Dawla is not connected to the land, rather it is connected to the ruling family or the ruling Umma, that is people of the same creed, religion, ideology, example, ideal, purpose and direction. There are no significant references to *Dawlat Al-Iraq*, or *Dawlat Al-Sham*, (the states of Iraq and greater Syria respectively) in pre-colonial Arabic usage. There is very little territoriality in the definition of the Dawla; the Dawla is the people who rule, and the political arrangements that bring them to power.

While the Umma is an ideal, example, purpose and direction that is permanent, and that, theoretically, demands that political bodies serve Islam as an idea and Muslims as people in return for legitimacy, the Dawla is a temporary arrangement that serves the ideal of the Umma, and its legitimacy is measured by serving those ideals, observing the teachings of Islam and the welfare of all Muslims, not only those under its authority. The survival of the Dawla is thus a utilitarian arrangement, a means rather than an end in itself.

The above is different from the papacy and the states of medieval Europe in the sense that there was nothing celestial in the Caliph, neither could the Caliph legislate. Virtually he had no religious powers; he could not ban people from having their own interpreta-

26. Despite heavy reference to its Lebanese identity, Hezballah's official discourse maintains that Lebanese national interests are and must be congruent with those of the whole Umma.

tions of religious texts. His was mainly an executive power, and while the Caliph could be theoretically or actually non-existent, the Umma still existed. The Caliph and the provincial princes and sultans were not seen as two kinds of authority, celestial and temporal, they were all of this world and they were both part of the same institution called the Umma. The Umma then could exist with or without a Caliph, in one Dawla or in many Dawlas. The Umma, as an idea, or as the purpose beyond the Dawla always exists, not in defining matters of worship, but in defining matters of political identity and relation with the other. The legitimacy of the Dawla then is measured not by the welfare the Dawla provides to its own inhabitants regardless of the rest of the Muslims or regardless of the ideal image of the Umma, rather it is measured by both, the welfare of its inhabitants as well as the welfare of other Muslims and the service of that ideal image. Thus, in theory, every Dawla in Islamic history had to be, or at least had to claim to be, ideological.

It is clear that such a definition of 'national interests' is rather vague and could amount in actual practice to nullity, since any elite at the top of any political arrangement, that is, any Dawla, can claim that its course of action is in the best interest of the Umma, and that the concerned elite is the most legitimate according to certain interpretations of the Quran and the Sunna. This is especially true given that up until the late twentieth century the two dominant sects, Ash'arite Sunnism and Twelvist Shiism, practically freed Muslim rulers from being susceptible to moral scrutiny and political mutiny by their subjects. Any policy could pass for legitimate and in the best interest of the Umma. However, while the Umma-Dawla system gives ultimate flexibility to Muslim kings and leaders in shaping their policies and competing with one another, it is far from vague or ineffective when it comes to Muslim versus non-Muslim conflicts. Then, the non-Muslim is a paramount threat and should be deterred and driven back. The most conservative and most 'liberal' Islamic sects agree on the illegitimacy of non-Muslim rule over Muslims, and the illegitimacy of any alliance between Muslims and non-Muslims against a third Muslim party. Such understanding undermines all treaties that are held between Muslims and 'infidels' against other Muslims. The argument here is not that such alliances did not take place in 14 centuries of Islamic history, nor that they were rare; however, the argument is that every time they happened they had a delegitimizing effect to different degrees.

The above creed is embedded in the Quran and the Sunna, and could be traced in the thought of more recent Islamic thinkers.

The Umma, as mentioned above, is an image, a construct that influences people's behaviour and around which emotions are rallied. The colonial redefinition of Arabs and Muslims into nation-states created a situation were Arabs and Muslims had two contradictory foci of loyalty, two mutually exclusive images to serve; one was the colonially imposed focus of loyalty, the nation state: Egypt, Jordan, Palestine, Qatar, Syria, Lebanon, etc and so on, and the other was the Umma. The Dawla of the Egyptians is completely different from the state of Egypt, it is a tool, a means to an end which is the Umma, while the colonially imposed nation-state of Egypt, is expected to be the end and purpose of a colonially constructed Egyptian nation.

Umma and Dawla in the Discourse of the Non-state Islamic Organizations

This section is not a detailed account of the history of Islamic movements; such a work has been done by many historians, and therefore falls outside the scope of this book. Rather, the purpose of this section is to mention a number of examples, from the nineteenth century up until today, of the discourses of Islamic non-state actors that indicate that they view themselves as Dawlas whose allegiance lies with the whole Umma. The following lines provide only an example of the discourse of various Islamic movements in the Middle East. While not a detailed study of the discourse of such movements, this section should suffice to provide the reader with keys that might help him understand the sense of identity expressed in such discourses. To avoid redundancy, I opted not to indulge in lengthy quotations from the speeches by the leaders of such organizations.

It might be curious why, if my main purpose was to understand the sense of identity of contemporary political actors in the Middle East, I spent more time explaining the theological trends in medieval Islam than dealing directly with the discourses of those contemporary political actors. It might also be curious why I am making the leap from the late thirteenth century up to the late nineteenth as if nothing much had happened in the 600 years in between.

The answer to the first question is simple; the purpose of this book is to explain rather than describe contemporary Islamic non-state organizations. It shall be shown that such organizations, which enjoy enough popularity in the Middle East for them to exist, recruit and operate throughout the region, see themselves as Dawlas in service of the whole Umma; non-territorial arrangements whose loyalty, allegiance and accountability are to all Muslim. They do not attempt to control the state apparatus, and if they do, they use it, or at least claim to be using it, not in the narrow interests of the citizens of that state, but in the interest of all Muslims. Not only did the political culture in which identity is based on the concept of the Umma define their political discourse, sometimes it also defined their structure and method of operations. Non-modern forms, that is, a mix of pre- and post-modern forms of organization, communication, and rules of conflict are applied. Such modes of thought and action cannot be understood without bearing in mind cultural norms, described above, even if they initially seem irrelevant.

It should be remembered that the paradigm in which such organizations operate includes an epistemology based on the interpretation of metaphor and the acceptance of an argument's truth because of its aesthetic or rhetorical value. Since the Umma is a text, an image, the interpretations of which are the Dawlas, the concerned organizations see themselves as interpretations, as manifestations of the same political entity. Therefore they lack the unitary pyramidical structure of traditional liberation or terrorist organizations. Some, like Hezballah and Hamas, have a strong structure, yet such a structure forms and disperses on call, where members of the organization conduct their civilian lives normally and are thus invisible until they are summoned for action. The whole structure is dissolved in society, yet crystallizes at will. Other organizations depend on a narrative, a number of arguments and impressions that are generated by everything from news bulletins to Friday prayers, communicated through the internet or through word of mouth. When rings of independent recruits are formed they are allowed much more freedom in decision making, within the network, than is the case with traditional terrorist or liberation organizations. This makes tracking down members much more difficult, as well as establishing clear lines of command and leadership.

As for the answer to the second question, regarding the five-century leap, I mentioned at the beginning of this book that at any one point in time people live in the shadow of ideas that are temporarily believed to be eternal. We have no way to prove that the above description of Islamic history and political thought was in fact true, but it is the image that is now predominant and effective in the minds and hearts of many Middle Eastern thinkers and politicians as expressed in their discourses. Rather than being a study of the past, the chapters on the formation of the canon, and the definitions of

Umma and Dawla, are a study of the present image of that past. Most of the violent non-state Islamic organizations that make the headlines today either operate in the Arab world or are led by people from the Arab world. And yes, in the Arab world, not in Iran, India or Turkey, but in the Arab heartlands of Islam, the current image is that the seven centuries between the fall of Baghdad and the modern era, were dark ages, characterized by intellectual and theological dormancy. Unlike what a number of Middle East specialists in Western Europe and North America usually think, very few in the Arab World see the Ottoman sieges of Vienna in the seventeenth century to have been the peak of Islamic civilization. It is the Abbasid Haroun Al-Rashid, rather than Ottoman Suleiman the Magnificent who's depicted in politics, as well as in arts and fiction, to be the symbol of the Golden Age. Moreover, to most Islamists, Arabs and non-Arabs alike, not even the Abbasids, but rather the short-lived quasi-republic led by the four elected successors of the Prophet, truly represented Islam's golden age. Therefore, as shall be shown below, the parts on the development of the Islamic canon up until the late Abbasid era were necessary to understand the references made in today's political discourses. They are definitely much more necessary for understanding today's political Islam than any theological development in the five centuries between Ibn Taymiyya and Ibn Abdel Wahhab.

For example, the two concepts could be found abundantly in the works of Jamaludin Al-Afghani. Afghani, also known as Jamaludin Al-Asadabadi, was a Persian-born Muslim thinker and agitator who travelled throughout the Muslim world in the late nineteenth century calling for solidarity and resistance against European colonialism. He is considered the intellectual godfather of many modern Islamic movements from the Muslim Brothers, established in Egypt in 1920s, to Al-Qaeda, established in Afghanistan in the 1990s. Some students of Middle Eastern political history interpret Afghani's ideas as a form of Islamic nationalism, that is, a call for some sort of Islamic political unity. They then interpret the later tension in his relation with the Ottoman Sultan as a sign of a change in his political view (for example, see Tibi 1990: 164–70). This is somewhat inaccurate; it involves reading Afghani through the lenses of European political terminology. What Afghani actually called for was the Islamic Bond (*Al-Rabita Al-Islamiyya*), the magazine he published while in exile in France was also called the Strongest Bond (*Al-Urwa Al-Wuthqa*). Both terms referred to his view that religion was the strongest political bond as opposed to nationalism. His main argument was not that

Muslim princes should necessarily act to form a united Muslim nation state; rather, they have to act, each in his own princedom, in the best interest of all Muslims regardless of their place of residence or citizenship. This argument is clear in that in sets the whole Muslim community as the point of reference, focus of loyalty and source of legitimacy for any individual Muslim prince regardless of the boundaries of his princedom. Afghani fell short of formulating the definition of the concepts of the Umma and the Dawla in the abstract wording presented in this chapter, yet it is quite easy to discern the meanings of the two concepts in his writings. The fact that he did not spend much time on the theoretical work of sculpting abstract definitions for the two concepts could be attributed to him taking the meanings for granted. After all, he was writing around the end of the nineteenth century when the meanings of those two words (Umma and Dawla) were still in the process of being changed to correspond to their European counterparts.[27]

The Muslim Brothers of the early twentieth century fully subscribed to Afghani's ideas on nationalism and Islamism. Apart from the Egyptian Nationalist Wafd Party, The Brothers might be the strongest and most important dissident movement in Egypt since its foundation in 1927 and up until Nasser's revolution in 1952. One could also safely say, despite the absence of accurate statistics, that they have been the largest civil, non-military, Islamic political organization in the Middle East for the rest of the twentieth century. Organization-wise, the Muslim Brothers was the mother movement of many Islamic groups that appeared later in the twentieth century, for example, the Islamic Group and the Islamic Jihad in Egypt, the latter of which became the international Islamic Jihad organization led by Ayman Zawahiri, who merged with Osama Bin Laden's Al-Qaeda in the 1990s; the Muslim Brothers in Syria, Lebanon, Jordan; and the Muslim Brothers in Palestine who later became the Islamic Resistance Movement (Harakat Al-Muqawama Al-Islamiyya: Hamas). In terms of ideology, the Muslim Brothers is one of two movements

27. See his article published in *Al-Urwa Al-Wuthqa*, 'Al-Jinsiyya wa Al-Diyana Al-Islamiyya' (nationality and the faith of Islam) and 'Madi Al-Umma wa Haderuha wa Ilaju Ilaliha' (The Umma's past and present and the remedy of its ailments) in Afghani, 4: 103–15. It is also noteworthy that, in an article titled 'Al-Khilafa' (the Caliphate), he summarizes the positions of Islamic sects on the issue of the Imamate in a manner quite congruent with the account provided here (Afghani, 4: 83). These three articles were published between March and October 1884.

to which most Sunni Islamic movements in the second half of the twentieth century Arab World, whether peaceful or violent, can be traced back, the other one being Wahhabism.

The Muslim Brothers belong to the tradition of *Salafiyya*,[28] which could be translated into the English 'Ancestor-ism'. The first argument held by this category of Islamic schools of thought is that the people's understanding of religion has been blurred by a set of superstitions and rituals that were not sanctioned by the Quran or the Hadith (sayings of the Prophet), nor by the biographies of the Companions. Salafis argued that no one could interpret the Holy Texts better than the Prophet, and no one could understand the Prophet's interpretation of the texts, as well as the meanings of his own words and deeds, better than the Prophet's Companions. The diversity of interpretations that created the great debates of medieval Islamic history was then substituted by an expanding body of texts; the Quran, the Hadith, the Prophet's *Seera* (his biography), and the biographies of his companions. In totality, those people were called the righteous ancestors (*Al-Salaf Al-Salih*), that is, the first Muslims whose understanding of the religion was the purest and least misguided.

One reason behind, and a consequence of, making such an argument is a drive to have a unified understanding of Islam among all Muslims by giving priority to the texts and figures on whose authority they all agree.

Another cardinal argument in the *Salafiyya* movement is the illegitimacy of any legislation that is not derived from the Quran and the Sharia. The idea that a state's constitution is the text of highest legal authority is unacceptable to Salafis, for that position is occupied by the Quran. Constitutions, if they are at all needed, are only administrative directives, whose interpretation and application should be subordinate to the interpretations of the Quran. In case the two texts are in conflict, the rule of the Quran and the Sharia overcomes that of the constitution and any positive body of laws that is derived from it.

28. *Salafiyya* here refers to a trend in Islamic political thought prevalent in the Middle East since the first fall of Baghdad in 1258. As a movement, it is the political expression of the theological school of Ashab Al-Hadith championed by Ibn Taymiyya, discussed above. The term as used here does not refer to the movement endorsed by Mohammad Rashid Rida, the Syrian student of Jamaludin Al-Afghani, in the first half of the twentieth century, though Rida's ideas correspond with the mainstream Salafi thought from which he took the name.

The position of the Muslim Brothers on the issue of the Umma is derived from this argument. Since the Quran is the highest constitution of all, all Muslims belong to the same political entity. As such, Muslims should require any government ruling over any portion of them to abide by the rulings of the same 'constitutional' text. Since each Muslim state derives its legitimacy from a 'constitution' that applies to all Muslims, the issue of whether the state actually abides by the rulings of the Quran or not is judged by all Muslims, not only by the Muslims under that state's jurisdiction. The reference of the state, then, is not its people; rather, it is the Quran as interpreted and understood by most, if not all, Muslims. Likewise, the loyalty of a citizen of an Islamic state does not lie in that state; rather, his or her loyalty is to the Muslim Umma, here meaning both the abstract principles of a textual guide-book, the Quran, and the multitude of Muslims who interpret such a text and follow its teachings.

Thus, just like in the writings of Afghani, the Muslim Brothers saw Islam as a political bond that transcends rather than substitutes modern states.[29]

As will be discussed later in the chapter on Arab nationalism, both Islamists and Arab nationalists found some congruence between the modern ideologies of nationalism and the ideas of the fourteenth-century Arab sociologist Ibn Khaldoun. Ibn Khaldoun established the concept of Assabiyya, which translates into something like the bond of kinship or tribal solidarity. To Ibn Khaldoun the ethic of Assabiyya had no moral or ideological content, it just meant that members of the same tribe or alliance of tribes would stand for one another. Ibn Khaldoun then argued that the stronger the bond of kinship is among a certain group of people, the more political and military power they could yield. Arab nationalists saw in Ibn Khaldoun's ideas a non-religious, pre-colonial expression of Arabism. Islamists accepted this congruence, only to emphasize that, like Ibn Khaldoun's

29. For example, in one of his messages to the members of his organization, Hassan Banna, founder of the Muslim Brothers, wrote: 'Oh, Muslim Brothers, listen: You are not a charity society, nor a political party, nor an interest group with limited aims, rather, you are a new spirit that animates the heart of this Umma, and brings it to life in the Quran. You are a new light that rises and disperses the darkness of materialism by the knowledge of God and a thundering sound repeating the call of the Prophet ... if you were asked: "what are you calling for?" say: "we call for the Islam that was brought to us by Mohammad, and government is part of it, and freedom is one of its teachings". And, if you were told: "but this is politics!" say: "this is Islam and we do not recognize these differences" ...' (Banna 1992: 110)

Assabiyya, Arab nationalism was but a sheer emotional force that holds no moral content. It refers to a group's coherence, but not to its purpose and direction, neither does it suggest anything about its form of government. That moral and constitutional content can either be imported from Europe, in the form of either liberalism or socialism, producing the corresponding types of nationalistic ideologies, or it can come from Islam.

As such the nation-states created in the modern times, and the nationalisms that come with them, are seen by the Muslim Brothers and other Islamists as new tribes. The feelings of togetherness the members of such tribes have for one another are only useful if they were guided by religion, that is, by some interpretation of the Quran, thus making the allegiance of these citizens lie with the whole community of Muslims rather than with their newly founded nations. This means that, to the Muslim Brothers, modern states can only become legitimate if they were transformed into Dawlas, that is, if they ceased to be nation-states.

This position finds it roots in the accommodationism of the Ash'arite interpretation of Sunni Islam, while the modern nation-states were considered evil. Just like bad Imams or Sultans, they were to be accepted as legitimate as long as they professed their allegiance to Islam. In other words, as long as those rulers of colonially created nation-states in the Middle East allied themselves with the whole Umma, their nation-states were to be accepted as modern Dawlas, and therefore as legitimate expressions of Islamic political identity.

This stance that attempts to accommodate Islamic and modern institutions governed a lot of the Muslim Brothers' politics from the 1920s up until today. After all, the movement itself was one of city dwellers who wore western suits yet frequented mosques.

The same line of argument could be found in the discourse of more violent organizations such as Palestinian Hamas and Lebanese Hezballah. Hamas sprang out from the Gaza chapter of the Egyptian Muslim Brothers, while Hezballah was created by veterans of the Islamic Revolution in Iran. Both organizations have their frame of reference in movements that lie outside the borders of the modern entities of Palestine and Lebanon. The dilemma of these two movements is, however, that they are fighting Israeli occupation of their territories. Land and territory must therefore feature strongly in their discourse, yet they still need to derive their legitimacy from sources different from nationalism. They also need to accommodate other secular movements with significant power within their immediate fields of operation; Fateh is a secular movement that has been working under the banner of Palestinian and Arab nationalisms for the second half of the twentieth century, and Lebanon has many non-Muslim groups with their political parties and international backing.

Nonetheless, despite all the factors pushing Hamas and Hezballah towards moderation, their discourse stays perfectly Islamic. They argue that the 'national' interest of both Lebanon and Palestine cannot but be congruent with that of the rest of the Islamic Umma; thus they argue that the existence of the modern states of Lebanon, and the modern structures of the Palestine Liberation Organization and the Palestinian Authority, in and by themselves, are neither good nor bad. Rather, how these states/entities are used, how the Palestinian authority or the state of Lebanon behaves regarding the main issues that concern Muslims today, is what matters in legitimizing or delegitimizing their existence. It is worth mentioning that some Arab governments used the same argument in attempting to accommodate the existence of the modern colonially created nation-state with the existence of the Umma. This, for example, had been an essential part of Saudi Arabia's legitimizing discourse since the establishment of the Saudi Wahhabi Alliance 200 years ago. The modern state of Saudi Arabia, which is bound by international law to be responsible for its own citizens, presents itself as a Wahhabi Islamic Dawla whose presence is destined to serve the most righteous interpretation of the Islamic Holy Texts. The same goes for Iran, where the internationally recognized state of Iran is legitimized internally as the beacon of the right interpretation of Islam, as embodied in Khomeini's theory of the rule of the scholar. Any action that contradicts this political discourse severely damages the legitimacy of the said states inside and outside their borders; the positions of both countries on Iraq are good examples.

As for Al-Qaeda, the examples of their political discourse where the concepts of the Umma and Dawla play crucial roles are innumerable. To mention only two, in a tape broadcast on Al-Jazeera on 2 November 2004, Bin Laden spoke of his plan of 'bleeding America to bankruptcy'. He portrayed the invasion of Iraq and Afghanistan as a trap set by Al-Qaeda for the Americans. He also described America's motives behind the invasions as a quest for oil, dominance, and, significantly, 'the replacement of an old agent with a new puppet' ('Full Transcript of Bin Laden's speech', Al-Jazeera.net, archives, 2 November 2004). Three years later, Mustafa Abul Yazid, the commander of Al-Qaeda forces in Afghanistan, said in a tape broadcast on Al-Jazeera on

24 May 2007, that one of the main strategies of Al-Qaeda was to 'globalize' Jihad, meaning to drag the United States and 'its agent [Arab and Muslim] governments' into a long war of attrition that would overstretch the Superpower into bankruptcy and political, if not military, defeat. He argued that the plan was working well in Iraq and in Afghanistan; the occupation of those two territories then becomes a triumph rather than a defeat in the discourse of Al-Qaeda. This might as well be brushed aside by some observers as propaganda to make the organization look stronger than it actually is. Nonetheless, the fact that it can pass as efficient propaganda indicates that, within the discourse of the organization, and for the most part of its target audience, territory and nation-states are not important; the destruction of the modern states of Iraq and Afghanistan does not really mean anything more than having imperialism destroy its own creatures. In a sense, it removes the barrier created between the colonial powers and the colonized population. The modern states created by Britain and France, and maintained by the United States, as part of a post-World War Two international system, are but a reorganization of colonial dominance, where the people are organized into states, making them much more controllable.

Moreover, Al-Qaeda's argument also presents a post-modern understanding of authority and sovereignty; sovereignty in Iraq and Afghanistan does not lie in the hands of the Karzay or Maliki governments, nor does it lie in the hands of the Americans, because neither the US nor its installed local governments could in fact control the situation in the these countries. Sovereignty is thus reduced to its basic meaning, the will of a group of people to obey another group of people more than any other. As such the spokesman/commander of Al-Qaeda was arguing that within Iraq and Afghanistan, his organization was more sovereign than the officially recognized states. Of course, the arguments of Al-Qaeda are not quite accurate; within Iraq and Afghanistan the organization is far from being the supreme authority. Nonetheless, the purpose of this section is to show how the concept of the Umma and the Dawla is present in the discourses of a spectrum of Islamic organization ranging from the most moderate to the most violent.

Much of the public sentiment in the Arab world could be understood in the light of the above, where actions which would initially appear to be in the interests of the concerned Arab state would be highly unpopular, while actions which appear to be against its national interests would be extremely popular. Such reactions are described in the western media and sometimes in western academia as irrational residuals of the past. Some modern-day political discourses and practical policies, in the United States and Europe, echo nineteenth-century colonialists in concluding that more occupations, globalization, and economic dependence would 'educate' Muslims out of their 'medieval' political identity. According to some modernists a democratic nation-state should be imposed on Muslims. The only problem, however, is that democracy cannot be imposed; it is an argument of compulsory freedom as contradictory as dry water. This will only add oil to fire, since it was colonization in the first place that created the problem. Others (dependency school and the left in general) would explain the anti-systemic movements in the region as expressions of economic deprivation and dissatisfaction with the current system of social distribution of values. These views, while accurate in diagnosing some essential reasons of anger and dissent in the Middle East, fail to explain why such dissatisfaction expresses itself in terms of belonging to an Islamic or an Arab Umma rather than in terms of class allegiances. It is a historical fact that neither liberalism nor socialism came anywhere near the popularity of Islamism and Arabism in the Arab world, both of which revolve around the concept of the Umma. While part of the phenomenon could be actually related to physical deprivation, culture and history have to be taken into consideration to explain the expressions of such deprivation. Reducing people to their physical needs is equally dangerous, for depriving men and women from choosing their own political form of organization, and redefining them into borders drawn by their historical enemies, is also a kind of deprivation, which alone, results in anger and rebellion.

The paradox of the Arab Muslim state, then, is that its very independence is the expression of it being under the power of colonialism; its very sovereignty is the sign of its servitude.

3
The Precious Nothing
A Theoretical Framework

INTRODUCTION

As mentioned above, it is not the purpose of this book to write the history of what are now 59 Islamic states, from the moment when Twelvist Shiism and Ash'arite Sunnism became the dominant determinants of political culture in the thirteenth century up until the modern era. It will also not be possible to write a detailed history of the past 200 years of the said countries in order to trace the usage of the concepts of Umma and Dawla in the political discourses of every political actor in power or opposition. Rather, this book is an attempt to contextualize and explain the current phenomena of the failure of Muslim nation-states and the rise of non-territorial Muslim organizations in global politics.

The sense of identity expressed in the modern interpretation of the native culture having been discussed in the two previous chapters, I shall focus in the coming chapters on the senses of political identity introduced to the region through colonial encounters. There shall be two points of emphasis: first, that the nationalisms of the region, as theories, are derivatives of, rather than opposites to, the colonial discourse, and second, that the theoreticians and politicians of such nationalist movements where continuously attempting to find a compromise that reconciles their nationalisms with the native sense of identity that revolves around the Umma.

To make these points, however, I need to present a deductive theoretical framework which I am claiming applies to all 22 countries in the Arab world, and then test that framework on sample cases which I think are more indicative than others. This chapter will then be purely theoretical. It is an attempt to extend the post-colonial argument that colonialism is a process whereby the colonizer redefines the colonized, to include the very structure of the colonially created nation-state.

The main argument here is that the very entity the colonized attempt to liberate, the very national self they try to assert in opposition to the colonial power, is but a colonial construct, a means of control and a tool of oppression. When a white man comes to the shores of Africa and calls the Africans black, he occupies language, for they are not black at all, it is he who is pale. The next step, after calling them black, is drawing a boundary and naming the place, say Nigeria. When the people who find themselves lumped together inside that magical circle recognized by the international community as a legitimate border try to struggle for their independence, they seldom realize that they are struggling for a name that is not theirs and trying to liberate an institution that was created to deprive them of liberty. The independence of a certain colony, then, rather than being a moment of salvation, is but a moment of internalizing servitude and accepting the name given to the natives by their colonial master; it is a moment of celebrating the chains, winding them over one's head and calling them a crown.

In the following lines I show how the above argument is a logical corollary of the main tenets of post-colonial theory. Later on, I will show how this happened to Arabs as well, and that the argument can apply to local nationalisms whose definition of the homeland is congruent with the colonially created borders as is the case of Egyptian Nationalism, or ones that transcend such borders as in the case of pan-Arabism.

POST-COLONIALISM AND NATION-STATES, A REVIEW

The usage of *post-colonial* theory in political analysis has been less frequent than in other disciplines such as literature and criticism. Nevertheless, it might be feasible to apply concepts that are mainly concerned with cultural processes to their political expressions. Despite the diversity of works in the field, most of the founding fathers of post-colonial theory such as Fanon, Cabral, Said, and others, agree on two main points:

1. They agree that the colonial process creates an identity problem for the native; an identity manufactured by the colonial master is imposed on him, one that is defined by the relation of servitude and subordination to his colonial master. The process of decolonization thus necessitates the liberation of the native from this colonially imposed self image, and its replacement with another of his own.

2. Most post-colonial theorists are aware of the native's role in accomplishing the colonial plan. Power is as much seductive as it is coercive; there is always this 'Khaldounian' tendency to imitate the victor, and to accept his perception of reality, including his perception of the native.

While the logic of power ... is fundamentally coercive, its campaign is frequently seductive. We could say that power traverses the imponderable chasm between coercion and seduction through a variety of baffling self representations. While it may manifest itself in a show and application of force, it is equally likely to appear as the disinterested purveyor of cultural enlightenment and reform. Through this double representation, power offers itself both as a political limit and as a cultural possibility. If power is at once the qualitative gap between those who have it and those who must suffer it, it also designates an imaginative space that can be occupied, a cultural model that might be imitated and replicated. (Gandhi 1998: 14)

This is politically expressed through different forms of native authorities, which, while retaining some form of cultural legitimacy due to their 'nativeness', act as middle men between the colonial master and the native population, as well as agents of 'modernization', that is, catalysts in a process whose aim is to transform the native into an image of his colonial master. The process of decolonization involves the restructuring of the native society in a manner that guarantees a shift of power away from those upper classes of the native population that assimilate themselves culturally and politically to the colonial power.

These ideas are illuminating when studying the political conditions in third world states after independence. Yet I argue that they are incomplete. Most early post-colonial theorists, especially the ones discussed below, talk of national liberation without any redefinition of the nation. The people/masses they refer to when discussing culture and resistance are the masses of the concerned colony. The name, the boundaries and the very existence of the state they are wishing to liberate and to whose masses they refer, is a colonial construct, and thus a colonial tool to facilitate domination. I am going to elaborate on this point in the coming few lines dealing with writers such as Fanon, Cabral, Said, Mamdani and Alexander.

In *Black Skin, White Masks* (1967) as well as in *The Wretched of the Earth* (1961), Fanon argues that colonialism is a state of mind as well as a political reality. He differentiates between native responses to the colonial encounter ranging from assimilation to resistance.

While total assimilation proves impossible, Fanon differentiates between two types of cultural responses: one is an attempt to retain the pre-colonial culture/identity, and the other is a progressive move towards a new post-colonial culture that is born out of the very process of resistance. According to Fanon, the first choice is self-destructive. To him, culture consists of the ideal expressions of the present conditions and activities of a nation, thus there is no such thing as a return to some form of custom; the pre-colonial custom is but an image, 'mummified fragments', of which only exotic dresses and artifacts remain. 'Culture has never the translucidity of custom; it abhors all simplification. In its essence, it is opposed to custom, for custom is always the deterioration of culture' (1961: 42). Such appearances only help to legitimize native elites while allowing them to pursue pro-colonial practices, thus it is an aspect of indirect rule rather than liberation. 'Culture is that fluctuating movement which they [the masses] are just giving a shape to and which as soon as it has started, will be the signal for everything to be called into question' (ibid.). Therefore culture must be the ideal expression of anti-colonial struggle.

There is no fight for culture which can develop apart from popular struggle. To take an example, all those men and women who are fighting with their bare hands against French colonialism in Algeria are not by any means strangers to the national culture of Algeria. The national Algerian culture is taking on form and content as the battles are being fought out, in prison, under the guillotine and in every French outpost which is captured or destroyed. (Fanon 1961: 43)

Fanon, however, does not provide any more description of national culture other than being anti-colonial. The only answer he gives to the question of identity, the native's main question vis-à-vis the colonizer, is resistance. Good cultural identity then is defined by being anti-colonial and conducive to national liberation. If a practice of the past pre-colonial era proves useful in the present-day struggle for independence, then this practice ceases to be custom, and becomes part of the culture of resistance which is the cornerstone of identity. Similarly, if a practice imported from the colonizer proves useful in liberation it ceases to be an act of assimilation.

Yet Fanon falls into a contradiction. While he asserts that the struggle for liberation is the main factor in the identity of the colonized, and while he maintains that decolonization is a process that involves the rejection by the native of the native's image imposed by the colonizer, he implicitly accepts the colonizer's definition of the nation. For example, in the quotation above, while Fanon talks about the formation of culture as colonial institutions fall, he still refers to Algeria, which is in itself a colonially created constellation of institutions. He implicitly accepts a colonial definition of the people living in that area as Algerians rather than a set of other possible identities belonging to the past or to the future: Arabs, Muslims, Sunnis, Wahranis, Bejawis, Shawiyya, proletarians, global citizens and so on. He talks similarly of Senegal, and Guinea, 'There will never be such a thing as black culture because there is not a single politician who feels he has a vocation to bring black republics into being' (ibid.: 44). The 'republics' then define the domain of the realities, the response to which forms the post-colonial identity. But the 'republics' are colonial, not post-colonial. Fanon similarly deals with Arab states; he asserts that Arab nationalism is a 'marvelous hymn' that is nevertheless meaningless, since the realities of the Arab *states* link them much more to the Mediterranean than to one another (ibid.: 40). Fanon does not see that these states are one aspect of colonialism and that the Mediterranean identity is one suggested by the colonizer. Rather, he sees it as a part of the present reality out of which the culture of resistance has to emerge. This contradiction in Fanon's thought, between defining the identity as anti-colonial while accepting the colonial definition of identity, is characteristic of many anti- and post-colonial discourses, especially in the Middle East.

While Fanon defines post-colonial identity by anti-colonialism, Marxist Cabral adds a class perspective to it. To him, everything anti-colonial is necessarily anti-imperialist, and everything anti-imperialist is necessarily anti-capitalist. He agrees with Fanon that identity develops along with everyday reality. But reality, that is, the infrastructure of identity, is dichotomous, and this dichotomy is reflected in culture:

Culture, the fruit of history, reflects at every moment the material and spiritual reality of society ... from this we see that all culture is composed of essential and secondary elements, of strengths and weaknesses, of virtues and failings, of positive and negative aspects, of factors of progress and factors of stagnation or regression. (Cabral in Williams and Chrisman, 1993: 61)

While Fanon mentions the domestic bourgeoisie, the compradors, who act as middle men between the colonial power and the colonized, and mentions their assimilation or hopeless aspirations of assimilation with the metropolis as part of the colonial arrangement, Cabral deals with them as part of the historical struggle defining the identity of the colonized. They are the negative aspect of culture, because their presence and their institutions of native authority are the superstructural expressions of an infrastructural relation of economic dominance within the colonized population. They become cultural agents of colonialism, itself a form of exploitation. Thus the struggle for independence must be a struggle against them as well as against the colonial power, making it a class as well as a national struggle. If the outcome of this class struggle is not determined by the process of liberation, the post-colonial state runs the risk of neo-colonialism under the rule of those installed and supported by the colonial power:

Recognizing this reality [the class chasm within the colonized society], the colonizer who represses or inhibits significant cultural activity on the part of the masses at the base of the social pyramid strengthens and protects the prestige and the cultural influence of the ruling class at the summit. The colonizer installs chiefs who support him and who are to some degree accepted by the masses; he gives these chiefs material privileges such as education for their eldest children, creates chiefdoms where they did not exist before...All this does not make it impossible that, among these ruling classes, there may be individuals or groups of individuals who join the liberation movement.... Preserving deep down the cultural prejudices of their class, individuals in this category generally see in the liberation movement the only valid means, using the sacrifices of the masses, to eliminate colonial repression of their own class and to re-establish in this way their complete political and cultural domination of the people. (Cabral in ibid.: 58)

While Cabral goes one step further than Fanon in determining the direction of the anti-colonial identity, he follows Marx and Lenin in seeing the liberated/prolitarianized state's legitimacy as a tool of social progress. National liberation, whose nation is undefined, should take place in colonies to gain control of the state apparatus, which will then proceed in the social distribution of values to the benefit of the 'productive forces in society' (Cabral in ibid.: 62). Thus, like Fanon, he implicitly accepts the colonially created state as the domain within which struggle takes place and as a tool to achieve social justice, rather than a colonially suggested identity against which struggle is conducted.

Cabral does not mention the role of culture in shaping the state's identity; the state's identity is its class bias and its anti-colonialism which he sees as one. Culture, however, helps to bring such a state about by supplying the movement with the emotional and spiritual fuel necessary for the struggle.

Culture is for the people an inexhaustible source of courage, of material and moral support, of physical and psychic energy which enables them to accept sacrifices-even to accomplish 'miracles'. But equally, in some respects, culture is very much a source of obstacles and difficulties, of erroneous conceptions about reality, of deviation in carrying out duty and of limitation on the tempo and efficiency of a struggle. (Cabral in ibid.: 63)

This view of culture (or the good part of culture, to be accurate) as fuel in effect reduces culture to emotions and denies the validity of the cultural perception of reality, especially if this perception was not congruent with the Marxist understanding of history and social reality. Such non-Marxist cultural perceptions of the world and their political expressions are then condemned by Cabral as negative aspects of culture. Cabral does not consider that such anti-Marxist trends might generate and harvest that cultural emotional fuel and rally people to their cause. If any anti-colonial expression of culture is necessarily anti-capitalist and thus Marxist, then, inversely, any non-Marxist expression of culture cannot be anti-colonial and therefore such expressions could be classified in the category of collaborating native authorities, that is, they are cultural tools in the hands of colonialism. The reactionary ideas that play into the hands of colonialism should not be expected to harvest that cultural emotional fuel mentioned above. Cabral does not consider the possibility that an anti-colonial movement can also be anti-Marxist. He does not see the link between the cultural perceptions of reality, which could very well be non-Marxist or even anti-Marxist, and the emotional fuel and will to sacrifice they generate. He does not see the relation between the cultural mind and the cultural heart. This is especially important in the Islamic world where a cultural perception of Nature and Man, namely Islam, is both anti-colonial and anti-Marxist, and it has been able to rally support, generate and harvest the will to sacrifice much more than any Marxist movement in the Middle East.

Mamdani joins Cabral in considering colonially installed Native Authorities' negative expressions of culture that play into the hands of colonialism. Mamdani argues that the 'native problem' was the main concern for white colonizers in Africa, mainly how to accommodate the dominance of a white minority whose existence depended on the submission and exploitation of a black majority. By enforcing tribal authority among the natives and creating territorial domains for different tribes, the white colonizers could ensure that black men, while still able to provide the white quarters with cheap labour, would be legally bound to their tribal authorities. They would be able to come to white quarters, but they would be unable to bring their families and reside there, creating a demographic imbalance and a political time-bomb. The 'Native Authority' arrangement also fragmented the colonized population in order to reduce the political threat posed by the natives' potential realization of the unity of their cause. The whites thus created a double legal system, one that offered European-style rights to white colonizers and kept them united and another which kept the blacks fragmented and exploited under the despotic authority of their tribes. Since native custom, the backbone of native authority, was unwritten, the Native Authorities were both the sources and executors of rules.

As its pioneers, the British theorized the colonial state as less a territorial construct than a cultural one. The duality between civil and customary power was best described in legal ideology. Legal dualism juxtaposed received (modern) law with customary law. But customary law was formulated not as a single set of native laws but as so many sets of tribal laws. Conversely, colonial authorities defined a tribe or an ethnic group as a group with its own distinctive law. Referred to as custom, this law was usually unwritten. Its source however, was the Native Authority, those in charge of managing the local state apparatus. Often installed by the colonizing power and always sanctioned by it, this Native Authority was presented as the traditional tribal authority. Where the source of the law was the very authority that administered the law, there could be no rule-bound authority. In such an arrangement there could be no law. (Mamdani 1996: 33)

Mamdani argues that this apartheid, originally thought to be unique to South Africa, is the essence of all colonially created states in the continent. On liberation, the state apparatus was deracialized, but the system of Native Authorities stayed intact under the banner of culture and authenticity. Whether the post-colonial state was 'conservative' or 'progressive', the despotic nature of the colonial structure stayed the same. While conservative states left the Native Authorities intact, their progressive counterpart attempted to homogenize the practice among different tribes, rather than abolishing it altogether (ibid.: 26).

Mamdani considers tribal authorities to be cultural institutions used by the colonial powers to solve the native problem and then inherited by the independent African states to consolidate their power. In other words he identifies Native Authorities with tribalism and thus considers it to be, in origin, part of the native culture. Yet it seems to me that there is a difference between the tribe as a pre-colonial native institution and the Native Authority as an institution created as part and parcel of the colony. Using the tribe as a tool of the colonial state changes the definition of the tribe. The functional change from pre-colonial sovereignty to colonial servitude entails an institutional mutation that should not be overlooked. While the ability of the tribe to make and execute rules vis-a-vis its members seems, at first sight, to be intact, its ability to make decisions vis-a-vis the 'other' is fundamentally curbed by the presence of the colonial state. In and by itself this fact changes the relation between the tribe and its members. The Native Authority, then, is a new institution which is different from, and whose essence is contradictory to, the essence of the tribe. Mamdani recognizes the alienation of the members of the tribe from their Native Authority, and he notices that such Authorities become targeted by national liberation movements which come from the cultural base of the tribe. To him, national liberation movements start as a series of civil wars within every tribe, using Cabral's wording, between the negative and positive aspects of culture. Mamdani sees this very fact as the reason behind the continuity of the bifurcated state after independence:

It is not enough simply to separate tribal power organized from above from tribal revolt waged from below so that we may denounce the former and embrace the latter. The revolt from below needs to be problematized, for it carries the seeds of its own fragmentation and possible self destruction. (ibid.: 24)

Because Mamdani does not see that while the tribe is part of the culture, the Native Authority is part of the colonial state, he attributes the continuity of the phenomenon of Native Authorities to the continuity of tribalism and the 'authoritarian possibilities in culture' rather than to the continuity of the state. Detribalization, rather than rejecting the colonial definition of the state, then becomes the remedy:

We are now in a position to answer the question, what would democratization have entailed in the African context? It would have entailed the deracialization of civil power and the detribalization of customary power, as starting points of an overall democratization that would transcend the legacy of the bifurcated power. (ibid.: 25)

The fact that tribes were called Native Authorities is part of the colonial redefinition of the colonized self, where the nation, which is but a map drawn by colonial officers, becomes the point of origin. The entities Mamdani seeks to democratize are the same entities Fanon seeks to liberate. It is my argument here that such entities were originally created in a manner that ensures their authoritarianism and submission. They are illiberatable and undemocratizable by definition. While a tribe might have been a natural pre-colonial focus of loyalty, the colonially created state and the Native Authority are not. If the subjects in a certain structure of power are not loyal to it, democracy means the disintegration and redefinition of that structure.

While Mamdani uses South African apartheid as a ruler against which to measure the form of colonial states in Africa, in *Unravelling Global Apartheid* (1996) Titus Alexander uses South Africa as an analogy by which to understand the international political system. Despite the fact that Alexander's work is not strictly academic, the analogy he uses is quite useful. Alexander argues that nation-states are but international forms of Native Authorities which supply the white centre of the world with cheap labour and raw materials, protect that centre from being demographically overwhelmed by third world immigration, prevent native populations from developing forms of resistance to the international political and economic system, fragment these populations with a rhetoric of nationalism and, through their monopoly on representing those populations in the international arena, mute the effect of the fact that they are the majority of the world; in other words, deny them the democratic privileges held by the citizens of the centre. To Alexander, nationalism is an equivalent to the claims of the African Native Authorities that they represent custom and authenticity; it is a claim to legitimacy that depends on manipulating national symbols while in fact it allows those authorities to serve as mid-way agents guaranteeing the continuity of global domination.

Cabral, Mamdani and Alexander explain political structures in terms of economic needs. While Cabral explains the existence of Native Authorities in terms of international capitalism, and while Mamdani explains it in terms of the necessities of the survival of the white minority in the newly established colonies, Alexander attributes global apartheid to protectionist trends in international capitalism, where international political settings contradict the conditions determined by Adam Smith as necessary for the theory of comparative advantage to work (see Alexander 1996: 41). Yet Alexander's work is more descriptive than explanatory. It would be natural for the white centre of the world to impose an international political system that assures its dominance, but there remains the question why and how the majority of the world helps sustain such a system. The answer provided by most writers to that question is concerned with the political systems and ruling elites in control of third world states. But the dominance of such groups is not explained and the state system itself is not brought into question. For all those scholars discussed above would agree that colonialism is a capitalist necessity, and that it involves a redefinition of the colonized by the colonizer, yet the acceptance by the local nationalists of this definition is not considered as a potential explanation for the political arrangements within and among states.

To understand the prevalence of global apartheid, one should understand the mechanisms that keep it running, and it is not run by the United States and its allies alone, nor would it suffice to say that the ruling elites in third world states are, all of them, at all times, self-interested, opportunistic, collaborators. The state system is a constellation of positions that renders the position holders, that is, the national leaders, most vulnerable. National leaders become hostages of their own power. I shall come to this point in the next section, when discussing the twin paradoxes of replacement and representation. Right now it suffices to say that while Mamdani's focus is inside the state, and Alexander's focus is outside the state, my focus is the state itself.

Since this is a study of the Arab world and since the redefinition of the colonized by the colonizer is its core issue, it is, of course, necessary to relate this work to Edward Said's. While Said's conclusions are the assumptions of this book, that is, his argument that the redefinition of the Orient is connected to European expansionism is accepted as a cornerstone of the argument made here, it is worth noting that my primary concern here is more about how Orientals deal with Orientalism than about Orientalism itself. I attempt to discuss the mechanisms and the implications of the acceptance or rejection by Arabs and Muslims of the definitions and redefinitions suggested to them by their occupiers. One should also point out that, despite using the concepts of post-colonial theory and the language of identities, ideas and cultures, this work is mainly about politics, and the main argument is that the acceptance of the colonially created state as a focus of loyalty and a determinant of identity curbs any effort to get rid of foreign dominance. There are also a couple of points about which to argue with Said: in the concluding chapters of *Culture and Imperialism*, Said talks about a new form of cultural resistance instead of the politics of identity. To him, anti-imperialist culture has ceased to be confined to nationalistic liberation movements; rather, it is produced by alienated individuals and anti-systemic transnational movements (Said 1993: 332). Said attributes the emergence of modern nationalisms and prejudices to imperialism, therefore resisting imperialism to him means also resisting the nationalisms/ collective prejudices that are but extensions and mirror images of it. But it would be a historical mistake to assume that the sense of togetherness felt by members of a certain tribe or followers of a certain religion was created by imperialism. The nationalisms created by colonization are only those whose foci of loyalty were the colonially created states, or whose ultimate purpose is to found a nation-state similar in form and content to the colonially created one, only with adjusted borders. It is important to remember that, especially in the Arab world, transnational anti-systemic movements, far from being transcultural, emphasize different forms of collective identity. Said's suggestion that anti-imperialist culture be the product of 'wanderers' is politically impossible and historically untrue, since there will be no focus of loyalty around which to rally. It could be understood that Said is making the post-modern argument that every discourse is prejudiced in favour of a collective, a group of people who serve the discourse and are served by it, and therefore Said reaches the post-modern conclusion that any discourse that wishes to avoid dominating others should not bear the signs of collective identities. But politics is a collective act. Therefore, having such prejudices seems to be an unavoidable evil.[1]

Aijaz Ahmad (1994) asserts that this 'wandering' is what makes Said and most post-colonial theorists part of the colonial discourse themselves. Ahmad argues that while they deconstruct western

---

1. Here I should warn the reader that, despite having explained the meaning of the Umma and Dawla in the previous chapters, and despite the fact that I am going to deconstruct colonially introduced identities in the Middle East, I am not trying to say that one is intrinsically more moral, fairer, or altogether better than the other. Various forms of Islamism, or modernism, like all political ideologies and institutions, will inescapably result in some people dominating others, and make it look like the natural order of things. I am only comparing the efficiency of the two identities, judging them by the criteria they set for themselves, and by the degree of internal contradictions they suffer.

discourse representing the third world, they are themselves westerners, or westernized scholars who represent the third world rather than letting it represent itself. Ahmad criticizes post-colonial theorists' choice of third world writings. For example, Salman Rushdie's writing is, to him, a western representation rather than a third world expression. Another criticism is Ahmad's remark regarding the ambiguity of the direction of the relation between colonialism and Orientalism:

Now if there is only this seamless and incremental history of Orientalist Discourse from Aeschylus to Dante to Marx to Bernard Lewis, then in what sense could one take the eighteenth century 'as a roughly defined starting point'? In other words one does not really know whether Orientalist discourses begin in the post-enlightenment period or at the dawn of European Civilization, whether in the period of the Battle of Plessey or in the days of the Battle of Troy. This then raises the question of the relationship between Orientalism and colonialism, in one sort of reading, where post-enlightenment Europe is emphasized; Orientalism appears to be an ideological corollary of colonialism. But so insistent is Said in identifying its origins in European antiquity and its increasing elaboration throughout the European Middle Ages that it seems to be the *constituting element*, transhistorically, of what he calls 'the European imagination'. In a revealing use of the word 'delivered', Said remarks at one point that Orientalism delivered the Orient to colonialism, so that colonialism begins to appear as a product of Orientalism itself, indeed, as the realization of the project already inherent in Europe's perennial project of inferiorizing the Orient first in discourse and then in colonization. (Ahmad 1994: 181)

It could be argued that the inferiorizing image of 'the other' is usually the product of violent contact. Orientalism could be tracked down to the wars between Greece and Persia. Colonialism, however, is an act of domination and redefinition of the conquered by the conqueror; the essence of colonialism, then, is to turn this inferiorizing image into an institutional reality. The paradox in Said's argument could thus be solved if this difference between pre-colonial and colonial Orientalism is taken into consideration. The inferiorizing image that shaped the imagination of pre-colonial Europe during frequent violent contacts with the East could have delivered the Orient to colonialism, that is, it could have become an element in defining the East both as a domain of special threats and as a host of special opportunities. However, the institutionalized redefinition of the Orient inherent in the colonial project helped to reproduce that image in more concrete forms in order to legitimize itself. It is clear that the second phase, that of colonialism, is the one that concerns us here.

However, the notion that the more frequent violent contacts are, the more hostile the image of the other is, is important in explaining the degree of hostility and contradiction between the Arab image of the self and the image imposed on it by colonial and neo-colonial powers. The Middle East, due to its geographical proximity to Europe, had the longest record of violent contacts with it. This resulted in the continuity and gravity of the chasm between European definitions of the Middle East and the way the Arabs and Muslims define themselves. When the European definition of the Middle East was imposed and institutionalized by colonial powers, it became more difficult for those Middle Easterners to express their own self-definition because of this chasm, and I argue that this task is impossible using the institutions installed by Europe. In other words, if people in the Middle East defined themselves as Arabs or Muslims, the institutional expression of such an image is impossible using the colonially defined institutions called the Arab states. The history of contradictory definitions between Arabs and Muslims on the one hand and Europe and Europe extended on the other is unparalleled in length or in the degree of violence with any other record between Europeans and other non-Europeans in Africa and Asia. Rome, Byzantium, the Crusades, Napoleon, the British Empire, Israel and the United States are usually mentioned in the same sentence in Friday prayers as different faces of the same coin. Imposing an institutional self-definition manufactured in Europe on the people of the Middle East is thus very risky. Among all colonially created states, which form 85 per cent of today's world, the Arab Islamic states are the weakest link.

The above argument about the incompatibility of European and Arab self definitions could be confused with what has now become a classic argument about the clash of civilizations. This of course should not be the case; Samuel Huntington's *The Clash of Civilizations* (1996), like a lot of work on modernization, sees traditions and cultures as independent variables that can, in and by themselves, hinder or enhance development, start and end wars, disrupt or maintain peace. This, as has partly been shown so far, is not quite accurate. It is not because of the difference in the way Arabs and westerners define themselves that the conflict breaks out, it is due to the difference in the way Arabs define themselves and the way westerners define Arabs, and the attempt by colonial powers to impose that definition of

Arabs on the Arabs that the conflict breaks out. The current hostility between trends in Arab Islamic culture and the West is created by the colonial impact, that is, it is initially the result of conflict, not the cause of it. Here I should emphasize the point made at the beginning of the chapters on the formation of Islamic canons: native cultures are not static residuals of the past. Rather, culture is always in the process of being created and recreated.

In Francis Fukuyama's *The End of History and the Last Man* (1992), the 'end' is but the end of the human intellectual dialectic. Such an end will leave western civilization, which, according to Fukuyama, is a rational body of thought, posed against its irrational rivals. Being but coincidental residuals of the past, such rivals are not going to intellectually/rationally compete with liberal democracy and are thus bound to fail. Huntington agrees with Fukuyama that there will be no competition, but a 'clash' (the word 'clash' is different from 'conflict', 'dialectic', and 'competition'). 'Clash' assumes the absence of direction, leadership and calculation, it assumes irrationality. This explanation of history (whether it ended or not yet) sets an independent variable (culture) that is inexplicable, is irrational and therefore negative. In that, the 'optimistic' Fukuyama and the 'pessimistic' Huntington are two faces of the same coin.

To sum up, the above briefing of the manner in which a number of post-colonial theorists tackled the issue of identity and liberation shows that in most cases the colonially created nation-state is taken for granted as the arena of liberation. It is to be liberated, democratized, proletarianized, or just humanized. The following section, which is a corollary of their work, will show that such an aspiration is impossible and contradictory.

THE TWIN PARADOXES OF REPRESENTATION AND REPLACEMENT[2]

As shown above, despite the diversity of the literature in the field, most post-colonial theorists agree on the assumption that the process of colonization involves a redefinition of the colonized by the colonial power. A colonially tailored image of the native centred on his relation vis-a-vis his colonial master is imposed on him. 'Half devil and half child', the native is measured against the standard White Man, whose burden is to civilize the child and kill the devil

2. With some editing, this section is part of my PhD dissertation, 'The Case of Egypt: A National Liberation Movement and a Colonially Created Government', Boston University, 2004.

using the necessary books and rifles. The native is then redefined in order to fit in the mould of the colonial image. A white mask, and a mask is a redefined face, is imposed over the original black face, to use Fanon's telling metaphor. In Timothy Mitchell's work *Colonizing Egypt* ([1985] 1988), colonialism means the forcing of the Egyptian reality to fit into an imagined ideal borrowed from Europe. To Mitchell, this has been the essence of the process of modernization in Egypt, where the old country becomes redefined, renamed and reorganized to fit an imagined European model. This kind of redefinition has been dealt with on the level of cultural processes such as literary representation, arts, education, and political discourse by a school of writers following the steps of Edward Said's leading works *Orientalism* (1978) and *Culture and Imperialism* (1993). The other level on which the process of colonial redefinition has been studied is the socio-economic level. Because colonialism is, in essence, a process of economic exploitation, a quest for raw materials, cheap labour, markets and a geo-strategic military edge over rival powers, a native class of middle men is created to facilitate the execution of these tasks. This shuffle of power relations within the colonized society creates a dilemma for the local bourgeoisie, who, economically, have common interests with the colonial power against the more deprived sections within their society, and politically have a common cause with those deprived sections against the colonial presence. Here I would like to be excused in going back to Fanon, as the contradictory relation between this bourgeoisie and the colonial power is insightfully described in chapters three and four of *The Wretched of the Earth* (1961). Fanon argues that, psychologically, there are two contradictory feelings of hatred and admiration on the part of the colonized middle class embodied in their need for independence and their quest for catching up economically and, in many aspects, culturally, with Europe.

The national middle class which takes over power at the end of the colonial regime is an underdeveloped middle class. It has practically no economic power, and in any case it is in no way commensurate with the bourgeoisie of the mother country which it hopes to *replace*. In its narcissism, the national middle class is easily convinced that it can advantageously *replace* the middle class of the mother country. But that same independence which literally *drives it into a corner* will give rise within its ranks to catastrophic reactions, and will oblige it to send out frenzied appeals for help to the former mother country. (Fanon 1969: 149, emphasis mine)

I have emphasized the words 'replace' and the phrase 'drives it into a corner' because they directly correspond to the two variables I am trying to link here, that is, the native elite's acceptance of the colonially imposed identity on the one hand and the military, political and economic failure of the colonially created nation-state on the other. The acceptance of the colonially defined nation, and the formation of a native government within the colonially drawn borders of such a nation, is an act of replacement of the colonial power, where the native elite takes not only the position of the colonial power, but regarding much of the issues on economy and security, performs its very same functions. This, I argue along with Fanon, 'drives it into a corner', where it loses the support of its constituencies as well as that of the colonial power. I'm going to take Fanon's argument one step further and deal with this dilemma in terms of two interdependent paradoxes: the Paradox of Representation and the Paradox of Replacement.

Socially, the native elites stand between the majority of the native population and the colonial power. They are relatively beneficent of the colonial economic situation, either as traders of raw materials, middle men in the provision of cheap labour or agents for the marketing of metropolitan products within the colony. Yet raw materials and cheap labour are not the only trophies of colonialism. Security is an extremely valuable commodity for a colonial power: security of international trade routes, security of foreign enterprises and businesses, security of European residents, including the military occupation forces and so on. The local elite then also becomes involved in the provision of such a commodity either by direct participation in security apparatuses or, due to their claim of representation, by creating a mirage of native participation and legitimizing the colonial structure of power. I shall return to this point on security later because of its special significance in the Middle East. At this point, however, it suffices to say that, to provide security efficiently, the native elites have to have some legitimacy among their own population. By their efficiency I mean that the native elite's provision of security should be less costly to the colonial power than direct occupation and policing by the colonial power's own forces.

Thus, while the members of a native elite are highly dependent for their social status on the stability of the colonial system of government, they are also dependent on their links to the rest of their own people because their 'native-ness' is necessary for performing all the functions mentioned above.

This position of the native elite, between the colonized population and the colonizing power, results in a paradox of representation. Any act of representation requires the consent of two parties; the party represented and the party to which the representation is done. Both have to accept the agent who does the representation. In the case of the colonial power and the colonized population, the two parties have contradictory agendas. The agent doing the representation must thus acquire the consent of two opposites.

This was clear, for example, in the case of the Egyptian national liberation movement in the early twentieth century. The mandate of the Wafd Party, spearheading the movement, and whose very name meant 'the delegation', was initially based on thousands of petitions signed by Egyptians from all social strata requesting British authorities to allow the 'delegation' to represent their case to His Majesty's Government in London. Sharif Hussein of Mecca, who, in 1916, led a rebellion against the Ottoman Empire in return for a British promise to establish an Arab Kingdom, insisted that Britain should recognize him as the King of the Arabs, and as the representative of the Arab nationalist cause. After the Kingdom of Iraq and the Emirate of Transjordan were formed, both sons of Sharif Hussein, Faisal I of Iraq and Abdullah I of Transjordan, competed for championing the Arab nationalist cause and to be recognized as such. Even later in the twentieth century, the Palestine Liberation Organization spent a good deal of blood and effort to secure its recognition as 'the Sole Legitimate Representative' of the Palestinian people. The recognition by Israel and the United States of such capacity was often cited by the Palestinian advocates of the Oslo peace accords of 1993 as one of the peace process's major achievements for the Palestinian nationalist cause.

This need to be recognized by two opposite forces infiltrates the very self of the middle man to become a need to accommodate two contradictory agendas, both of which are *his own* and vital to him too. For any representation problematizes the representative who simultaneously becomes himself as well as someone else, and when the interests of the representative and those whom he represents diverge, the representative has to lose either part of his identity, his independent existence or his capacity as a representative. In other words, the native elite becomes sandwiched between its interests as a dependent bourgeoisie and its interests as a group of natives.

This paradox of representation then leads to another paradox, that of replacement. The contradiction mentioned above is solved by a strategy of replacement, where the native elite replaces the colonial power. And replacement, like representation, is a contradictory process; it simultaneously involves elements of continuity and discontinuity. While the native elite tries to get rid of the colonial presence, such as the military occupation, it keeps the colonial relation of dependence that fulfils its members' socio-economic interests as middle men. Replacement is an attempt by the native elite to solve the conflict it suffers due to its position in between the two opposite forces of the native population and the colonial power. To the native population, it offers the promise of liberation, symbolized by legal independence, formal, or sometimes only nominal, sovereignty as well as the end of military occupation; to the colonial power, it offers to secure the vital colonial interests, such as the safety of international trade routes, the safety of colonial enterprises, the safety of European residents, and all other regional geo-strategic interests of the colonial power. All of these functions require the keeping of law and order by a state apparatus. Thus the colonially created state embodies this doctrine of replacement. In the case of the Egyptian nationalist movement, this could be seen in the February declaration of 1922, the constitution of 1923 and also the treaty of 1936. It is also present in the logic of the peace treaty between Egypt and Israel signed in 1978, where Israel withdrew from the Sinai Peninsula on the condition that the Egyptian government would keep it as a demilitarized buffer zone and provide Israel with fuel. In the case of Jordan it could be seen in the meeting between Laurence, Churchill and Abdullah I in 1921, where Abdullah was required to secure the southern borders of the French domain in Syria from attacks by 'anti-French Arab Terrorists' in return for an Emirate and possibly a throne under French mandate in Damascus (see Abdullah's rationale in accepting the deal, in his words, quoted in Mahafza 1991, 1: 147). In Iraq the constitution of the Hashemite Kingdom and the 1931 treaty with Britain fit quite well into the pattern; the new constitution of Iraq written after the American invasion in 2003 emphasized that the Iraqi army would join the 'multi-national forces' in their war on terror. In Palestine the 1993 Oslo accords and the creation of the Palestinian National Authority in 1994 with the principal commitment to crack down on terrorism is also an example. Israel needed security and the Palestinians needed independence; the logic of the peace process was thus to create a Palestinian independence that guaranteed Israel's security and so on.

However, this strategy of replacement is likely to fail because the fulfilment of the national elite's commitment to one party threatens its ability to fulfil its commitment to the other. Keeping the infrastructure of the colonial relation creates economic and political grievances among the masses in addition to the unfulfilled promise of getting rid of foreign occupation. On the other hand, that promise, in and by itself, creates a target against which public anger is directed. This, in turn, jeopardizes law and order, and the socio-economic settings whose protection is the essence of what the native elite has to offer to the colonial power. Hence the paradox is that when the native elite decides to replace the colonial power in controlling the colonially defined state, they are required, as governments, to keep peace and security by protecting the status quo, and, at the same time, they need a legitimacy that can only be harvested by promising to change that very status quo. It is clear how each task is apt to frustrate the other.

This failure is then expressed in different forms. The form that concerns us most here is that which involves an outright rejection of the colonially created nation-state and its nationalism. Significant numbers from the same social strata that previously used to form the constituencies of the nationalist movements that accepted the colonially created state start joining such rejectionist rival movements. Once such loss of ground takes place, the leading elite, whether a national liberation movement or a state government, will find it difficult to control the population, and thus it loses credibility as far as the colonial power is concerned.

This double failure is therefore the inevitable result of the colonial origin of the concerned nation-states. From late nineteenth century and up until World War Two, the colonially dictated constitutions and sets of 'international' treaties between the colonial power and the local elites were the birth certificates of such states. Such documents embodied the colonial deal; the colonial powers grant independence to the local elites and the local elites grant the colonial powers dependence in return. From World War Two on, the international system established under the auspices of the United States, and whose main institution was the United Nations, continued to play the role of the now defeated British and French Empires. The newly independent third world states were trapped in three concentric loops: economic dependence, which resulted in military vulnerability, both of which were legalized by a set of international laws, and the influence of the United Nations Security Council. Colonial and neo-colonial powers still use those three loops to keep their former colonies in line. The degrees of freedom and wealth they grant to their followers vary from one case to another. Of course a third world state's share of global power and wealth does not depend solely on how much of it is granted by the Superpower, yet the role of the Superpower in determining the degree of power and wealth cannot be denied.

Here I would like to go back to a point I mentioned at the beginning about the production of security. While colonial powers could want different things from different colonies, security has always featured strongly on their wish list when it came to the Middle East. It is easy to see why: the Middle East is simply in the middle. It controls much of the world's trade routes, it is also rich in raw materials, and finally it is densely peopled with a population that has lately become much more youthful than that of its colonial masters. In the following section, I shall show how this aggravates the dilemma of the colonially created Arab nation-states, rendering them the weakest link among other states of similar origin.

THE PRECIOUS NOTHING

It is the classical argument of dependency theorists and neo-Marxists that the international economy resembles to a great extent a closed system of national capitalism where the poor countries are the workers, providing mainly raw materials and cheap labour, while the rich countries at the centre are the organizers and owners of the means of production. This system is maintained by colonialism and neo-colonialism where states created by the colonial powers are destined to continue to behave as colonies as far as the economy is concerned. Now, however, the international economy is becoming less and less labour intensive. What importance, then, do these third world states still have?

As mentioned above, one thing left out by dependency theorists is that cheap labour and raw materials are not the only trophies of colonialism and necessities of global capitalist economy. Security is one of the most, if not *the* most, vital raw material provided by the colonies and by their heirs, third world nation-states. Looking at the economies of those states, one can see huge bureaucracies, the biggest branches of which are security apparatuses. In the Arab world, countries have tens of them: one Arab country has 22 security apparatuses; another has 26; an Arab semi-state, or a state-to-be, already has 11. Sometimes the ratio of security personnel to normal citizens is as high as one policeman for every 15 citizens. But that's not all; people working in non-security government institutions do not actually work. Hiring huge numbers of men and women in government bureaucracies is not simply a mistake; rather, it is a measure of producing security. These people do nothing, but this 'nothing' is what they get paid for; this 'nothing' is extremely precious and necessary for the international economy to work. If you were working in a government bureaucracy, you would not want to rebel since the lightest punishment you would get is simply losing your job. In countries where for every one working citizen there are almost five citizens under the age of 15, most of whom are probably his or her children, that is a serious threat. The traditional colonial deal stipulates that third world countries, especially those which are geographically situated on the strategic routes of international trade, are structured so as to pacify their own populations. In return, they get loans and grants from the countries in the global economic centre. As the international economy becomes less and less labour intensive, third world countries are required to provide only security and raw materials to the global economy. If you're an Arab reading this book in English, you're probably a member of the Arab upper middle class and if you looked into your personal and family histories, you would realize that you made it into this elite by serving the international economy one way or another, either by working in one of the princedoms of the Persian Gulf, the good salaries of which come from selling the principal raw material in today's world; by working in the government apparatuses, providing the world with security and order one way or another; or by directly working in institutions financed by the United States and European countries. It could be argued that many Palestinians prospered from working for the PLO, and that the PLO could be anything but a provider of security to the capitalist world. This is partly true, but it should be noted that a significant percentage of the PLO's income came from the Gulf, and that organizing the Palestinian people made them less of a security problem to many Arab countries, which could now deal with a recognized organization instead of suffering from networks of scattered fighters here and there. In a sense, even the PLO was a provider of security, if compared to its 'chaotic' alternative. The immediate class interests of the Arab elite are thus congruent with those of the colonial power, that is, both benefit from the production and consumption of security.

But if we define security as this 'precious nothing' that is produced by the third world and consumed by the first, it is understandable that the more Arabs produce it, the less its western consumers will want to pay for it. This is true for any good, but it is truer in the case of security; first because it is 'nothing', that is, it is intangible. Like good health, when it is abundant it is taken for granted, and only when absent is it missed and appreciated. As time passes, it becomes more and more difficult for the United States government, for example, to convince its constituencies to pay money for dictatorships around the world because they just keep their peoples from revolting. It becomes even more difficult, precisely because those dictatorships do a great job in making a revolt seem extremely unlikely. The imperial centres would want to pay less also because security is one commodity that is better produced by a dead worker than by a living one; surely dead men do not bite. Through the International Monetary Fund and the World Bank, the capitalist centres of the world keep advising the colonially created states, the producers of security, to produce it at a lower cost, that is, to cut government spending and employ less people who do nothing. If they do not succeed, and unrest and terrorism break out, they will be considered failed states; everything from embargo to invasion becomes possible.

Some members who belong to the Arab elite then feel threatened; their historical job as providers of security is being questioned by their employers who think they can do it better. Some members of the elite decide to stop producing security altogether, and thus you have producers of insecurity, that is, 'terrorists'; others keep trying to convince their employers that they still can do a good job, and excel in pacifying their own people at lower costs. Looking at the current situation in Iraq, for example, Arab governments would very much like to see the Americans drown, yet they would not want to see the resistance win. Rather, they would want the American installed Iraqi government to pacify the Iraqi people on behalf of the Americans, but in their absence. In a sense, this new five-year-old Iraqi state reminds other 80- and 70-year-old states in the region of their childhood and predicts their destiny.

Moral judgments aside, one could look at global terrorism as an international workers' strike. Unsatisfied with their share of global wealth and power, the producers of security decide to refrain from producing it, thus producing insecurity. Like workers, they have demands, some of which are political and some economic. Despite the outrageous degree of violence involved, strikes are not revolutions.

The demands are mainly reformatory. The use of a cultural rather than a socialist language serves more than one purpose; it helps recruit more people to the cause, and it relieves the said insecurity-producing organizations from radical demands. It leaves some space for negotiations between them and global capitalism. For example, the demands of most such organizations in the Middle East, at least declaredly, are the American withdrawal from the Middle East, the liberation of Palestine and the establishment of Islamic Sharia as the only source of legislation in Islamic countries. Such demands are much less radical than the demands of, say, the Soviet Union, which involved radical changes in the ownership of the means of production world-wide and an inversion of the international balance of power.

One last point remains to be made: there might be a tendency to explain the above condition of Arab states being sandwiched between the demands of their own populations and those of their patron colonial and neo-colonial Superpowers using the classic arguments of the realist school of international relations theory, rather than attributing the problem to the colonial structure of the state. That is to say, Arab states suffer the above dilemma because, like all third world states, they would like to have a better share of international power and wealth, yet have very few bargaining chips. The longer they are stuck in this dependent position the graver their legitimacy problem grows, which in turn renders them more dependent on their colonial patrons and so on, in a vicious circle of weakness and instability. The advocates of this argument often mention the cold war in support of their theory – it is normal, they say, to see similarities between states installed by Britain and France in the inter-war period, and the regimes supported by the United States in the post-cold war period, because the balance of power in both cases was severely tilted against the interests of Arab regimes. On the other hand, such states, having stayed more or less the same during the cold war, had much more power and freedom, and did not suffer from the dilemma mentioned above. As such, the advocates of this balance-of-power argument come to the conclusion that the dilemma of Arab states is more conditional than structural.

A closer look at the Arab states during the cold war might provide us with an answer to this balance-of-power argument. It is true that the cold war window allowed for a mirage of freedom for those pseudo-independent entities as third world leaders played the two Superpowers against one another. It is also true that during the cold war, especially among Arab intellectuals, faith was partially restored in the modernist project that was introduced by Europe. The two world wars seemed to prove that the liberal capitalist version of European humanism had failed, while socialism seemed to offer another version of European humanism that was anti-capitalist and therefore anti-imperialist. Thus several forms of socialism seem to have offered Arab intellectuals an alternative, non-colonial form of modernity that they could embrace without being accused of betraying their identity to the alien invader. Clumsy attempts to hammer out an 'Arab Socialism' were abundant, and in the cases of Egypt, Syria and Iraq, such sketchy theories were elevated to become state ideologies.

However, the structures that were created by colonial liberal powers like Britain and France remained more or less the same under Arab socialist nationalist rule. In a sense, the differences in structure between the Arab nationalist socialist state of the cold war, and its liberal colonial predecessor, paralleled the differences between European socialism and European liberalism. That is to say, the differences were trivial if compared with the similarities. Both ideologies, and therefore both corresponding state-types, were European in origin. They both shared the same philosophical roots in European humanism, the same political roots in nationalism, and more or less the same relation to the other, that is, they were Eurocentric and therefore colonial. By Eurocentrism I here mean the tendency to apply theories that are derived from the European historical experience to understand the histories of non-Europeans, disregarding the differences. When such a paradigm informs the minds of European, as well as native state builders elsewhere, the outcome is a set of institutions that are more in harmony with Europe than they are with their immediate historical, geographical and demographical contexts. Hence the argument that nationalist socialist states that emerged after the end of classical colonialism and thrived during the cold war were nonetheless colonial in their structure, in their function, in their discourse and in the very logic that brought them into being; a logic of a native that wants to be like the master. A closer look at the discourses of such states will reveal that, despite their apparent comfort during the cold war, they still faced the severe legitimacy dilemma described above. The two variants of Arab Nationalism, socialist and liberal, pro-East and pro-West, still had to be reconciled with the native culture, and especially with the notion of the Umma. The tension between Arab states and their populations in both camps of the cold war was not less than the tension during the interwar period, except in cases where the leaders could portray their policies and institutions as acting in the best interest of the Umma. The huge popularity of Nasser's regime, for example, stemmed from his confrontations with the colonial powers and support of other Arab and Muslim nations, rather than from his domestic policies or ideological statements.

This argument will be expanded below when dealing with Arab socialist nationalism. At this point it suffices to say that it was a half-way solution. It was a hybrid of everything: partly modern, partly traditional, partly secular, partly Islamic, partly socialist and partly bourgeois. The only aspect in which these states were not hybrids, though, was their dependence. Those countries were as dependent during the cold war as they were before it and as they became after it. It is true that they sometimes had the option of shifting their dependence from one side to another, but that did not change the reality of their dependence. The war of 1967, which was the first and almost fatal blow to the Arab cold war regimes, is a good example. When both Superpowers seemed to agree that Israel should survive, regardless of the wishes of their Arab nationalist allies, be those Egypt and Syria, allies of the Soviet Union, or Jordan, an ally of the United States, they were all defeated and no drastic action was taken by either one of the Superpowers to ease their humiliation. One could list a number of similar examples where the wills of the two Superpowers were reconcilable, causing the ever dependent Arab states to suffer. This can include the civil war in Lebanon and the Iraq-Iran war, the ending of which was far from being a priority on the agenda of either one of the two Superpowers of the time. Another point to be made is the fact that none of the Arab states could make use of the Superpower rivalry to break away from the three aforementioned loops of economic dependency, military vulnerability and international law up until the end of the cold war. With the Soviet Union tottering to its end, and with the United States advancing to the strategic areas from which the Soviets withdrew, the final blow of Arab nationalism and cold war pseudo-independence came with the second Gulf war of 1990–91.

Not much actually changed in the structure of the Arab states after 1991. They continued to be providers of security, selling to any Superpower that would buy, but the rate that what was now the only Superpower was willing to pay became much less after the cold war ended (there was no competition in the market of buyers;

no one else wanted to buy Arab security). So while the structure stayed the same, only the new terms of buying security changed. The share of international wealth and power and the extent of political concessions that the United States was willing to offer the Arabs in return for the existence of their security providing states became much less. For example, with regards to political and military behaviour, the United States' position on the Arab-Israeli conflict, its inclination to practise classical colonialism through direct invasions, its tendency to use sanctions and military attacks on Arab states increased significantly after the cold war. Yet decision makers in the United States still expected those Arab governments that were not under attack to manage to control their populations. Of course, with the events of September 11 such an assumption proved erroneous; it is significant to point out that most of the perpetrators of that terrorist attack came from countries that were close allies of the United States.

The paradox of replacement thus became much more visible at that point. It was difficult during the cold war to say that one regime was a pure agent of the United States or the Soviet Union, because any Arab regime, while an agent to someone, and while facing serious legitimacy problems internally, was not an agent to the same power all the time nor all the way. From 1991 onwards, it was quite easy to see how Arab states were states of vassalage.

Accordingly, the argument presented here is that Arab states failed because they were bound to. Their failure was a function of their colonial build-up. They were created to mediate between two contradictory identities. The native of those two identities entails that all political arrangements in the abode of Islam should take into consideration the well-being of the whole Umma. Such entities would then produce security and raw material only if the share of Muslims from international wealth and power was satisfactory. Such an identity was therefore, by definition, anti-colonial, though not necessarily anti-capitalist. The other identity of the two was one that revolved around, and legitimized, colonially created nations that were economically dependent on and militarily vulnerable to the colonial and neo-colonial powers of the day. Each one of those entities was created in such a way as to guarantee the ongoing production of raw materials and security regardless of what happened to other entities. Actually, the mere fact that such entities were states, abiding by the international law, obliged them to behave in that self-serving manner. This self-serving manner, in line with nationalism, directly contradicted the Islamic notions of Umma and Dawla explained above.

If, for example, Egypt declared war on Israel because the latter invaded Lebanon, it would be as much a legitimate act according to the current interpretations of Islamic Sharia as it would be illegal according to international law. The state of Egypt, on the other hand, inactive during the Israeli invasion of Lebanon in 1982, presented its position to the international community as an example of its abidance by the rules of international law, as any decent nation-state should. But it also tried to sell the same inaction to the Egyptian people, as being the wisest policy in the interest of the Lebanese and the Palestinians.

The problem is that this attempt to reconcile two contradictory agendas, which we have chosen to call the paradox of replacement, is bound to fail. The more Egypt produces security, the less threat it poses to Israel, the less leverage it has vis-a-vis Israel, and that in turn reduces the legitimacy of the Egyptian government and pushes some Egyptians to form non-state organizations to act where the Egyptian government has failed to take action. Moreover, as such organizations are formed, causing the Egyptian government to lose control over increasing numbers of its citizens, the Egyptian government loses credibility vis-a-vis the international community, including its neo-colonial patrons. It should be stressed that the above pressures exerted from the international community and by the people of Egypt against the Egyptian government, are independent of the type of that government. They will always be there because they stem from the fact that Egypt is a state, not because its government is leftist or rightist.

Looking at the events in the Middle East through these conceptual lenses serves two purposes: first, it helps us situate the role of the native culture in the conflict, not as a cause, but as a catalyst; second, once the terms of the conflict are made clear, attempts at a working compromise can become more fruitful.

THE LEAST LIKELY CASES FOR FAILURE: EGYPTIAN AND ARAB NATIONALISMS

In the next chapter I shall take, as a sample for such failed compromises, the Egyptian nationalist movement and the Arab nationalist movements in the Levant. Egyptian nationalism was an early example of nationalism developed purely around colonially created states, while Arab nationalism was the basis of the establishment of the states of Iraq, Syria and Jordan, and it also underlined Palestinian nationalism.

Egyptian nationalism was more likely to succeed in reconciling native and colonial agendas than any other local nationalism in the region. Egypt could easily be presented as a natural nation-state. It has always enjoyed some form of administrative unity, even when it was part of a larger Empire. From the very beginning there was an attempt to deny the links with Islam and Arabism, and to construct an image of an Egyptian nation whose history was perfectly parallel to that of western European nations; a Pharaonic antiquity to parallel the Greco-Roman antiquity, an Islamic age of faith to parallel the Christian middle ages, and a bright secular modernity that came to Egypt with the French Expedition (1798–1801). However, this pure form of Egyptian nationalism had to converge again to meet with Arabism and Islam, in order to compete with rising tendencies among the constituencies of the Egyptian nationalist movement. This discourse eventually collapsed because of the difference between the modernity of the colonizer and the modernity of the colonized. When Egyptian nationalists came to power, they realized that the state they came to rule could scarcely be the naturally and historically ordained expression of Egyptian nationhood they expected it to be. Rather, the very structure of the state was that of a colony. Egyptian nationalism had been a Franco-British creation, just like the Egyptian bureaucracy, army and territory had been manufactured to occupy and control the people of Egypt, rather than free them. This contradiction caused the ultimate failure of the Egyptian nationalist liberation movement and its giving in to Arabism with the revolution of 1952.

The discourses of Iraq and Syria, on the other hand, had been pan-Arab from the start. Local Iraqi or Syrian nationalisms were never real contenders for power in those two countries. The discourse of Arab nationalists has been always plagued with the attempt to reconcile the factual sovereignty of the colonially created state with the imagined, or aspired, sovereignty of the 'Arab nation'. According to that discourse, any sovereign Arab state would only be legitimate if its purpose was to dissolve itself in a larger imagined entity, an idea that is not at all far from the conventional concept of the Islamic Dawla. It has also been the task of Arab nationalist thinkers to reconcile the idea of that aspired secular Arab nation, based on race or language as they copied it from reading German and Italian nationalist thinkers, with that of the Islamic Umma. Thus the concept of the Umma infiltrated their ideology twice: first by advocating the existence of an Arab Umma, and then by reconciling that Umma with the pre-existing Islamic Umma. The concept of the Dawla also infiltrated Arab nationalism twice: first in reconstructing the territorial colonially created Arab states as Dawlas in service of the Arab Umma, and then in reconstructing the imagined, or awaited, united all-encompassing Arab state as a Dawla in the service of the Islamic Umma.

In general, Arab nationalism represented the aspiration during the cold war that the secular modernist project which first came to the Middle East with the colonial powers could actually work. No real changes were introduced to the structure of the colonially created state. There was only an attempt to legitimize such states by representing them as products of a natural historical development of an imagined non-Islamic Arab nation. When the cold war ended in the Iraqi bloodbath, Arab nationalists relapsed into the traditional Islamic alliances and discourses. Saddam Hussein added the phrase 'God is Great' to the Iraqi Flag, and Syria's two Assads, father and son, consolidated their alliances with Islamic, non-Arab Iran. Iraqi society, organized in the form of a colonially created nation-state, albeit with an Arab nationalist ideology, lost the confrontation with the creators and sponsors of that state. Iraq fell and the whole political system was dissolved. Yet the same Iraqi society was able to exercise considerable military and political pressure when organized as a multitude of non-state, non-sovereign and non-territorial entities. The State of Syria, facing similar but milder pressures than those faced by Iraq before the American invasion, resorted to sponsoring such non-state organizations in Lebanon and Iraq. The triumph of Hezballah against Israel in 2000 and 2006, when contrasted with the failure of the Syrian army to regain the Golan Heights, highlighted the failure of the nation-state and the apparent efficiency of the Dawla.

While in Iraq, the state was replaced by various Dawlas, and in Syria, the state co-existed with and depended on Dawlas acting around it, Arab governments who did not move closer to Islamic defiance, like Saudi Arabia, Egypt and Jordan, provided organizations such as Al-Qaeda with quite significant numbers of supporters, and with its three principal leaders, Bin Laden, Zawahiri and Zarqawi respectively.

In the following chapters, it will not be my purpose to tell the whole story of these two cases, but rather to present some examples that show, first, the colonial origin of those nationalisms, and second, the failed attempts by the nationalists to reconcile the native and the colonial senses of identity. It is obvious how the second point naturally flows from the first. As colonial states were created to serve colonial interests, and as nationalisms were manufactured to legitimize such states and thus make them more efficient in controlling the conquered populations, local leaders had to make various attempts to reconcile the colonially created nations in the Middle East with the Islamic Umma. These attempts included the reinterpretation of Islamic texts confining it to its private spiritual aspects and quarantining it out of political organization and practice, the redefinition of Islam as a secular cultural product of the concerned Muslim nations' genius, such as the Arabs, and the representation of the colonially created nation-states as Dawlas whose existence would benefit the whole Umma in the long run, even when the immediate colonially dictated policies of such states seemed to contradict the welfare of Muslims outside their borders.

Other than the fact that the two nationalisms discussed here cover the majority of the region's population, I chose to deconstruct Egyptian and pan-Arab nationalisms, rather than, say, Jordanian or Qatari nationalisms because those two nationalisms constitute what political 'scientists' like to call 'least likely cases'. That is, the hypothesis presented in this chapter about the colonial origins of the nationalisms in the Middle East is least likely to be true when applied to Egyptian and pan-Arab nationalisms. Most historians from both sides of the colonial divide seem to agree that Egypt is the most 'authentic' of the Arab states. It has been an undivided administrative unit for hundreds of years; it has its rich, non-Arab, non-Islamic Pharaonic inventory of symbols, around which a sense of Egyptianness could easily be woven. And there was at least a full generation at the beginning of the twentieth century that saw Egyptian nationalism as the genuine antithesis of British colonialism. The same goes for Arab nationalism, the movement spearheaded anti-western and anti-colonial popular revolts from the 1920s on and during the cold war. Pan-Arabist regimes fought several wars against the remaining settler colonial state in the region, Israel. Finally, Iraq's latest battle with the United States as a sovereign state was fought under an Islamized version of Arab nationalism.

Thus, if the hypothesis made in this chapter passed the test of those two types of nationalisms, it could easily be concluded that the hypothesis is probably true for all other nationalisms in the region.

4

The Colonial Origins of
Egyptian Nationalism

INTRODUCTION

As mentioned in Chapter 3, the cases in this chapter are but examples. Egypt was chosen because it was one of the cases where my hypothesis was least likely to be true. If I can show that Egypt as we know it today is but a colonial construct, and the Egyptian nationalism and the Egyptian nation-state around which it revolves were structured in such a way as to guarantee Egypt's dependence and weakness, then a similar argument can be made about any other Arab or Islamic state with greater ease.

Carl Brown cites the late eighteenth century as the era of the first contacts between Muslims and colonial Europe. He mentions three dates in which the three major Muslim Empires suffered devastating defeats by Europe: the battle of Plassey in 1757, which was a turning point in the history of the British domination of the Indian subcontinent, ruled by fragmented remnants and heir states to the Muslim Mogul Empire; the Treaties of Gulistan in 1812 and Tukmenchay in 1828 in which Iran, again in a state of decadence after the fall of the Safavid dynasty in the previous century, suffered considerable territorial losses to Russia; and the Treaty of Kuchuk Kaynarja that ended the Crimean war between the Ottoman Empire and Russia, where the former surrendered vast territories to the latter (Brown 1990: 84).

Nonetheless, the date of choice here will be 1798, the year of the Napoleonic invasion of Egypt. This was the first modern colonial attack on the heartlands of Arabs and Muslims in the Middle East. The last time French soldiers had been seen on Egyptian shores was during the late Crusades of the thirteenth century. The Napoleonic invasion, which expired in only three years, had long-lasting effects. A failed British attempt to invade Egypt followed in 1807, and a push towards modernization resulted in an ever-increasing European influence due to colonial competition for control, and local attempts to balance interventions from one European power with interventions from another. The Napoleonic invasion could therefore be considered one of the major triggers of modernization in the Middle East; the political side of modernity of course being the establishment of nation states.

Moreover, the discourse and policy of the French occupation forces, and their native appointed government in Egypt, provide us with a pattern that would reappear in every official discourse in Egypt, and to a certain extent in the rest of the region, for the following two centuries. From the very beginning, the invaders and their appointed government presented three arguments in an attempt to legitimize the political system installed by the colonial power. The first was to evoke, or even create, a secular Egyptian nationalism according to which the French invasion would become an act of liberation. The second was to attempt to reconcile the native Islamic culture with the invasion, and the third was to present the French invaders as Muslims, their ideologies being the most modern expression of Islam's essence. As mentioned above, native elites would be using all three arguments to legitimize the existence of the colonially created states they led for the following 200 years in one form or another.

FRENCH EGYPT

On 1 July 1798, as the French were landing in Alexandria, a declaration by the invading forces was being distributed and read aloud to the people of the Mediterranean city. Jabarty, the Egyptian Scholar at Al-Azhar University, and the chronicler of the event from the Egyptian side, cites the declaration in full. The Arabic text that he cites was the document the people of Egypt could read or hear of as news bearers roamed their streets to let them know of the impending attack. The declaration read:

In the Name of God the Most Gracious the Most Merciful, There is no God but Allah, He has neither son nor partner in his power:

Oh, Sheikhs, Imams, Judges ... and notables of the country, tell your people that the French are faithful Muslims too, and the proof of that is that they invaded Great Rome and destroyed the seat of the Pope who had always incited the Nazarenes [that is, Christians] to fight Islam, then they headed to the Island of Malta, and they ousted the knights [of Saint John] who used to claim that God demanded them to fight the Muslims. (Jabarty 1997, 4: 66)

This religious bribe, similar to George Bush senior's argument that the United States had no quarrel with the Iraqi people, is common in the discourse of conquerors. However, the point to note here is that the Expedition recognized Islam as being the main determinant of political affiliation, and avoided any direct assault on the religion as such. At another point in the declaration, the religious bribe is mixed with another, more worldly one, as the values of the French Revolution are set out:

All people are equal before God, the only thing that distinguishes them from one another is their rationality and their merit, and there is a contradiction between the Mamlouks [on the one hand] and reason and merit on the other. What distinguishes them over others so that they could rule Egypt alone, and enjoy the best of things in it, [the best of] pretty concubines, Arabian horses and delightful houses ... With God's help, from now on, let no one of the people of Egypt despair of reaching higher offices ... the Ulama, the notables and reasonable people among them [among the people of Egypt] shall run affairs, and by that the whole Umma will be better off. (ibid.: 67)

This is the first reference to the Umma in the declaration; clearly the reference here is to the people of Egypt, not the whole Umma of Muslims. This is made clearer by the next line:

Long time ago there were great cities, wide canals and thriving commerce in the Egyptian lands and nothing destroyed all of this other than the greed of the Mamouks and their oppression. (ibid.)

However, the reference here is left to be deduced from the context. A more direct sentence including the term '*al-Umma al-Misriyya*' with the intended meaning of an Egyptian nation in the modern French sense of the word appears towards the end of the declaration; we shall cite that in a moment. At this point, however, it is worth noting that the propagation of the liberal values of the French Revolution was coupled with a change in the political system; the formation of a political bureaucracy, manned by the intellectual elite of the conquered province. 'The Ulama, the notables and the reasonable people' are promised higher ranks and offices in an anticipated administration. This link between the creation of an imagined nation of locals and a colonially created native administrative authority, later destined to become a state apparatus, is characteristic of modern Middle Eastern history.

After the religious/cultural and worldly/political bribes the dictations of the declaration become clear, the language becomes militaristic, no longer organized in preamble-like paragraphs but in numbered articles, making it clear that the army of the French Republic meant business:

Article one: All villages located in a circle of three hours from the places by which the French army passes, must send delegates to the commander in chief so that he knows they have obeyed, and that they have raised the banner of the French which is white, blue and red.

Article two: Every village that rises against the French army will be burnt down.

Article five: It is the duty of the Sheikhs, the Ulama, the judges and the Imams to keep doing their jobs, everyone of the locals should safely stay in his house; Prayers will be held in mosques as usual. All Egyptians should thank God the Almighty for the fall of the Dawla of the Mamlouks saying in loud voices: May God preserve the majesty of the Ottoman Sultan, may God preserve the majesty of the French army, may God curse the Mamlouks, and may God take good care of the Egyptian Nation [al-Umma al-Misriyya]. (ibid.: 66–9)

This last recommendation regarding what the Egyptians should say in prayers is a French modification of the Islamic tradition of praying for the current Sultan during Friday sermons. The mentioning of the name of the Sultan in Friday prayers has been, throughout Islamic history, the sign of the popular recognition of his authority. If a preacher at any mosque refrained from mentioning the name of the sultan, it signified rebellion. Moreover, the name of the officers in charge of local authority in any given Islamic province were to be mentioned in sequence after the name of the Sultan, from the most powerful to the least. The attempt by the French to mention the French army after the name of the Sultan in Friday prayers, far from being an optional rhetorical song of praise for the occupation, was an instruction to the Friday prayer leaders/guides to recognize the authority of the French. The fact that the name of the French army was mentioned after the title of the Sultan indicates the recognition by the French of the nominal authority of the Ottoman Sultan over Egypt, that they were ruling Egypt in his name. The declaration issued by the Sultan that later arrived in Egypt rallying Muslims to fight the invaders, and making clear that the French were no Muslims, thus severely damaged the credibility of the French discourse in Egypt.[1]

Finally, as previously mentioned, the term *al-Umma al-Misriyya*, in the sense of an Egyptian nation, was being used for the first time in

1. For the Ottoman rallying calls to the peoples of Egypt and the Levant mentioned see Jabarty (1997, 4: 59–63).

the Arabic language. The equivalent to the phrase here dictated to prayer guides by the French occupation, *Aslaha Allahu hala l-Ummati l-Misriyya* (God take good care of the Egyptian nation), had been *Aslaha Allahu hala l-Muslemeen* (God take good care of the Muslims) or any similar formula to that effect. Ironically, even today, common Friday prayer sermons in Cairo seldom refer to anything like *al-Umma al-Misriyya*, and after praying that God offer good guidance to the rulers of Muslims, the traditional prayer is still the one used before the French invasion.

Nonetheless, the term '*al-Umma al-Misriyya*' did not go out of usage, nor was it without effect. Not only was the introduction of the term the beginning of a process that attempted to create an Egyptian nation, but also a process where the meaning of the word 'Umma' changed in Arabic usage to mean 'nation' in the secular modern European sense. The new meaning of the term coexisted with its old traditional usage whose meaning was discussed in the previous chapters. This coexistence might have caused much of the later confusion in the studies concerned with political identity in the Middle East. It also represented the struggle, in language as well as in parliaments, villages and open battlefields between those two self-definitions (Islamic Umma versus local nation) and the patterns of local and international behaviour they entail.

Despite all these bribes, however, Cairo revolted against the French twice. The first revolt took place while Napoleon was still in the city, as soon as the French decided to collect taxes. The revolt was led by sheikhs from Al-Azhar. They made the argument to the people of the city that the French were infidels, and that therefore they didn't have the right to collect taxes from Muslims. The sheikhs also stated that their colleagues, who cooperated with the French and formed the first Diwan (native authority, the administrative body created by the French to run the domestic affairs of the province), were traitors (for the documents, declarations and events of the first revolt, see Jabarty 1997, 4: 122–31).

In narrating the events of the first revolt, Jabarty, who was by no means a revolutionary, and who later, as a renowned Sheikh of Al-Azhar, joined the Diwan and had good relations with the French, still referred to the occupiers as 'the infidels' and to the rebels as 'the Muslims'. When Jabarty does not use the term '*kafara*' meaning infidels, he uses the term '*al-ifrinj*', meaning the Franks, one used to refer to all western Europeans in the times of the Crusades. Nowhere does he use the term 'Egyptian' in the nationalist sense. Moreover, he associates the local Christians and Jews with the invaders, with no sense of nationhood whatsoever.[2]

After the first revolt, Napoleon, with the consent of the collaborative Sheikhs of the Diwan, issued another declaration to the people of Cairo, hinting that he had superhuman powers, and that he was in fact the awaited Mahdi of the Muslims, he even ventured to state that 20 verses of the Quran referred to him:

Declaration from General Bonaparte to the people of Cairo: There are corrupt people amongst you who incited you, they all perished. Oh, Ulama, and prayer guides, let the people know that those who fight me by their own free will won't find sanctuary in this world or in the hereafter. Could there still be a man so blind not to realize that Fate himself [in Arabic, 'fate' is masculine] directs all our deeds? Is there still such an unbeliever who doubts that everything in this world is under the power of Fate? Let the people know, that from the beginning of creation, it was written [that is, destined] that after the destruction of the enemies of Islam and the fall of the Cross, I'd come from the far west to fulfil my duty. Tell the people that the Noble Quran literally stated, in more than twenty verses, that which took place, and it also explained that which will happen in the future. It is in my power to hold each one of you accountable for what he feels about us in the depth of his heart, because I know everything, even that which you have not revealed to anyone. And the day will come when everyone clearly sees that I am guided by heavenly commands, and that everything humans do will avail them nothing to overcome me. (An Arabic translation of the statement by Bonaparte, published in Courier D'Egypte, p. 82, quoted in Jabarty 1997, 4: 133–4)

2. For example, when the French retook control over the central quarters of the city after the revolt, Jabarty wrote: 'and at night, the Franks entered the city like a flood, passed in the streets and alleys with no one to stop them, as if they were demons or soldiers of the devil' (Jabarty 1997, 4: 127). Also the following description of their capture of Al-Azhar mosque is one often cited in later Egyptian historical narratives:
   'They [the French] tied their horses to the Qibla [a decorated wall in the mosque pointing to the direction of Mecca, the direction worshippers face while praying], they destroyed the lanterns, the lamps, the libraries and the writers' corners, they threw copies of the Quran to the ground, they excreted on them and trampled them with their feet, they drank liquor then threw their empty glasses around the mosque' (ibid.: 129). Summing up the events of the revolt, Jabarty writes: 'and they [the French] slaughtered many people, they threw them in the Nile. In those two days and the days that followed many people died whose numbers are known only to God, and the infidels persisted in their aggression and stubbornness and they did whatever evil they wished to the Muslims' (ibid.: 131). Also, on the relation between local minorities and the French see ibid.: 190.

Along with this marvellous declaration, Bonaparte, who was convincing the Egyptians that 20 verses from the Quran really referred to him and making a Murji'ite argument about fate, established another, more sophisticated political system for Egypt. The executive native authority of Al-Azhar sheikhs which he established on the eve of his conquest of the city was expanded to include a semi-legislative body of 60 sheikhs, notables, merchants, Copts, three French citizens and a French commissioner. This 'Grand Diwan' then elects a smaller Diwan of 14, an executive body, meeting every day to run the administrative affairs of Egypt. However, Napoleon's approval of the elected members was required before they could take office. As commander in chief of the occupying forces, Napoleon also decided how much the members of the Diwan should receive in salary.

What matters most to us in this study is the pattern that was established during this event and that continued to influence the history of the Middle East later. Napoleon chose members of the local elite, created a colonial setting in which they had political and economic stakes, chose to recognize them as representatives of the Egyptian people. Yet the very system through which such representation was supposed to take place was designed to prevent them from any true representation. They were required to perform the contradictory task of accommodating the interests of the French with the emotions of the Egyptians. Their power depended totally on them being accepted as mediators by those two opposite sides of the colonial equation: the occupiers and the occupied. To the people of Egypt the declarations of the Diwan always started with Islamic verses and expressions, and they always ended by stating that calm would be best for Muslims and for Islam. However, between the beginning and the end, the representatives of the Egyptian people had to somehow squeeze in and legitimize the colonial situation in which they were operating. Their claim to represent and control the people, that is, their native-ness, was the main reason why Napoleon was willing to lend them some power and recognition, yet his lending them such power and recognition greatly damaged their legitimacy.[3] This loss of

3. The first Cairo revolt was a demonstration of such loss of legitimacy as the rebellious Sheikhs of Al-Azhar almost accused the members of the Diwan of apostasy. During the second revolt, Sheikh Bakri, a member of the Diwan, was beaten, and his turban and gown torn for being a collaborator. His daughter, who was said to have had relations with the French, was killed. Members of the Diwan were aware of such loss of legitimacy throughout: when Napoleon asked Sheikh Sharqawy and Sheikh Sadat to wear tricolour gowns, they refused because 'that would damage our respect among the

legitimacy, in turn, led the French to loose interest in the local elite as a viable political tool to control the population. We shall see the same pattern repeated with the British. They would create a local elite of landowners, exert pressure on the Ottoman administration in Egypt to establish representative bodies through which that local elite could claim to represent the People of Egypt, manufacture an Egyptian nationalism that legitimized the economic and political rise of such an elite, and then entrust that elite with the same task the French tried to delegate to the Diwan, that is, to accommodate colonial interests with the native emotions, beliefs and political culture.

What happened during the first revolt was repeated during the second revolt after Napoleon conducted a failed assault on Palestine and left Cairo to his second-in-command. An Ottoman attempt to retake Cairo was crushed by the French, yet it was supported by a massive popular rebellion in the streets of the city. The revolt was threatening enough for General Kleber to order the shelling of the entire city centre using his heavy artillery positioned in Saladin's high fortress on the Muqattam hill. The only point worth noting regarding this second revolt might be that, while the first revolt took place against French tax collectors, the second revolt was in fact in support of and led by Ottoman tax collectors who were sent to the city as the Ottomans were anticipating they could retake it. Despite the fact that the taxes were quite burdensome to the Cairene merchants, they did support the Ottoman officials against the French. The events of the second revolt cast doubt on some analyses that see the first revolt as an uprising in protest of tax collection rather than against occupation.

BRITISH EGYPT: THE SKILFULLY CONSTRUCTED AUTOMATON[4]

The French left Egypt under the military pressure of an Ottoman British alliance in 1801. After a period of unrest, Cairo came under the rule of an Albanian officer from the Ottoman army, Mohammad

---

Muslims'. After an angry fit, Napoleon is reported to have settled for having them wear a tricolour badge. Jabarty reports that they used to put it on whenever they met the French and take it off when walking in the streets or meeting Muslims. (On these events and other representations of the second revolt see Jabarty (1997, 4: 321–54).)

4. With some editing, this section and the ones that follow till the end of this chapter are taken from my PhD dissertation, 'The Case of Egypt: A National Liberation Movement and a Colonially Created Government', Boston University, 2004.

Ali Pasha. We will not include a detailed account of his reforms; his extended reign of almost half a century has been the subject of many studies. What matters most to us here is to investigate the ideological, economic and political roots of Egyptian nation building and Egyptian nationalism.

From 1517 when the Mamlouk empire fell to the Ottoman Sultan Selim II, and up until the French evacuation of Egypt in 1801, Egypt's political and economic affairs were determined by a taxing system called '*iltizam*', literally 'commitment'. The Ottoman treasury demanded a fixed amount of money in annual taxes to be paid by the province of Egypt; it then delegated to the local administrators of Egypt the task of collecting that amount. There was no mechanism, however, by which to monitor the amount those local administrators actually collected from the peasants. The Mamlouks, the caste of Muslim Caucasian warrior-slaves who came to rule Egypt and the Levant by the time of the late Crusades in 1261, and stayed in power until the Ottoman conquest in 1517, formed the crux of this stratum of local administrators/tax collectors under Ottoman rule. Mamlouks did not own the land of Egypt, for the land was formally owned by the Ottoman Sultan, but they were given usufruct rights over lots of agricultural land in return for that fixed amount of money expected by the Ottoman treasury. It was therefore customary that they collected much more money from the peasants (the *fellaheen*) than the amounts they were supposed to render to the central treasury and they lived off the difference. This pattern was replicated on a local level, since the Mamlouks delegated tax collection to another lower level of tax collectors, who would in turn charge the peasants for a higher tax than the one they paid to the Mamlouks, and so on. The end result was that the money reaching the treasury of the Egyptian province and the treasury of the Ottoman Empire was much less than the money actually collected from the peasants, the agricultural surplus having been sucked away by chains of tax collectors. The military and economic failure of the Mamlouks in fending off the French invasion made it easier for Mohammad Ali to get rid of them. The 'Massacre at the Citadel' is often cited by European historians fascinated with Oriental despotism, and by Middle Eastern historians fascinated with European Machiavellism. Mohammad Ali invited the Mamlouks for a celebration at the Citadel, the headquarters of Egyptian rulers since Saladin built it in the eighties of the twelfth century, on the occasion of him sending his 16-year-old son with an army to fight the Wahhabis in Arabia. As soon as they arrived, they were led to a passage with a dead end and massacred. In doing that Mohammad Ali ended 500 years of Mamlouk influence in Egypt. He was then able to centralize taxation, generating more surpluses yet collecting less tax from the peasants. His system of monopolies was thus the most significant attempt to establish public ownership of the means of production in the Arab Middle East. He used the agricultural surplus from his monopolies to reinvest in agriculture, build a modern army and start some industrial projects. He also started a trend of commercial farming as he introduced cotton to the Egyptian economy. His vast and modern army proved to be the most competent within the Ottoman Empire, the Sultan Mahmoud II used it more than once, in the war against the Wahhabi Movement in Arabia, and in Greece. Mohammad Ali's industrial modernization project drove him to seek expansion and a conquest of Sudan and an attempt to expand towards Syria followed. The latter put him in confrontation with the sultan. The war between the sultan and Mohammad Ali in Syria was crucial in the history of both Egyptian and Arab nationalisms, for it allowed for European intervention in Egypt and the Levant, as well as for weakening central Ottoman authority vis-a-vis local elites which were becoming more and more dependent on Europe. Such elites would later raise the banners of Egyptian and Arab nationalisms in the region. Mohammad Ali's army, in a series of victories, conquered Palestine, Lebanon and Syria and fought its way through Anatolia until it reached Kotahya not far from the Bosphoros. The Sultan, weakened by Mohammad Ali's attacks from the south and worried about the Russians in the north and northeast, resorted to Britain and the European powers, who did not want to see the Ottoman Empire vanish, nor a strong state, established on the routes to India.

In 1838, as the relations between the Ottoman Sultan and Mohammad Ali were strained. Britain and Turkey had signed a treaty cancelling monopolies all over the Sultanate, including Egypt, of course. France accepted the treaty the same year.[5]

5. Nearly a hundred years after these events, Rafei comments that France accepted the treaty cancelling monopolies because 'it apparently was in accordance with principles of humanity' (Rafei, *Asr Mohammad Ali* [The Age of Mohammad Ali], 1951, 2: 295), meaning free trade and human rights of property. He does not mention France's colonial economic interests in Egypt nor that the collapse of the system of monopolies and the strong central government in Cairo would provide both French and British businesses with opportunities, and that those economic opportunities would in turn provide pretexts for political intervention.

In 1840, Britain, Russia, Prussia, Austria and the Ottoman Empire signed the Treaty of London demanding that Mohammad Ali withdraw his troops from all of northern Syria, to the south of Acre, where he would be allowed to have the southern Syrian province (Palestine) for the rest of his life and his dynasty would be able to retain Egypt as a hereditary kingdom under the sovereignty of the Ottoman Empire. If in ten days he refused, Palestine would be withdrawn from the offer and he would only have Egypt. If in another ten days Mohammad Ali refused, he would face an all-out war with the signatories to the treaty. The Pasha of Egypt was informed of the terms of the agreement while the British Armada was besieging the coasts of Egypt and Syria. Article 5 of the appendix concerning the Egyptian question stated that all the *firmans* (decrees) and laws of the Ottoman Empire would be influential and active in Egypt and Palestine (Rafei 1951: 318). This of course meant extending the system of capitulations, as well as the effects of the 1838 Anglo-Turkish treaty to Egypt and thus the collapse of Mohammad Ali's monopolies. The Treaty of London was then seconded by the Firmans on 13 February and 1 June 1841 which stated that all treaties that had been signed and that would be signed by the Sublime Porte would be active and influential in Egypt.

In allowing the Pasha to retain his governorate yet preventing his troops in northern Syria from reaching Istanbul, and in allowing the Sultan to keep his Sultanate yet preventing his troops from regaining Egypt, the 'even-handedness' of the Treaty of London weakened both sides by keeping them apart, vulnerable and, most of the time, in need of foreign intervention by European powers.

Despite the various tricks Mohammad Ali used to avoid fulfilling his obligations according to the treaty of 1840, his defeat eventually resulted in the gradual privatization of much of the economy. Mohammad Ali had introduced commercial crops into Egypt, most significantly cotton. This tied the Egyptian economy to that of Europe, yet under his system of monopolies, trade with Europe allowed him enough surpluses to establish substantial military and political power as well as start some industrial projects. The privatization of the economy, coupled with the already established links to Europe, eventually contributed to increasing dependence and indebtedness. In fact, as will be shown below, the relation between privatization and indebtedness was circular; privatization increased indebtedness, which the Egyptian government, advised by the British and French councils, attempted to remedy by more privatization. The continuous acquisition of land by private individuals gradually resulted in the emergence of a landowning elite.

Apart from paving the way for increasing foreign investments and creating a national elite, on the international level, the 1840 treaty created the notion of an independent Egypt, and, accordingly, it redefined who the Egyptians were. Rafei's description of the treaty, given his typical Egyptian nationalism, is very telling:

The Treaty of London was the fundamental document regarding Egypt's international standing from 1840 till the outbreak of the World War in 1914. For it specified Egypt's position and created an international independent entity, and elevated its status from a *Welaya* [province] like any other of the *Welayat* [provinces] of the Ottoman Sultanate to an independent state whose independence was conditioned by Turkish sovereignty. Egypt had already achieved her independence in the first Syrian war that ended with the peace of Kotahya[6] 1833, yet, from the point of view of international law she was but a *Welaya* that legally had no privilege over the other Ottoman *Welayat*. But the Treaty of London, which deprived Egypt of the fruits of her victories and limited her independence with many constraints, recognized that Egypt had an international position independent from Turkey, since it made Egypt's rule hereditary in the dynasty of Mohammad Ali. And it is known that the acquisition of the [hereditary] right of government, especially in that era, was an aspect of independence and sovereignty. This means that the Treaty of London recognized Egypt's independence under the condition of Turkish sovereignty, and it was no more in Turkey's right or the right of any other country to jeopardize this independence that was now guaranteed by an international treaty. (Rafei, *Asr Mohammad Ali* [The Age of Mohammad Ali], 343).

The argument here is that the agreement of 1840, which Mohammad Ali was made to accept under the threat of military force, was exemplary of the links between three elements: the Egyptian, non-

6. The Peace of Kotahya was an understanding between the Sultan of the Ottoman Empire and Mohammad Ali, the rogue, but still Ottoman, governor of Egypt, whose troops had controlled Syria and advanced into Anatolia. The terms of the understanding were that Mohammad Ali would withdraw from Anatolia in return for the Sultan appointing him as governor, *Wali*, of greater Syria, the province of Adna, added to Egypt, Hijaz and Crete which Mohammad Ali already had. Nevertheless, Mohammad Ali would still only be an Ottoman governor/Wali, loyal to the Sultan. Despite the advantages Kotahya gave to Mohammad Ali, it was not internationally guaranteed. Legally, it was an internal unwritten understanding between the Sultan and one of his employees. The Sultan could have gone back on his obligations any time he felt the power to do so.

Turkish, non-clerical national elite; British colonial policies in Egypt; and the idea of Egypt as we know it today, as a separate entity whose relative independence from the Ottoman Empire is internationally recognized. The colonial redefinition of the natives of the Nile Valley is not merely cultural, but political. Such a redefinition, seen by Rafei as a step towards the political expression of Egyptian nationhood, was actually part of the colonial process, tightly linked to the economic and military domination. The very same treaty he considers to be the basis for Egypt's independence implied that the land in Egypt be privatized, that foreign capitulations be extended to the country and that the army be reduced from half a million to 18,000 soldiers. Clearly, Egypt's dependence on Europe was the condition of its independence. Such a structural contradiction in the nature of the Egyptian nation and/or state continued up until 1952, when it gave way to Arab nationalism under Nasser.

Now, the rulers of Egypt, weakened by the collapse of the monopolies system and the limited army, knew that their only guarantee against Ottoman attempts to take back the privileges they had was to lean on the European powers which guaranteed their autonomy since 1840. They also needed a local group of Egyptians whose loyalty would lie principally with them rather than with the Ottoman Sultan. Egyptians, in the Napoleonic meaning of the word, now owned some land and thus were fit for such a role. Mohammad Ali's two successors, Said and Ismail, began admitting non-Turkish Egyptians into the state apparatus. During the reign of Said, who started the tradition of borrowing from Europe and constructing colonial projects, Egyptians were promoted to become middle- and high-ranking officers in the army. Most of those promoted were the sons of the local governors, medium-size landowners who were the main beneficiaries of the land privatization projects.

Said's famous speech, quoted by Urabi[7] in his memoirs and in Rafei's history, belongs to this context, that is, the policy of the Khedives of Egypt to find some local support and international guarantee to maintain their special status within the Ottoman Empire.[8]

7. Ahmad Urabi was an Egyptian officer who led a revolt against the autonomous Ottoman governor of Egypt, Khedive Tawfiq, in 1881–82. His rebellion, however, led the Khedive to ask for British military intervention and the occupation of the country.
8. Said made this speech in front of many of the Turkish princes, whether from Mohammad Ali's family or other high-ranking Ottoman officials: 'Brothers, I have studied the conditions of this "Egyptian people" through its history, and I found it oppressed and enslaved by other nations of the earth, many

Ismail, Said's successor, who was more enthusiastic regarding increasing his privileges vis-a-vis Turkey, endeavoured to establish a semi-parliament. On 19 November 1864, Egypt had a consultative body, *Majlis Shoura al-Nuwwab*, of 75 members chosen and elected from the *umdas* (provincial governors and chiefs of villages), notables and sons of the influential families in the country. Though this council did not have enough power when it came to real matters such as finance and war, its mere presence gave the impression that Ismail was a legitimate ruler of an independent state, he also paid a lot of money in order to have the title of 'Khedive' (a higher rank than the normal Wali, which was held by his predecessors Mohammad Ali, Abbas I and Said).

This class of landowning Egyptians, which was gaining more power, whether in the semi-legislative council, the bureaucracy or in the army, was clearly dependent on Europe, as mentioned above, yet it was naturally desirous of increasing its powers. This desire expressed itself in the landowners' support for Urabi's movement. The Treaty of London created a delicate balance of power between the Khedive and the landowners, it also reduced the Egyptian army to military insignificance. Nonetheless the small army of 18,000 troops it allowed to survive still functioned as a vehicle for middle class, non-landowning Egyptians to ascend up the social ladder. The Urabi revolt, named after the Egyptian army officer who led it, Ahmad Urabi, started as a dispute between Egyptian and Circassian officers in the army, but became a movement for reducing foreign intervention in the country.

---

states came to rule it consecutively, like the Hittites, the Assyrians, the Persians, even the peoples of Libya, Sudan, Greece and the Romans. This was before Islam, and after it, the conquering states (*al-Dowal al-Fatiha*) took it over, like the Umayyads, the Abbasids, the Fatimids of the Arabs, and the Turks, the Kurds and the Circassians, and more than once France has raided these lands until it occupied in the beginnings of this century by the time of Bonaparte, and since I consider myself an Egyptian, I have to bring up (educate/raise) this people, and edify it until it is suitable to serve its country in a good manner, and not be in need of foreigners. I have prepared myself to make these views of mine clear in words and deeds' (Said, son of Mohammad Ali, quoted in Rafei, *Asr Ismail* [The Age of Ismail], 1932, 1: 36). Some of the Turkish princes were angered by the speech, for equating them with other invaders. Yet it is interesting to point out that while Said used the word 'enslavement' to describe pre-Islamic invasions, and the word 'raid' to describe France's attacks, he used the positive sounding word '*Fateh*' to describe the Islamic empires. Moreover, the contradiction in his speech becomes clearer when he declares that he 'considers himself an Egyptian'.

While the Egyptian nationalist narrative depicts Britain's intervention in 1882 as an act directed mainly against the Egyptian nationalist movement – the class of local governors and middle-size landowners who supported Urabi – British policies after occupation seem to run against that argument. The British deprived the landowners from assuming direct power from the Khedive. Part and parcel of such political change would have been to rearrange the financial dealings with Europe, which might have jeopardized the interests of European creditors. Once that and Britain's imperial routes were secured, little harm, political or economic, was done to the national elite. In fact Evelyn Baring, Earl of Cromer, Britain's high commissioner in Egypt, the author and builder of '*Modern Egypt*', argues that when it came to strengthening the local elite, the British occupation performed Urabi's programme, only with greater skill (Cromer [1908] 1962: 608).

As an elite whose political and economic interests converged with European policies was created, the colonial choice of who will represent the whole native population of Egypt was made. Thus, the redefinition of the land and people of Egypt into an Egyptian nation did not stop at the creation of internationally recognized Egypt in 1840. Rather, it continued into choosing which section of the population was to represent that colonially created entity. Here it is useful to turn to Cromer's *Modern Egypt*. To Lord Cromer, the redefinition of Egypt and Egypt's government was a clear objective:

Although, I will not venture to predict the goal which will eventually be reached, I have no hesitation in expressing an opinion as to that which we should seek to attain. So far as can at present be judged, only two alternative courses are possible. Egypt must eventually either become autonomous, or it must be incorporated into the British Empire. Personally, I am decidedly in favour of moving in the direction of the former of these alternatives...All that we have to do is to leave behind us a fairly good, strong and – above all things – stable government, which will obviate anarchy and bankruptcy, and will thus prevent the Egyptian question from again becoming a serious cause of trouble to Europe. We need not inquire too minutely into the acts of such government. In order to ensure its stability, it should possess a certain liberty of action, even though it may use that liberty in a manner which would not always be in accordance with our views. But it is essential that, subsequent to the evacuation, the government should broadly speaking act on principles which will be in conformity with the common place requirements of Western Civilization. The idea, which at one time found favour with a section of the British Public, that Egypt may be left to 'stew in its own juice', and that however great may be the confusion and internal disorder which is created, no necessity for European interference will arise, may at once be set aside as wholly impracticable. It is absurd to suppose that Europe will look on as a passive spectator while a retrograde government based on purely Mohammedan principles and obsolete Oriental ideas, is established in Egypt. (ibid.: 903)

He also states that:

What Europeans mean when they talk of Egyptian self government is that the Egyptians, far from being allowed to follow the bent of their own unreformed propensities, should only be permitted to govern themselves after the fashion in which Europeans think they aught to be governed. (ibid.: 874)

Cromer writes a whole section at the beginning of his book about 'the difficulty of ascertaining Eastern opinion' (ibid.: 5–6). He is not referring to differences in language; rather, he is referring to differences in culture. He cannot possibly see the opinions of the native population, except with great difficulty. To him the native way of thinking is irrational and they are therefore incapable of forming an opinion. In 'The Dwellers in Egypt' and the following chapter, 'The Moslems', Cromer makes clear that Islam, and maybe the biological qualities of the Egyptians, prevent them from thinking rationally.

The British occupation rendered great benefits to the Egyptians; any rational thinking would lead them to appreciate that. Any opposite feeling could be attributed to Islam, that is, irrationality,[9] or simply a form of ingratitude, that is, immorality.[10] But to Cromer, his mission was one of education and civilization; his duty was to transform the population of Egypt from such a backward Islamic position to one of modernity and rationality. After thirty pages of describing

9. Cromer juxtaposes Islam and rationality, defined by seeking material gains, as opposites, yet he is optimistic that the latter will eventually overcome. 'In truth, religious conviction, backed by racial prejudices and by the sympathy generally entertained amongst Orientals for a theocratic form of government, may for a while wrestle with personal interest and political associations, but chances are that, if the struggle is continued, religious conviction will get a fall' (ibid.: 592).

10. 'The want of gratitude displayed by a nation to its alien benefactors is almost as old as history itself. In whatever degree ingratitude may exist, it would be unjust to blame Egyptians, for following the dictates of human nature. In any case, whatever be the moral harvest we may reap, we must continue to do our duty, and our duty has been indicated to us by the Apostle St. Paul: We must not be "weary in well-doing"' (ibid.: 909).

how uncivilized Islam was as a social code, Cromer mentions the following:

Nevertheless, there is one saving clause, which serves in some respect as a bond of union between the two races. Once explain to an Egyptian what he is to do, and he will assimilate the idea rapidly. He is a good imitator, and will make a faithful, even sometimes a too servile copy of the work of his European caretaker. His civilization may be a veneer, yet he will readily adopt the letter, the catchwords and jargon, if not the spirit of European administrative systems. His movements will, it is true, be not un-frequently those of an automaton, but a skilfully constructed automaton may do a great deal of useful work. This feature in the Egyptian character is of great importance in connection with the administration of the country. (ibid.: 579)

An independent Egypt would then be a 'skilfully constructed automaton', one that had been educated and directed by Britain and one that would be grateful to it. To administrate the country, then, Cromer needed someone who was native by birth but European by culture, someone whose language, logic and way of thinking Cromer could understand. This translator of cultures would be fit for representing the Egyptian population. For any other representation would discredit Cromer's missionary claims. Naturally, those among the native population who would accept the colonizer's logic would be those whom the colonizer's logic benefits most. While those landowners whose financial affairs the occupation improved were not, by any means, the majority of the Egyptian population, they were taken by Cromer as representatives of that silent majority. It is worth noting that Cromer keeps referring to Britain's main mission in Egypt as one whose aim is to benefit the *fellaheen* (the peasants), the most downtrodden and oppressed, yet of all the people he knew in Egypt, he never mentions the opinion of a *fellah*, or the way by which a *fellah's* opinion or preferences could be known to him.[11] Cromer only assumes what the *fellah* might want.

In the next section I will show how the leaders of the Egyptian national movement of 1919 were just the right people whose logic Cromer would accept. I shall also highlight their relation to Islam,

11.   'It has been the misfortune of the English in Egypt that the classes who, under their political programme, most benefited by British rule, were those who were least of all able to make their voices heard, the *fellaheen* are, politically speaking, ciphers, they are too apathetic, too ignorant' (ibid.: 610).

in the sense that they attempted to find that impossible compromise between Islam and their new born nationalism.

AHMAD LUTFI AL-SAYIDD: THE THEORIST OF EGYPTIAN NATIONALISM

Ahmad Lutfi Al-Sayidd was the main theorist of Egyptian nationalism; his ideas inspired most of the leaders of the Egyptian nationalist movement that dominated Egypt's political life from the turn of the twentieth century till Nasser's coup in 1952. He starts his autobiography *Qissat Hayati* (My Life Story) with the following lines:

I was raised in a pure Egyptian family, that knows no other homeland but the Egyptian homeland, finds no pride except in Egyptian-hood and does not belong [holds no loyalty] except for Egypt, that blessed [kind] land in which civilization grew since the most ancient of times, and that has enough natural wealth and ancient honour to achieve progress and glory. (Lutfi Al-Sayidd 1998: 11)

On 15 January 1872, Ahmad Lutfi Al-Sayidd was born to an Umdeh (belonging to the *Shaikh al-Balad* medium-size landowners class, that benefited most from the privatization of land after dismantling Mohammad Ali's system of monopolies, as mentioned above) who also held the title Pasha, in the village of Burqeen in Lower Egypt. He learned the Quran at the *kuttab*, the traditional mosque-school of the village, then, on a friend's advice, his father sent him to a government elementary school in his home governorate of Daqahliyya (one of those started by Mohammad Ali, then endorsed as part of Ismail's dependent modernization project) instead of Al-Azhar. After finishing elementary school in 1885, he joined the Khedivite School (high school level) in Cairo. Then, in 1889 he joined the School of Law (ibid.: 19). In 1893, while he was still a student at the School of Law, he went to Istanbul along with the Khedive, and there he met Jamal-ul-din Al-Afghani who, after being exiled from Egypt, was staying in Istanbul, hosted by the Caliph.

While some scholars of Egyptian nationalism such as Charles Wendell assert that Lutfi Al-Sayidd did not learn anything from Al-Afghani, it is apparent that by that time, he still had pro-Islamic loyalties to the Khedive and to the Ottoman Empire; his shift away from Al-Afghani's ideology came later on, when his career and socio-economic status were at stake. It is true that there is no trace of Al-Afghani's ideas in Lutfi Al-Sayidd's work and that, more often than not, his work runs directly opposite to those ideas, yet one has to remember that Al-Sayidd wrote all of his work after the great shift in his career took place. In 1894 he finished Law School and was appointed in various low and middle-ranking government posts, and in 1896, he had thought, along with some of his friends, to form an association whose aim was to liberate Egypt from English occupation. It was around this time that he met with the young Mustafa Kamel,[12] the rising figure of pro-Ottoman, anti-British resistance in Egypt who also was on very good terms with the Ottoman Khedive. Mustafa Kamel told Lutfi Al-Sayidd that the Khedive knew everything about the association and endorsed it. The members of Lutfi Al-Sayidd's association, including himself, became part of Al-Hizb-Al-Watani (the patriotic party led by Mustafa Kamel, under the nominal leadership of the Khedive himself). The party's ideology of pan-Islamism and endorsement of the Caliphate is almost an extension of Al-Afghani's ideas. Even the code-names used within that party were telling about its ideological tendencies, the Khedive was referred to as Al-Sheikh, and Mustafa Kamel was referred to as Abul-fida (literally, the father of sacrifice, but the expression actually means the patron of self-sacrifice or simply the one who would sacrifice himself), and Lutfi Al-Sayidd was called Abu Muslim[13] (ibid.: 29).

The Khedive asked him to go to Switzerland and stay there for one year to acquire Swiss citizenship on the grounds that it might give Lutfi some legal protection as he resisted the British occupation. Lutfi

12. Mustafa Kamel was a young Egyptian of Turkish origin, who spearheaded the civil resistance to the British occupation of Egypt. He was a staunch supporter of the Ottoman Empire and the Islamic identity of Egypt. His political position was to refuse negotiation with Britain until it withdrew from Egypt, and to attempt to find support among other European powers, especially France, to the cause of liberating Egypt and returning it to Ottoman sovereignty. He was on good terms with Abbas II son of Tawfiq son of Ismail son of Mohammad Ali, the Khedive of Egypt at the beginning of the twentieth century and up until the outbreak of World War One. Mustafa Kamel's version of Egyptian anti-colonialism, was overshadowed by that of Lutfi Al-Sayidd, on the basis of which the independent Egyptian Kingdom was declared after the defeat of the Ottomans in World War One.

13. The codename refers to Abu Muslim Al-Khurasani, the secret agent of the Abbasids, who organized their supporters in Iran and Iraq, and was secretly able to raise an army much larger than that of the Umayyads, before leading it in a series of battles starting in Persian Merv and ending in Abu-Sir west of the Nile, where the last of the Umayyad Caliphs was killed, and the Abbasid Caliphate was declared, first in Koufa then moved to Baghdad.

went to Switzerland and stayed there for most of 1897. He attended lectures in law and philosophy at Geneva University, where he also met Mohammad Abdu. Abdu was another student of Al-Afghani. He was a sheikh trained in Sunni Islamic jurisprudence, he had supported the Urabi revolt, and therefore became an enemy of the Khedive and his family. In his earlier years he advocated Afghani's ideas, and co-edited a magazine called *Al-Urwa Al-Wuthqa* ('the strongest bond' referring to Islam as the strongest political bond among Muslims). Nonetheless, he gradually moved more and more towards the camp of the colonial powers, as he advocated a programme of liberation by education and argued against the absolute powers of the Khedive. He later became a friend of Cromer's, who forced the Khedive to allow him to return to Egypt, appoint him as a judge, and then as the highest religious and legal authority in the country: Great Mufti.

By the time Lutfi Al-Sayidd and Abdu met, the latter had already established good relations with the British. The Khedive, who never had good relations with Abdu, whether before or after Abdu's change of heart towards the British, was not happy with this new friendship between Al-Sayidd and Abdu. When Lutfi returned to Cairo, he was informed, again by Mustafa Kamel, of the Khedive's position. Lutfi seemed affected by Abdu's ideas on resisting occupation by education. In his last report to the Khedive, he wrote that he should head a movement of public education. After eight years with little political significance, and almost no contact with either the Khedive or Mustafa Kamel, Lutfi resigned from his government post and started in 1905–06 establishing the newspaper *Al-Jareeda* and the Al-Umma Party (ibid.: 32–3).

Lutfi Al-Sayidd mentions that the idea of forming the party and the newspaper came to him during the Aqaba dispute between Britain and the Ottoman Empire. The British claimed that the seaport town of Aqaba, situated at the tip of the Aqaba bay between modern-day Egypt, Palestine, Jordan and Saudi Arabia, administratively belonged to Egypt, while the Ottoman Empire claimed it did not. Almost all Egyptian newspapers supported Turkey, with considerable religious fury, despite the fact that the British were, strategically, claiming a city that would be advantageous to Egypt. Yet the public sentiment seemed to identify with the Islamic bond between Egypt and Turkey, rather than with an Egyptian national interest so present in the colonial discourse of the British (on the Egyptian pro-Turkish reaction see Cromer [1908] 1962: 591–2, Lutfi Al-Sayidd 1998: 38, and Wendell 1972: 235). Lutfi Al-Sayidd thought of establishing an association of *A'yan* (landowners and notables) in Egypt to oppose both Turkey and Britain, and call for the establishment of an independent, democratic and liberal Egypt. It is worth noting that those were quite the same objectives Cromer had declared as the ultimate policy of the occupation. Al-Sayidd wrote that the establishment of *Al-Jareeda* came to represent those who have real interests in the country, 'whom Lord Cromer used to claim had no issue with the occupation!' (ibid.: 39). He put an exclamation mark at the end of the previous sentence to express his disagreement with Cromer's argument; in a sense the party was formed to 'tell' Cromer that those with real interest in the country were 'not' satisfied with the occupation. The point I would like to draw attention to here is not whether Lutfi Al-Sayidd was true about his party's opposition to the occupation, but rather what kind of opposition and what kind of alternative to occupation he was advocating. For replacing an occupying force definitely includes opposing it, yet it also includes accepting much of its programme. I would also like to point out that, unlike Mustafa Kamel's Al-Hizb-Al-Watani, whose policy was not to have any negotiations with the British unless they withdrew from Egypt, Hizb-Al-Umma was formed precisely to address the British, as well as establish the notion of an independent liberal democratic Egyptian nation on the basis of the treaty of 1840 (see ibid.: 38–42).[14] The resemblance between the definitions of Egypt held by the party and that held by Cromer

14. The contrast between the names of the two parties 'Al-Umma' and 'Al-Watani' is also telling of their political orientations. The name of the Al-Umma Party involves an attempt to make a shift in the meaning of the concept of Al-Umma. The term, which previously referred to the community of Muslims, was now the term which referred to the Egyptian people as an Umma. Al-Hizb-Al-Watani, however, used the word 'Watan', which means 'homeland', to refer to Egypt. Egypt is simply a geographical location whose inhabitants belong to the Islamic Umma and should regain the Watan, (the homeland) they lost to a non-Muslim power – that is, they are not an Umma by themselves. It should be remembered, as mentioned above, that the expression 'Egyptian Umma' was first introduced into the Arabic language by Napoleon in 1798. The point here is that the Al-Umma Party, right from its name, was accepting the colonial redefinition of Egypt. If the Egyptians were indeed a nation, they would first need to be convinced of that very fact; they should learn their own nationalism. Not only did they have to learn that they should demand a government of their own, but also they should learn what kind of government they should demand. The teacher in both cases would be Europe and, in many cases, the occupation force itself. The acceptance of the notion of Egypt thus led to the acceptance of the whole colonial logic. See Lutfi Al-Sayidd's high esteem of Cromer below.

could easily be seen in Lutfi Al-Sayidd's work. Cromer juxtaposes the rational modern Egypt brought about by occupation to the irrational medieval Islamic Egypt. Lutfi Al-Sayidd makes the same juxtaposition:

We say this, and avow it before Allah and all Mankind, that the Egyptians must not, in the interest of the country, make religion, under these circumstances, the basis for their political acts. They must repudiate today, as they have in the past, any accusation of religious bigotry [al-Ta'assub al-dini], i.e. pan-Islamism and fanaticism. For they have found out that this accusation was one of the major pretexts employed by the British for remaining in Egypt, and that they are still making use of it up to the present moment. (Lutfi Al-Sayidd, Al-Jareeda, 21 October 1911, translated by and quoted in Wendell 1972: 233)

Not only does Lutfi Al-Sayidd accept the course of modernization suggested by the occupation, he openly mentions that that acceptance is the condition for achieving independence. Sticking to the Islamic 'irrationality' is a pretext for the occupation to stay. The remedy is to rationalize the Egyptians away from such 'bigotry' so as to convince the occupation of their merit. The twist in Lutfi Al-Sayidd's logic here is that he denounces the Egyptians' attachment to Islam as a form of socio-political organization, because that leads to the continuation of occupation, rather than denouncing the fact that the British would continue their occupation because the Egyptians made a choice that did not suit the occupation's taste, paradigm, or political and strategic interests. It seems to be an underlying assumption in Lutfi Al-Sayidd's passage that as long as the Egyptians are religious bigots then it remains within the right of the British to occupy them until they are civilized, which is the same logic mentioned above by Cromer.

Charles Wendell, who considered Lutfi Al-Sayidd the fruit of Egyptian 'evolution' due to contact with Europe through the nineteenth century and the first half of the twentieth century, states that Islam was a nightmare to both the European statesmen and to Lutfi Al-Sayidd (Wendell 1972: 231). Lutfi Al-Sayidd called those of the Egyptians (the vast majority according to his own calculations) who adopted Islamic political loyalties, 'the mob' or the 'unsophisticated' (Lutfi Al-Sayidd, Al-Jareeda, 2 September 1912, quoted in ibid.):

Lutfi admitted the existence of a dilemma of his own at the very moment he took a decisive step forward out of the nineteenth-century impasse. He sees very clearly the irreconcilable differences between the ancient Umma and the

Egyptian Umma he was celebrating, and he had given his wholehearted allegiance to the latter. Yet even he had to confess that the 'common people' (al-'amma) were still more attracted to the medieval ideal of the Umma Muhammadiyya than they were to that of their own nation, if indeed they were aware that such a thing existed. Circumstances placed Lutfi in the curious position of a liberal nationalist who had to defend the idea of Egyptian nationhood, not merely against western critics but also against fellow-Egyptians who rejected the concept in favor of other loyalties. Therefore his less obvious mission in journalism was to assist in the creation of the nation he was simultaneously addressing. (ibid.)

In another article Lutfi Al-Sayidd wrote in 1912, he asserted that utilitarianism was the only basis on which political action should be taken.[15] The problem with this is that he accepted the self-definition suggested by the occupation, that is the Egypt he is preaching in the quotation above. Egypt, represented by its middle-class landowners, was financially benefiting from occupation, and Lutfi Al-Sayidd recognized that. What the British were doing was good, good for the Egypt they created that is, not good for the Ottoman Empire or for the Islamic Umma, nor was it good for the social classes within Egypt who were loyal to the Ottoman Empire and the Islamic Umma such as the Khedive, and the *effendis* (urban students, who had been losing job opportunities to foreign employees put in their place on the advice of the British High Commissioner) or the peasants. Utilitarianism involved two processes of learning from one's colonial master. It is a western philosophy learned by Lutfi Al-Sayidd and taught by him to his people, and if colonially created Egypt was to be the focus of loyalty, utilitarianism would be an argument for, rather than against, the policy of the occupation. Accepting utilitarianism, then, meant learning how to perform the function of the occupation, to accept

15. Lutfi Al-Sayidd wrote: 'It seems to me that what renders this pan-Islamic credo self contradictory is that attempt to make differences in religious beliefs the basis for political action in the affairs of this world. This is a dangerous credo. We have shown why it is dangerous on every opportune occasion, and we agree with those who say that only the vital principle of utilitarianism is suitable for adoption as a guiding principle for political activity. We believe categorically that making utility the basis for action is a credo which does not conflict with the monotheistic [Islamic] faith. Let people act as they wish in actual life for their own benefit, with the proviso that they do not legalize the forbidden, nor forbid the legal, and that they comport themselves in conformity with the teachings of their religion, which commands the good and forbids the evil' (Lutfi Al-Sayidd, *Al-Jareeda*, 1 September 1912, quoted in Wendell 1972: 230).

the occupation's logic, which was the only way by which occupation could be convinced of the Egyptians' merit.

The above congruence between the logic of Lutfi Al-Sayidd and Cromer led Lord Lloyd, the British High Commissioner in Egypt (1925–29) to state that the Umma Party was actually created by the latter:

Cromer had for some time been at work upon a policy, calculated as he thought to offer a much more sober and effective check to the nationalist Party's [Mustafa Kamel's Al-Hizb-Al-Watani] campaign. He knew that there was in Egypt a large number of moderate minded men of influence and standing who did not by any means welcome the activities of Mustafa Kamel and his fellow workers. Equally patriotic, they were more broad-minded and far-sighted, and they desired to achieve political progress by more cautious and constitutional methods. He had been endeavouring to procure among them some form of active organization by which their views might be propagated and their aims promoted. As a result of his efforts there was formed in October 1907 a new party – the party of the nation – 'Hisb-el-Umma' with its own newspaper, *El-Jerideh*. (Lloyd 1934, 2: 50)

After such a change of heart, Lutfi Al-Sayidd held much higher posts than the ones he held during the eight years previous to his career in *Al-Jareeda*.[16] When the first delegation, 'Wafd', was formed by

16. Egypt was declared a protectorate on 18 December 1914. In 1915 Lutfi accepted an appointment from Sultan Hussain Kamel as public prosecutor of Bani Suwaif, and later in the same year, the post of director of the National Library, replacing the German scholar, Arthur Schaade. It was in this favourable environment that he found the time to begin his translation of Aristotle. In November 1918 Lutfi resigned from the National Library to join the Wafd, the delegation of Egyptian nationalists who advanced the cause of Egyptian independence after World War One. Right after the 1919 Revolution, he returned to the National Library and remained there until 1925. In 1922 he drew up a programme for the university conceived as a faculty of humanities and sent his proposal to King Fouad. The King approved the programme, adding that the government was planning to found a new university which could presumably incorporate the older institution as its faculty of humanities. In 1925, Lutfi was appointed chancellor of the university-to-be. The foundation stone was laid by the King himself on 7 February 1928. In June that year, Lutfi became the Minister of Education until the fall of the cabinet in October 1929. In 1930 he was recalled as chancellor of the university. In 1937, with the increasing influence of Young Egypt and the Muslim Brothers, he resigned because the government refused to establish a police force inside the university; he had argued that too much political rivalry existed among the students and that there was too much activism on campus.

members of the Egyptian Legislative Assembly to ask the British High Commissioner for permission to go to Paris to represent the Egyptian cause to the world, Lutfi was the only member of the delegation who was not a member of the Legislative Assembly.

A BRIEF ACCOUNT OF THE RISE AND FALL OF EGYPTIAN NATIONALISM

The argument here is that the very individuals, who, in terms of ideology and in terms of political action, led the Egyptian nationalist movement that culminated in the 1919 revolution, were those who met Cromer's criteria, and were brought into politics by the consent of the colonial power, rather than against its will. Not only did these individuals come from the class of large and medium-size landowners who were brought into Egyptian politics by the colonial intervention of the nineteenth century, but also their own individual interests became intertwined with the colonial presence in Egypt. Ahmad Lutfi Al-Sayidd was given here only as an example. The same could be said about Saad Zaghloul, the archetype of the Egyptian nationalist hero, speaker of the Legislative Assembly created by the British occupation, and leader of the Egyptian revolution of 1919. The same is also true about his successor Mustafa Al-Nahhas. They were all anti-colonial hard-line students, yet once they started looking for a position in the colonially created political institutions of Egypt, they seemed to have accepted the colonial discourse. Moreover, there was a dialectical relation between the formation of those personal socio-economic interests and the adoption of the colonial discourse; their social position led them to accept the colonial logic and that led the colonial officers to accept them as representative of the Egyptian people which in turn bettered their socio-economic standing. Those members of the elite were accepted by the colonial power as representatives of the majority of the Egyptian population precisely because their discourse was more like that of the colonial power than that of the majority of the Egyptians.

In the following sections, I shall show how this paradox of representation led to the paradox of replacement where these representatives

---

Introducing university police to campus would have offended many political parties including the ones in power. At the end of that year he became, conveniently enough, Minister of Interior. Then he returned to the university in 1941. Finally he left to take a seat in the Senate, and became president of the academy of Arabic language until his death on 5 March 1963 (Wendell 1972: 218–21).

of the people of Egypt helped create an Egyptian independence that secured the interests of the occupation. I shall also show how such a colonial deal was bound to fail because it depended on reconciling two irreconcilable agendas and identities.

The Drafts of 1917–18

As World War One approached its end, Egyptian officials were worried about their legal position. Egypt had legally been part of the Ottoman Empire, its status was guaranteed by the Treaty of London in 1840, and the various *firmans* given to Ismail by the Sublime Porte. The British occupation in 1882 did not have any legal definition. Then, in 1914, Egypt was severed from the Caliphate and Britain gave Prince Hussain Kamel the title of Sultan and declared Egypt a protectorate. British protection was a military rather than political measure and it was a temporary one taken due to the necessities of war. Egyptian officials recognized the awkwardness of their position. Egypt was no longer part of the Ottoman Empire, it was not part of the British Empire and it was not an independent state. It was called a Sultanate but its independence was not recognized by any other nation including Britain. The famous 13 November 1918 visit, which the Speaker of the Legislative Assembly and, later on, leader of the Egyptian nationalist movement Saad Zaghloul and two of his companions paid to Sir Francis Reginald Wingate, the British High Commissioner in Egypt (1917–19), was not the first attempt by Egyptian government officials to determine their position vis-a-vis Britain. Actually, attempts were being made all through 1917 (see Lasheen 1971, 2: 86–91). Due to the sensitive situation during the war, and the fact that most Egyptian officials owed their positions to the consent, if not the endorsement, of the British High Commissioner, most of the proposals, understandings and drafts were not officially presented to the British government. One important exception was a proposal drafted by Hussain Rushdi, the Prime Minister under Sultan Hussain Kamel, and the man who played a crucial role in facilitating the country's administration under British protection. It was up to his government to keep Egyptian pro-Turkish and anti-British sentiments, that had expressed themselves on various occasions before World War One (the Taba incident 1906 and the War for Tripoli in 1911, for example) from causing serious trouble to the British occupation during the war.[17] Rushdi's position was

17. About Sultan Hussain Kamel and his Prime Minister Hussain Rushdi, the famous pro-Ottoman Iraqi poet Ma'rouf Al-Rasafi wrote in verse 'I used

crucial enough to all parties so that he could present his proposal without risking the loss of his office. On 9 July 1917, Rushdi showed his draft to Saad Zaghloul. The main points in the draft were the following: Britain would recognize Egypt's government as a constitutional monarchy headed by a hereditary sultan and assigned ministers. The autonomy of the sultan should be gradually increased. The Legislative Assembly would have the power of issuing legislations that should be ratified by the sultan and must not contradict Egypt's foreign commitments (the capitulations). The sultan would not be allowed to have representatives abroad other than the representatives of Britain; however, he would have the right to receive foreign representatives in Cairo. Britain would have the right to occupy any part of the land of Egypt, and the Egyptian government would partially pay for such an occupation. The commander of the Egyptian army would be British. There would be a British financial councillor whose permission must be taken for any act of government spending as well as British councillors in each ministry who have the right to advise yet not to supervise (Lasheen 1975, 2: 87–8, Zaghloul's Notebook 31, 1755, and Ramadan's edition of Zaghloul's diaries 1987–98, 6: 221–5).

Rushdi presented his draft to Mr William Brunyate, the British councillor at the ministry of justice, who reported it to the British Foreign Office. Lenient as this draft was, the British government was extremely unwelcoming with regards to discussing Egypt's future before the end of the war (Lasheen 1975, 2: 101–2, *Kahmsoun 'Am ala Thawrat 1919* [50 years since the Revolution of 1919], 81–6, Zaghloul, Notebook 28, 1500, 1508–9, 1518, and Ramadan's edition of Zaghloul's diaries 1987–98, 8: 41, 53–5, 73).

On 9 August 1917, in light of Hussain Rushdi's proposals, Ahmad Lutfi Al-Sayidd and Saad Zaghloul decided to draft an alternative proposal for an agreement between Egypt and Britain in which Egypt's situation would be defined. The broad lines of the draft are mentioned in Zaghloul's diaries. Egypt would become a hereditary constitutional monarchy. The sultan would practise his powers through his ministers, who would be accountable to an elected legislative

---

to think that all baseness was divided among the two Hussains of Egypt, until the shameless hand of treason added a third Hussain to them from Hijaz', referring to Al-Sharif Hussain Ibn Ali, father of King Abdullah I of Jordan and Faisal I of Iraq, and leader of the Arab Revolt alongside the British in World War One (Rasafi 1975: 59–64).

council. Britain would retain the right to occupy the Suez Canal region and the three major cities therein, Port Said, Ismailiyya and Suez, whenever there was a threat to its imperial communications. Egypt would have the right to defend itself with its own army, but in case of actual threat, Britain had the right to intervene. Egypt would only have the right to sign economic treaties with other countries, that is, no political or military pacts. Egypt would have no embassies abroad and British embassies elsewhere would represent them. British employees in the Egyptian government would stay in their posts until their contracts expired then they were to be replaced by Egyptian employees. In return, Egypt would promise that, in case foreign expertise was needed, only British candidates would be considered. And lastly, the commander of the Egyptian army would be British (Zaghloul, Notebook 31, 1762–1763, Ramadan's edition of Zaghloul's diaries 1987–98, 11: 232–3, also see Lasheen 1975, 2: 89–90).

There are a couple of points that are worth noting about the two drafts mentioned above. While at first sight the two drafts seem quite different, a closer reading would make the differences diminish. While Rushdi's draft allows Britain at all times to occupy any part of the land of Egypt, Zaghloul's draft allows Britain to intervene for Egypt's protection, whenever threatened. Yet Zaghloul leaves to Britain the definition of both intervention and threat. British military intervention on Egyptian soil is not conditioned by an Egyptian request or even permission to Britain. This actually meant that Britain had the right to decide, with no constraint whatsoever, why, when, how and for what period to occupy Egypt. The second difference is about the accountability of the sultan; here Zaghloul's draft gives more power to the native Egyptian landowning elite over the Turco-Egyptian Pashas represented by the Sultan. However, both would be equally dependent on Britain given the other constraints mentioned in the draft. Other than that, the two drafts only differ on the issue of British councillors, their authorities and the number of British employees in the Egyptian government. Thus the real differences between the drafts of Zaghloul and Rushdi are not actually about functions, they are about who will perform those functions. It is worth noting that this was the declared goal of the British occupation according to Cromer and the rest of the British High Commissioners in Egypt. It was clear in the British colonial discourse that Britain's task was to raise, educate and train Egyptians who could exactly do the job Britain was doing. The logic of replacement is thus common to both colonial and nationalist discourses, as is clear from the above drafts.

Moreover, these two drafts, with only a few changes, became the two alternative programmes that defined the two camps, the 'extremists' led by Zaghloul and the 'moderates' led by Rushdi and his Minister of Education Adli Yakan, right after the 1919 revolution. These drafts also became the basis for Egypt's independence in 1922.

However, for the time being, the British government was not ready to accept that the time for replacement had come, that the Egyptians were mature enough to break from their colonial patrons, and Rushdi's draft was dismissed, while Zaghloul had not declared his own to the British in the first place.

The Revolt and the Delegation

At the famous meeting between the three Pashas and the British High Commissioner in November 1918, the conversation as reported by two different historians, Rafei and Ramadan, could be easily described as an attempt by the three Pashas to prove to their interlocutor how deserving they, and the nation they represented, were of the power they sought (Ramadan 1968, 1: 88–91, Rafei 1955, 1: 93–7, and 'Wingate's Report on 24 November', Public Record Office: FO/371/3204, Document No. 15, in *Kahmsoun 'Am ala Thawrat 1919* [50 Years Since the 1919 Revolution], no pagination). In doing that, they started the first steps towards replacement. The idea was to replace the protectorate with Egyptian independence and an alliance between Britain and Egypt in which Egypt would preserve Britain's interests. When Saad Zaghloul laid out the terms of Egypt's aspired independence he actually offered more than what he had offered in the draft of 1917; the Egyptian government would secure the colonial routes to India, Britain would have the right to reoccupy the Suez Canal in the event of war or in case its imperial communications were threatened, Egypt would be an ally of Britain and it would provide Britain with troops in case they were needed (Rafei 1955, 1: 96–7).

When Wingate asked the three Pashas about their representative capacity, they said they were elected members of the Legislative Assembly (yet the last elections which that Legislative Assembly went through were the very first elections that brought it into being).[18]

18. The Legislative Council was very much a club of medium-size and large-size landowners as well as the 'enlightened' Sheikhs of Mohammad Abdu, that is, the same combination Cromer saw fit to represent Egypt. To run for elections for the Legislative Council the candidate had to pay at least £20 in land taxes (see Lasheen 1971, 1: 161, footnote 5).

Wingate said that they were only three members and thus they could not claim to represent the opinion of the whole body, let alone the whole nation.

A couple of hours later, according to what they had planned with Zaghloul three weeks earlier, Prime Minister Hussain Rushdi and his Minister of Education Adli Yakan visited Wingate, asking for permission to travel to London as a formal delegation in order to discuss Egypt's status, and they too were dismissed, on the basis that Britain was not ready to discuss the matter right now, and that while they could actually go to London they would not be able to discuss any of the serious matters until Britain was done with the post-war arrangements. Thus the representative capacity of both formal and informal delegations was rejected by Wingate. This drove them to prove how representative they were. Having done their best in proving their colonial qualities through the offers they made, they were now led to show how native they were, meaning how effective they were in controlling the native population.

On the evening of the same day the three Pashas met and formed a delegation of seven, the first Wafd, adding Mohammad Mahmoud Pasha, Ahmad Lutfi Al-Sayidd, Abdul-Latif Al-Makabbati and Mohammad Ali Allouba Pasha. The seven members were to be presented to the rest of the members of the suspended Legislative Assembly who would then express the recognition of the seven as representatives of the assembly, and thus of the whole nation.

The text presented by the delegation to the members of the Legislative Assembly, by the signing of which they would recognize the delegation's mandate, was quite interesting. It read:

We the undersigned, delegate their excellencies Saad Zaghloul Pasha, Ali Sharawy Pasha, Abdul Aziz Fahmi Bey, Mohammad Ali [Allouba] Bey, Abdul-Latif Al Makabbati Bey, Mohammad Mahmoud Pasha, and Ahmad Lutfi Al-Sayidd Bey, and whomever they choose to add, to work, with peaceful means, whenever possible, for Egypt's independence, in accordance with the principles of freedom and Justice, *whose banner the state of Great Britain and her allies hold high*, and for which they [Britain and its allies] support the freedom of nations. (Rafei, 1955, 1: 102, emphasis mine).

The paradoxical and contradictory nature of the political discourse expressed in the above statement was apparent even to a conservative historian such as Rafei. The wording was so typical of Hizb-Al-Umma: peaceful negotiations with Britain, with the spirit of learning from the occupation. No signatures could have been collected on a document that praised Britain and its allies 'While the Umma's Jihad and her suffering of occupation are but consequences of Great Britain's policies since 1882' (Rafei 1955, 1:103). Rafei also emphasizes that the delegation did not even mention 'complete independence', a phrase that would clarify that any form of autonomy or limited 'national authority' would fall short of the aspirations of the Egyptian people.

It was on the almost violent intervention of three members of Al-Hizb-Al-Watani who visited Zaghloul at his home that the wording was changed;[19] the phrase on Britain was omitted and the phrase 'complete independence' was added (Rafei 1995, 1: 102–8 and Vatikiotis, *The Modern History of Egypt*, 1969: 255). Before the signature campaign started, however, Zaghloul and the Wafd sent a number of letters to Wingate asking for permission to leave for London. On 1 December 1918 Wingate refused to give permission and issued a statement that any remarks or demands Egyptian officials wished to communicate to the British government should be communicated to him, and that such demands should be consistent with the British declaration of the protectorate in 1914. This second refusal by Wingate outraged the Egyptian officials. Despite the generosity of their offers and the various guarantees they put on the table that they would serve Britain's interests, and despite the fact they were proving their acceptance by the native population through the signatures campaign, the British government still did not recognize them as representatives or potential alternatives that could take its place in Egypt. It was at this point that Zaghloul and the Wafd, along with Hussain Rushdi, Adli Yakan and even the Sultan himself, started to adopt a more radical approach towards the colonial power, eventually demanding full independence, the withdrawal of British troops from Egypt, asserting the international nature of the Egyptian question and therefore insisting on addressing the Peace Conference in Paris instead of the British Foreign Office. It is difficult to assert the hidden

19. Abdul Maqsoud Mutawalli, Mustafa Al-Shourbagi and Mohammad Zaki Ali, the three members of Al-Hizb-Al-Watani, were so loud in their attacks on Zaghloul that he reminded them they were in his house, at which point Mohammad Zaki Ali cried that it was the house of the people. Due to the flexibility of Arabic language, the phrase, which originally meant that the house was built from the people's money and that Zaghloul had little title to it, could nevertheless be used by Saad Zaghloul to render symbolic significance to his house, calling it ever after '*Bait Al-Umma*', the house of the nation! (see Rafei 1995, 1:102–8, also see Vatikiotis 1969: 55).

intentions of the individuals leading the movement, yet the fact that these were not the original demands of the elite, as shown above, and the fact that, after they were recognized as representatives of the Egyptian people, these radical demands were abandoned, as will be shown below, make such demands look like a tactic to gain recognition rather than a strategy to gain independence.[20]

On 3 December Zaghloul refused to negotiate on the basis of the declaration of the protectorate, and on 6 December the Wafd (the delegation) issued a statement to the people of Egypt to the effect that the Egyptian question was an international question that should be discussed in the Peace Conference in Paris on the basis of President Wilson's 14 points and the right of self-determination (Ramadan 1968, 1: 102–3). The Wafd also made it clear that it was not demanding permission to go to London; rather, it was now demanding the right to go to Paris. And instead of recognizing Britain's right to occupy the Suez Canal or any other part of Egypt, the Wafd's statement mentioned that it was demanding full independence and sovereignty for Egypt in return for guarantees (instead of military occupation) to preserve the interests of the European powers (instead of Britain) (Ghurbal 1952: 55). The Wafd then started sending petitions, appeals and different kinds of messages to George Clemenceau and Woodrow Wilson explaining how Britain was not allowing the Egyptians to voice their opinions among free nations.

The programme on 6 December was very much like the strategy of Al-Hizb-Al-Watani. The programme of Mustafa Kamel's popular party had been to counterbalance Britain's power with that of other European powers, to internationalize the Egyptian question as much as possible on the one hand, and to support the Caliphate, on the other. However, by the end of the war it was apparent that the Ottoman Empire would not survive and that it would not be able to retain its Arab provinces. Al-Hizb-Al-Watani then had to rely on the first half of its strategy: internationalization, and postpone the second half regarding Islamic unity.

It was at the programme on 6 December that the signature-collecting campaign gained enormous momentum. The campaign

20. Mohammad Hussain Haikal reports that he met Lutfi Al-Sayidd in Zaghloul's house and asked him whether the Wafd really believed that demanding British withdrawal and the right of self-determination was prudent. Lutfi clearly told him that it was but a bargaining tactic to facilitate the only practical solution, which was to conduct direct negotiations with the British in London (see Haikal 1951, 1: 82).

was a great success, it first started with the signatures of the members of the Legislative Assembly, then it was passed to government officials, then it was passed to ordinary citizens.

Two remarks can be made about the first signature campaign. First, the acceptance of the colonial logic, as opposed to the 'immaturity' of the rest of the population, helped Zaghloul and his colleagues become members of the Legislative Assembly in the first place, that is, it helped them gain the acceptance of the colonial masters as representatives, their nativeness by contrast to the foreignness of the occupiers helped them gain the acceptance of the population. The second point is that the people of Egypt signing the petition were actually giving support to a programme other than the original programme of the Wafd. The difference between the discourse of 6 December and the discourse maintained by the Wafd during negotiations with Britain before and after that date is typical of the contradictory double talk used by the nationalist elite to gain recognition from two opposite parties: the native population and the colonial power.

A series of events involving the resignation of the Egyptian government and the insistence of the Wafd on taking the Egyptian case to the international community after having been denied its representative capacity by Britain led to the latter's decision to send Zaghloul and the Wafd members into exile on 8 March 1919. On 9 March, a country-wide revolution broke out. Public enthusiasm was such that republics were being declared in villages, railways were destroyed to prevent the British troops from sending reinforcements to rebellious towns, and neither the government nor the British military could control the situation. The British response was typically colonial, with hundreds of civilian casualties throughout the country.

The revolution led to a fact-finding mission, which eventually had to negotiate with the members of the Wafd. The negotiations led to the splitting of the Wafd into two groups, moderates under the leadership of Adli Yakan, and extremists under the leadership of Zaghloul. The moderates accepted a unilateral declaration of independence by Britain; when Egypt was granted such an independence and elections took place, the extremists, though nominally still rejecting it, decided to run for the elections, thus accepting the de-facto British redefinition of Egypt.

The 1922 Declaration

The 'Declaration for Egypt' of 28 February 1922 stated that Britain recognized Egypt as an independent sovereign country, and that British protection of Egypt ended, that the Egyptian foreign ministry would be reopened, that a parliament and a constitutional government would subsequently be formed. Nevertheless, there were four reservations on the above points: Britain retained the right to use all means to protect its imperial communications and the routes to the East; it also had the right to protect Egypt against internal and external dangers, and it had the right to protect foreign interests and European residents in Egypt. Finally, the status of Sudan was unaffected by the declaration; the state of affairs there would still be regulated according to the 1899 treaties between Egypt and Britain. It is clear that while protection formally ended, Britain still retained the right to protect whatever it perceived as needing protection in Egypt. The main function of the national elite here was to facilitate the protection through the formation of a government and a parliament. The declaration was in fact handing over a small portion of the colonial power to the native elite (resigning the special status of foreign advisers in ministries as well as the financial and judicial councils). Negotiations about handing over more power to the Egyptians were thus dependent on how well they use the power already handed to them.[21] The parliament and the government were formed, among other things, to negotiate an alliance treaty

21. In one of his messages to his government, the British High Commissioner in Cairo, Viscount Allenby stated that 'it was one of the most important aims of the British policy to win Egypt's friendship, if we were not willing to prove in deeds that we trust the Egyptians, I think that it is impossible to make them cooperate with us' ('Allenby's letter to Curzon on 17 November 1921' in Shafiq, *Hawliyyat Misr Al Siyassiyya: Tamhid, Al Juz' Al Thani*, [Egypt's Political Annals: Introduction, Part Two] 1927 452). Trusting the Egyptians is a concept that merits some attention. Allenby summarized the problem as being a matter of trust: as far as the offers the Egyptians were making to guarantee British interests, handing them power was mainly a matter of trusting that they would keep such promises, that is, the promises themselves were satisfactory to the colonial power. The strategies of the nationalist movement and of the colonial power converged, yet each party did not 'trust' the other party enough to believe that the agendas were in fact the same. The use of the expression 'trust' also implies a notion of succession and replacement. The way in which trust is handled, that is, the institutions through which the transfer of power takes place from the colonial power to the native elite, guarantees that that trust will not be violated.

between Britain and Egypt. Successive Prime Ministers of Egypt such as Zaghloul, Yakan, Tharwat, Mohammad Mahmoud, Sidqi and Nahhas, all accepted that the basis of such an agreement would be to accommodate Egypt's independence with Britain's interests. Shortly after the declaration was issued, on 15 March, Egypt's independence was declared, Sultan Fouad became King Fouad, and Abdul Khaleq Tharwat became the first Prime Minister of independent Egypt. The first function of the new government was to assume the powers in the Ministry of Interior that were, up to that point, in the hands of the British Military Authority.

In 1923 a constitution was passed, and the Wafd ran for election and won. The history of Egypt then becomes an alternation between the Wafd, which now only consisted of the extremists who nominally rejected the 1922 declaration, and practically accepted it, and the moderates of the Constitutional Liberal Party who accepted the declaration nominally and practically. A pattern of competition for representation led both sides to attempt to prove to the British they were quite up to the task of preserving colonial interests in the country. The records of the negotiations they held with Britain and the drafts they produced from 1922 till 1936 show striking similarities. Finally, in 1936, Italy was surrounding Egypt from east and west (the kingdom then included both today's Egypt and today's Sudan; it thus bordered Libya from the northwest and Ethiopia from the southeast, both of which had been invaded by Italy). Britain found it expedient to conclude a deal with the Egyptians, for its delegation of power to some local elite in times of war would cut the costs of policing a rebellious Egypt. The treaty of 1936 was reached.

The 1936 Treaty

In his speech on the Day of National Jihad on 13 November 1935, Mustafa Nahhas, Zaghloul's successor to the leadership of the Wafd, explained his party's programme as follows:

It should be known that the situation in Egypt now completely differs, both legally and emotionally, from the situation in 1914 when the First World War broke out. Egypt will not accept today that her sons be taken to the battlefield, that her crops be confiscated, her money be spent and her barracks, seaports and airports be used by sheer force and against her will. Yet she would sincerely welcome protecting herself with everything in her control, cooperating with her ally (Britain), with her own free will and choice, and in her capacity as a free country, enjoying complete sovereignty and full independence. ('Nahhas'

Speech on the Day of National Jihad', published in *Al-Ahram* on 14 November 1935, quoted in Ramadan 1968, 1: 778)

The logic of replacement is very clear in the above passage; Egypt would refuse to provide Britain with military needs if that was imposed on it by force. In Nahhas' language, this meant that Egypt would refuse to provide those facilities if that took place before a decisive treaty was reached with the representative forces in Egypt, that is, with Nahhas' Wafd. Yet if such a treaty was reached, Egypt would perform, by its own free will, exactly the same tasks that it would have been made to perform by force of occupation.

In his speech, Nahhas was also appealing to both audiences: the Egyptian native audience to whom he was promising independence and sovereignty, and the British audience to whom he was promising an alliance through which all the benefits of occupation would be preserved by Britain.

Another remark about Nahhas' speech is that it took place four days after a declaration by Sir Samuel Hoare, the British Foreign Secretary at the time, where he stated that the current situation between Egypt and Britain was sufficient, and that, under the declaration of 1922, Britain retained the right to use all the military facilities in Egypt. Hoare's declaration meant that Britain was going to depend directly on its forces located in Egypt in case of war, and that it was willing to perform the colonial tasks on its own, without the help of native representatives. Nahhas' speech mentioned above came as a response to Hoare's declaration, part and parcel of a series of nationwide protests that involved violent attacks against British troops all around the country (Rafei 1987, 2: 214, 215, and Ramadan 1968, 1: 782). The point here is that the above deal of replacement described in Nahhas' speech was, at the time, the most radical demand he could present; this conciliatory speech was the peak of his confrontational programme.

The speech's logic was the essence of the 1936 treaty. The text of the treaty, just like the drafts of 1917 and 1918, revolved around the concept of creating an Egyptian independence that would preserve British interests. Article 7 of the 1936 treaty stated that Egypt was committed to facilitate the usage of its land, sea and airspace by the British forces in the case of war, the imminent danger of war or in any 'sudden dangerous international situation' (Article 7, 'The Treaty of Alliance', *Al-Qadiyya Al-Misriyya 1882–1954* [The Egyptian Cause 1882–1954], 461). The same article also stated that it would be the duty of the Egyptian government to take all legal and administrative measures necessary for the provision of the above facilities. It also specified that such legal and administrative arrangements would include the declaration of martial law, a state of emergency and instituting strict censorship on news coverage.

As for the permanent British presence in the Suez Canal area, the 1936 treaty allowed for two military bases with 10,000 troops to stay in the area; it also allowed for an indefinite number of British battalions to be relocated to the west of Alexandria, for eight years, a measure designed to avert an expected Italian invasion from Libya. The British Royal Air Force would also have the permanent right to use Egypt's airspace for training (clauses 2, 13, 18 of the appendix to Article 8 of the Treaty of Alliance, *Al-Qadiyya Al-Misriyya 1882–1954* [The Egyptian Question 1882–1954], 462–7).

Just like the previous drafts from 1917 to 1930, the treaty of 1936 stated that the British troops would stay in the Suez Canal until the Egyptian army was able to defend it on its own (Article 8). The treaty also specified that the Egyptian army would be allowed to buy only British arms and ammunition. Thus the development of the Egyptian army to the level by which it could defend the Suez Canal was controlled by the British decision whether or not, and to what extent, to equip the Egyptian army. It was also left to the judgment of Britain to decide whether at any point the Egyptian army was efficient enough to defend the canal. Article 5 of the treaty committed Egypt not to take any position vis-a-vis foreign countries that was not consistent with the policy of Britain. Article 12 stated that it was the responsibility of the Egyptian government to preserve foreign lives and properties in Egypt. It is significant that that obligation was part and parcel of the treaty that guaranteed Egypt's independence (*Al-Qadiyya Al-Misriyya 1882–1954* [The Egyptian Question 1882–1954], 461 and 470). Again, the meaning of this commitment and how well it was carried out was left to the judgment of Britain. In addition to the military articles, The treaty of 1936 had the same effect as the declaration of the protectorate in 1914 with the only difference that much of the functions were now carried out by the Egyptian government. The logic of replacement thus needs no further elaboration in the 1936 treaty, where the function of the Egyptian government, police force and army was to preserve the British interests, and it was up to the British government to judge how much the Egyptians merit to be entrusted with such duties. The

1936 treaty was thus an expression of Cromer's idea of an Egypt that would be as independent as an automaton.

The Fall of Egyptian Nationalism

By tracing the events of the 1919 revolution up to the signing of the 1936 treaty, the discourse the national leadership used to address its constituencies and the discourse addressed to the colonial power, three arguments could be made: (1) the drafts, and the documents that defined Egypt's independence, were presented by the leadership of the nationalist elite and guaranteed the continuation of the colonial relation. Moreover, they made the continuation of the colonial relation the main condition for independence – the whole state was defined and structured in a manner that would guarantee its functioning as a colony; (2) these documents were reached through competition among the ranks of the native elite, who competed to prove to the colonial master, with whose power they wanted to be entrusted, how trustworthy they were in guaranteeing colonial interests; (3) the national leaders also competed over how much control they could exert over their native constituencies; their discourse with the masses naturally contradicted their discourse with colonial power, yet their appeal to the masses was part of their appeal to the colonial power, that is, that controlling the masses was a tactic in the strategy of proving their abilities to colonize the country rather than liberate it.

Studying the negotiations between the Wafd and Britain, in comparison with the negotiation between the British and the Constitutional Liberals, one realizes that there was no real difference between the suggestions of the two parties. Yet the Wafd's position was more difficult than that of the Constitutional Liberals, because the Wafd always came to power on the basis of making two contradictory promises, one to the Egyptians and another to the British. Once the Wafd came to power it was bound to violate either one of the two promises or both.

Before 1936, the Wafd was always brought to power due to an understanding with Britain that it would be able to convince the Egyptians to accept British suggestions regarding an alliance treaty. The Wafd's pre-election promises prevented it from doing so. While the Wafd's rejection of British suggestions might have increased its bargaining power in opposition, in government these rejections allowed the British to use the loopholes of the 1922 Declaration of Independence as well as the loopholes of the Egyptian constitution to oust the Wafd from power. After 1936, the treaty itself was used to exert pressure on the Wafd when in power. Nahhas' unilateral cancellation of the treaty in October 1951 brought the Wafd face to face with its structural contradiction. The Wafd's position in power was dependent on that treaty, on the Egyptian constitution and the Declaration of Independence; the cancellation of these documents would have practically entailed open confrontation between the Wafd and the British. The Wafd's structure as a party led by a colonially created elite, concerned with occupying positions of power in a colonially created institution called the Egyptian Kingdom, made such an open confrontation impossible. Unable and unwilling to turn into a guerrilla resistance movement, the Wafd was trying, with apparent futility, to fight the British with the Egyptian police, that is, fight the British with institutions the British had created. The state the Wafd was trying to liberate was itself a measure of occupation.

In a sense the Wafd was much less powerful precisely because it was in power. Every time the Wafd was ousted from power its failure vis-a-vis the colonial power was exposed. The ultimate expression of the Wafd's historical failure was expressed in the burning of Cairo on 26 January 1952. On 25 January the British troops in the Suez Canal attacked the headquarters of the Egyptian police in the city of Ismailiyya and massacred them. Outraged policemen in Cairo, supported by students demonstrated in the streets of the capital on the 26th and by noon the demonstrations had turned into an all-out arson spree. The Wafd government, being blamed for its strategy of fighting the British troops with the Egyptian police, lost control of the situation. The demonstrators, along with the organizations Young Egypt and the Muslim Brothers, demanded that all-out guerilla warfare be waged on Britain, and that the government should end its monopoly on armed resistance (on the demands of Young Egypt and the Muslim Brothers, as well as their paramilitary agenda against Britain, see Sharqawi, 41 and Naseef 2002: 26).

Unlike some accounts that portray the event as a conspiracy against the Wafd, looking at the pattern of the burnt buildings as well as the testimonies of the people involved in the event, it seems likely that the burning was an expression of the population's dissatisfaction with the whole socio-political system in which the Wafd operated. After 26 January, it was obvious that the Wafd's ability to fulfil any promise to the colonial power had been totally lost.

The consequences of the strategy of replacement as far as the Wafd's constituencies are concerned, were dire. Some scholars, such as Gershoni and Jankowski, suggested that the emergence of anti-Wafdist movements in the late 1930s and the early 1940s was the result of the increasing number and politicization of the Egyptian educated urban middle class (Gershoni and Jankowski 1995: 7–15).

That middle class had been active throughout the first half of the twentieth century; the change was not in the degree of the youth's politicization, but in the direction of their political choices. Before concluding the 1936 treaty the Wafd almost monopolized the majority of that social stratum. Under the Wafd, this urban middle class used to lead Egyptian workers through establishing contacts with trade unions as well as Egyptian peasants. The social backgrounds of non-Wafdist movements such as the Society of Young Egypt, the Society of the Muslim Brothers and the various communist groups came directly from the same stratum whose support was monopolized by the Wafd; a core of educated urban youth leading workers and peasants. The fact that such movements rejected the entire ideological, political and economic settings advocated by the Wafd, the fact that all rejected any form of compromise with Britain, the fact that none sought to resist Britain using the state apparatus created by Britain, and finally the fact that the membership of these societies skyrocketed right after the Wafd signed the 1936 treaty with its clear logic of replacement, makes it likely that the formation of these groups was an expression of the Wafd's loss of legitimacy among its constituencies. Though all non-Wafdist movements rejected the capitalist settings in Egypt, the fact that the social background of the members of these groups were almost identical suggests that they were formed primarily as a manner by which to deal with the question of national liberation rather than as a strict expression of economic grievances.

Of these opposition groups the most significant in terms of numbers were Young Egypt and the Muslim Brothers, both of which rejected the colonial identity of Egypt and embraced some supra-national ambition, either towards the Islamic or the Arab communities.

The movement of the Free Officers, which brought down the whole system, was formed by army officers belonging to these non-Wafdist groups. Many of the officers came from the communist organizations, the Muslim Brothers and Young Egypt. Some even moved from one movement to another until the coup of 1952. The burning of Cairo, and the coup of the Free Officers six months later, brought to an end the trilateral combination of Egyptian nationalism, economic dependency and parliamentary rule leading to negotiations with Britain, which were the essence of the strategy of replacement. In essence, the Wafd was not being punished for what it did; it was being punished for what it was. The very elements that caused it to exist, that is the functions of representation and replacement, were the very elements that caused its doom, and that is the paradox. The automaton Cromer wanted independent Egypt to be had a structural defect, for it was built over the body of a people who, like any other people, was very much alive, and whose movement contradicted the movements for which the automaton was built. Ultimately Cromer's automaton had to be taken apart.

EGYPTIAN NATIONALISM AND THE UMMA

It has been shown how the Egyptian nationalist movement attempted to reconcile itself with the programme of the pro-Ottoman Al-Hizb-Al-Watani in 1919 in order to harvest the popular support it needed for the purpose of proving its representative capacity to Britain. Yet it remains a historical fact that Egyptian nationalists, unlike Arab nationalists, made little effort to incorporate the concept of the Umma, in its Islamic sense, in their ideology. Moreover, many Egyptian nationalists including Zaghloul and Lutfi despised any notion of Arab or Islamic unity.[22] After all, the Egyptian elite was attempting to replace a Turkish elite that had ruled the country for centuries under the banner of Islam and the Caliphate. It is interesting, while tracing the failure of Egyptian nationalism and its loss of favour by the 1940s, to see what rival forces gained the grounds lost by the Wafd and its supporters. The Muslim Brothers and Young Egypt both held strong Islamic and Arabist inclinations. The Free Officers, many of whose members came from either one of the two aforementioned organizations, also had strong supra-national tendencies. It should also be remembered that, while the burning of Cairo might have been the main expression of popular anger at the Egyptian liberal nationalist political system, the direct cause of that system's downfall was its astounding defeat in the Palestine war of 1948. The army, which brought down the monarchical system, disbanded the parliament and eventually adopted pan-Arabism as a state ideology, was first alienated from the system during this war.

22. Unlike Lutfi Al-Sayidd, who fought the idea of pan-Islamism without directly hitting at the religious texts of the Quran and the Hadith that imply it, Zaghloul comments on one of the most frequently quoted texts of Hadith that calls for the solidarity of all Muslims, by saying that the Hadith leads to 'hated fanaticism and exposes one to overwhelming dangers' (Saad Zaghloul quoted in Lasheen 1971, 1: 59, also see Lutfi Al-Sayidd, *Al-Jareeda* quotation on pan-Islamism above).

The war had accentuated Egypt's position as a state of vasselage and its inability to oppose one British policy of creating a national home for the Jews in Palestine, let alone fight off Britain.

It has been mentioned above that the elites in the Arab world tried to deal with the notion of the Umma by either keeping Islam separate from politics or by portraying nationalisms and nation states as modern forms of Islamic Dawlas. The classical Egyptian nationalists opted for the first, while Arab nationalists opted for the second of those two options.

Before moving to the next chapter to discuss Arab nationalism, one should make a final note about the Egyptian episode. Egyptian nationalism as presented by the classical Wafd Party received fatal blows in 1948 and 1952; it never again became a serious political force in Egypt. From 1952 up until 1977, Arab nationalism gradually became the state ideology in Egypt.

Egyptian nationalist discourse has sometimes been resorted to by President Anwar Sadat and his successor Hosni Mubarak, especially when they were driven to make decisions that contradicted the interests of other Arabs and Muslims. Slogans such as 'Egypt above all' were not uncommon during the peace negotiations between Egypt and Israel in 1977–78 or during the second Israeli invasion of Lebanon in 1982, to mention but two examples. Such positions have been correlated with the rise of Islamic movements as the main opposition groups in today's Egypt.

Nonetheless, since it became an ally of the United States in the second half of the 1970s, more often than not the Egyptian regime has been attempting to portray its pro-western policies as being in' the best interests of Arabs and Muslims. Waging war against Israel in defence of an Arab country under attack is out of the question, not only because such an act might harm Egypt, but because by harming Egypt it might harm the overall fighting capacity of the Arabs and Muslims. Egypt's advocacy for peace with Israel or for the presence of American troops in the region is explained as being in the best interest of everyone in the region. On the other hand, Egypt's diplomacy towards the United States is based on attempting to achieve political influence by having the latter delegate the securing of its interests to the Egyptian government. Thus, while blunt Egyptian nationalism has somewhat subsided in favour of a tone which is more conciliatory with the notion of the Umma, the logic of representation and replacement is still quite easy to track in today's Egyptian political discourse.

5
Arab Nationalism

INTRODUCTION

Arab nationalism produced a number of states in the region, the study of the constitutions and institutions of which would render this book impossibly long and descriptive. While the previous chapter on Egyptian nationalism did discuss the institutions of the Egyptian state, this chapter will be more theoretical, trying to trace the paradoxes of representation and replacement in the discourses of Arab nationalists.

As mentioned in Chapter 1, to some nationalist social scientists, nations are but discoveries. That is, sentiments of national togetherness have existed from time immemorial among a certain group of people; these feelings are muzzled by superstition, local tyranny, or foreign influence, until they find their most perfect expression around the time of some national enlightenment/revolution and the establishment of the nation-state. This view was definitely present among Arab nationalists. It can be found in everything, from poetry to party pamphlets. However, with a closer look at the literature of Arab nationalists, one sees that there was more to it than this simple assertion.

As a middle ground solution between European modernity and Arab-Islamic tradition, Arab nationalists were looking for some legitimacy from both modern European and pre-colonial Arabic sources. Thus there was an inherent contradiction in the Arab nationalist doctrine. On the one hand, Arab nationalists were quite aware that the concept of nationalism, and the above understanding of the development of national sentiments from pre-history up until its culmination in a nation-state, came to them from Europe. On the other hand, they had to prove that such sentiments existed among Arabs and that Arabs were aware of them before they contacted modern Europe, that is, before colonialism. Arguing that the Arabs only became aware of their national identity at Europe's instigation would have credited Europe, rather than the Arabs, for the emergence of Arab nationalism. Moreover, like in any proper nationalist narrative, foreign domination should feature negatively. No self-respecting nation could owe its national existence to the teachings of another. Therefore, in the Arab nationalist narrative, Europe's colonial intervention must feature as an obstacle rather than a cause for the expression of national identity. Arab nationalists, with a few important exceptions, did not want to make Islam the basis of political association, nor did they want to make European teachings the basis of their national awareness. They were therefore in search of non-European, non-Islamic, yet still Arab, texts and events that might offer them some indication of a pre-colonial national sentiment.

This led Arab nationalists to reinterpret their history where they used to read nationalism into anything that might have remotely resembled it. Expectedly such readings were not always methodologically sound. For example, the writings of Al-Jahiz (775–868 AD), a literary critic of the ninth century, by which he attempted to reassert the supremacy of the Bedouin Arab traditions in poetry against the new trends spearheaded by Arabized Persians, were often cited as an indication of some sort of Arab national awareness. Similarly, the works of Ibn Khaldoun (1332–1406 AD), the fourteenth-century sociologist, on tribal solidarity as the basis for the rise and fall of princedoms, were of exceptional value to Arab nationalist theorists. Ibn Khaldoun was an Arab Muslim, yet his interpretation of history did not refer to any divine order. He therefore looked like a secular Arab scientist from the middle ages who recognized tribal (Arab nationalists read that as ethnic) solidarity as the basis of political association. The problems of the Arab nationalists' interpretation of Ibn Khaldoun in the sections on Arab nationalism during the cold war will be discussed in what follows.

What concerns us here is to mention that the trend of reinterpreting history to assert the existence of national sentiments continued to cover events as recent as the nineteenth and twentieth centuries. Mohammad Ali's reforms and his relative autonomy in Egypt, his son's expansionary wars in Syria, the Wahhabist movement in Arabia, the formation of Arab literary societies in the latter days of the Ottoman Empire, and the Arab Revolt against the Ottomans in 1916, were all lumped together as early expressions of Arab nationalism.

Since Wahhabism has been shown to be a classic Islamic movement in Chapter 1, and since recent scholarship has shown that Mohammad Ali, an Albanian officer of the Ottoman army, never really promoted any Egyptian or Arab nationalist programmes, and that his was an overwhelmingly Ottoman programme of reform and modernization (see for example Fahmy 1997: 239–42 and 306–15), I shall here concern myself with the last two events mentioned above. I shall expand on the formation of the Arab literary/political societies before World War One and on the discourses of the Arab Revolt of 1916. In both cases, the discourse of Arab nationalists was different from the European blueprints they were trying to imitate in that it was a hybrid of modernist and Islamic discourses. This mix corresponds as expected to the attempts of such nationalists to reconcile colonial and native agendas.

Another reason for focusing on the societies and the revolt is that, for most of the twentieth century, the version of Arab nationalism generated by the societies was to dominate the discourse of leftist Arab nationalists while the discourse of the Arab Revolt was to dominate right-wing conservative Arab nationalist regimes. In the following lines I underline the colonial influence in the genesis of those two branches of Arab nationalism and the logics of representation and replacement inherent therein. I will also try to show the various intellectual attempts to reconcile the idea of the Arab nation and nation-state with those of the Umma and the Dawla discussed at the beginning of the book.

While the work of the societies did not culminate in a fully mature political movement or in the establishment of a state, the Arab Revolt resulted in the establishment of four Arab states.[1] Therefore, the

---

1. The Arab Revolt, which took place against the Ottomans during World War One, resulted in the establishment of the short-lived kingdom of Hijaz in western Arabia, under the kingship of Sharif Hussein Ibn Ali, the ruler of Mecca and the leader of the revolt. In 1924 this kingdom fell to the forces of Abdul Aziz Ibn Saud, the Wahhabi leader from the eastern parts of the Arabian Peninsula who then established the modern kingdom of Saudi Arabia. Another short-lived Arab kingdom was established in Damascus under Faisal, son of Hussein of Hijaz. That kingdom fell to the French who invaded Damascus in 1920. Faisal was then appointed King of Iraq by the British. This third offspring of the Arab revolt lasted till 1958 when a communist-nationalist body of officers brought it down to establish the modern republic of Iraq. Finally, in 1921 a princedom was established in the area east of the Jordan River, bordered to the west and to the east by the British Mandates in Palestine and Iraq, and by the French Mandate in Syria to the north. This was the princedom of Transjordan, and Faisal's older brother, Abdullah, was appointed its Emir. Initially this was a temporary arrangement, since the British promised Abdullah that if he could secure the southern borders of the French mandate in Syria against Arab resistance, Britain might use its good offices with France to establish him as King of Syria under mandate. Britain's promise never came true, Abdullah's reign in Transjordan lasted for the rest of his life, and of all the Sharifian Kingdoms produced by the Arab Revolt, his is the only one that survives today as the Hashemite Kingdom of Jordan.

logic of representation and replacement could only be traced in the
intellectual discourse of Arab nationalists from the societies, while
it could be traced in the political programmes of the Arab Revolt.
In other words, the members of the Arab literary societies were not
official representatives of the Arabs. They were not allowed access
to any representative political office; nonetheless, they were representatives in the cultural sense. By basing Arab nationhood on
European criteria, they were partly addressing the Europeans. They
were attempting to convince a European audience that according to
European definitions of nationhood, Arabs deserved to be treated as a
nation. This intellectual middle ground between Arabs and Europeans
corresponded to the political and economic middle ground enjoyed
by the local elites which was later on institutionalized in the creation
of the nation-state.

The leaders of the Arab Revolt, on the other hand, presented
themselves from the start as official representatives of the Arabs.
Sharif Hussein, the Ottoman governor of Mecca and the leader of
the revolt, insisted on being addressed by the British as the King of
Arabs. It will be shown below that this representation, just as in the
case of the Egyptian nationalists, directly led him to the paradox of
replacement. The price of Britain addressing him as the King of the
Arabs was for him to act as a vassal king for Britain.

PRELUDE: OTTOMAN MODERNIZATION AND DISINTEGRATION

By the end of the eighteenth century, the tax system in greater
Syria[2] was similar to that in Egypt. The government required a fixed
amount of tax the collection of which it delegated to local notables,
who collected more money than they were committed to pay to the
Ottoman treasury and lived off the difference. The same pattern
was repeated as the notables themselves delegated power to lesser
tax collectors, who collected more from the peasants than they had
to pay to the notables, and so on. This system was called *'iltizam'*
(commitment) in Egypt and was called *'Muqata'a'* (allotment of land,
that is to notables and lesser tax collectors) in greater Syria. At the
beginning of the 1830s Mohammad Ali started his campaign in the
Levant, where his son and brilliant military commander Ibrahim was
able to control the area and redesign its administration.

2. By greater Syria I here mean the area which includes modern-day Lebanon,
    Syria, Jordan and Palestine, as well as parts of northern and western Iraq.

Syria was different from Egypt in that it had a considerable number of Christians who, unlike Egyptian Copts, had centuries-long relationships with Europe. Moreover, the topography of Syria, where human settlements were concentrated in mountainous ridges depending on local wells for irrigation and water supplies, made it easier for local dynasties to resist central authority. While Mohammad Ali could easily wipe out all political opposition in Egypt and apply a strict system of agricultural, commercial and industrial monopolies, his son had to rely to some degree on local allies in Syria. Those allies did not have the same agenda; both Muslims and Christians welcomed Ibrahim's initial policies of alleviating taxes and ending compulsory conscription. However, as Ottoman and European military pressure increased on Mohammad Ali's armies in Anatolia and the Levant, Ibrahim had to go back on his previous policies and began collecting taxes and conscripting Syrians. This instigated a rebellion just before his final withdrawal to Egypt in 1840.

The ten years of Ibrahim's reign did, however, leave a mark. Even before Mohammad Ali's defeat and the implementation of the Treaty of London in 1840, the Ottomans had decided to move along the lines of Mohammad Ali's policies, to modernize the administration, rid themselves of local tax usurpers and centralize power.[3] This was the Tanzimat period.

Since its establishment, the Ottoman Empire was but another example of the traditional agricultural Islamic empires of the late middle ages and early modernity. It was a typical Dawla in the sense discussed in Chapter 2. That is, it was not fixedly sovereign or territorial. Stability in the empire depended on delicate balances of power among the various political formations within it. This was more apparent in greater Syria, Iraq and Arabia than in Egypt due to the diversity of the population. In Egypt the population was mainly made of peasants and city dwellers, most of whom were Sunni Muslim, with tribalism playing a relatively minor part in the politics of the Ottoman province. Syria Iraq and Arabia on the

3. The Tanzimat period (1839–76) during the reign of the two Ottoman Sultan's Mahmoud II and Abdulmajeed II was also a movement for western education, by sending more officers of the Ottoman army to Europe and/ or getting European instructors to train them at home. The two most influential documents of the Tanzimat were the Hatt-i Sharif of 1839, and Hatt-i Humayun in 1856. The Tanzimat came to a halt during the rule of Abdulhamid II (1878–1909). However, the movement was resumed by the Young Turks who were in control of the country from 1909 till the fall of the empire.

other hand, hosted lowland peasants, semi-settled mountain tribes, desert nomads, inland city aristocrats, port merchants and a nascent bourgeoisie.

Culturally, while Egypt's population were Sunni Muslims and Orthodox Copts, the Levant's population were Sunnis, Shiites, Druz and Alavids among Muslims, as well as significant numbers of Maronite, Catholic and Orthodox Christians. Ethnically, the Arab, Kurdish, Turkish mix was more evident in the Levant than in Egypt. In addition to those groups, Janissaries, Sipahis and other military castes from Istanbul, along with the appointed governors, 'Walis', of the provinces usually took part in the continuous making and unmaking of political arrangements and power balances in the region.

Again, like a typical Islamic Dawla, while the balances of power in the provinces were the source of authority, allegiance to the Islamic Caliphate in Istanbul was the source of legitimacy. In its push towards European-style modernity, the Ottoman government during the Tanzimat period was gradually moving from being a Dawla to becoming to nation-state. This move collided with the native culture and with forms of political organization described above, which in turn resulted in separatist tendencies among the groups constituting the empire, including nationalist tendencies among the Turks and the Arabs. Accompanying this process of cultural alienation was a process of economic dependency on Europe. Since this is not a detailed study about the fall of the Ottoman Empire, I shall give only one example of how modernization led to the triple outcome of alienation, dependency on Europe and disintegration.

Al-Samawa, the epical desert between Iraq, Syria and Arabia, has been home to many Arab tribes since the pre-Islamic era. Raiding the rural areas of the Euphrates valley and the highlands of Syria and Palestine, establishing tribal control over them and eventually settling there, was a common practice until the twentieth century. Raids were managed by a system of tribal protection of villages or through agreements between the governors of the various cities and the elders of the tribes. By the time of the Tanzimat vast pieces of land were thus controlled by the tribes in the context of 'Masha', a system of common tribal property of land. Allotting land to tribesmen was within the exclusive authority of the tribal chief. When a tribe increased in numbers it naturally expanded and settled in more villages, either through agreement or through conflict, depending on the local balance of power. This system strengthened the traditional bonds between the tribesmen and their chiefs in both tent and hut.

However, these bonds of socio-economic interdependence were broken by the introduction of *Tapu*, a system of registered private land ownership. The differentiation between state-owned and private-owned land was considered necessary for modern economic planning in the Ottoman Empire. Thus undefined tribally controlled lands had to be defined and assigned to a known owner accountable to the state (to replace the 'committed' tax collector of the older *iltizam* system). Such an owner was usually the tribal chief. This changed the nature of the relation between the tribesmen and their chiefs from interdependence to one-sided dependence. Chiefs were now economically and politically independent from their tribesmen. Their political, social and economic status was guaranteed by legal ownership of land rather than by the fighting power of their tribesmen. The latter were thus turned into serf-like peasants. Added to the above, and, partly because of it, a process of urbanization was taking place throughout the late nineteenth and twentieth centuries. Tribesmen and peasants were thus exiled from their geographical as well as cultural context. They lived in mud huts and slums in the outskirts of great cities.

On the other hand, the tribal chiefs of the mountains and local notables of the cities did not enjoy their new found authority, for registering the lands made it easier for the central government to interfere in their affairs. They were independent from the government, yet quite vulnerable to its wrath. It should also be noted that the Tanzimat also involved a set of regulations that facilitated trade with Europe, and led to the commercialization of agriculture. The newly founded landowning elite, which Britain and France helped create in Egypt, was created in Syria by the Tanzimat; and like their Egyptian counterparts, they had reasons to fear Istanbul and long for Europe.

Thus, the trend of modernization and centralization, despite a temporary halt during the reign of Abdulhamid II (1878–1909), understandably contributed to the disintegration, rather than the salvation, of the empire. The Tanzimat also involved the allowance of more and more European commercial and cultural infiltration of the Empire. Missionary schools were established in greater Syria, Catholic, Protestant and Orthodox. The Capitulations, a system of economic facilitations and legal privileges granted to Europeans in the Ottoman Empire to invite foreign investment, also meant that European businesses thrived, thus enhancing relations between local dynasties and European economic and political circles.

Unlike classical colonial patterns in, for example, sub-Saharan Africa, the missionaries and the companies in the Middle East only succeeded in converting Christians. That is, most of the conversions took place from local denominations of Christianity to either Catholicism or Protestantism. It was from amongst those Christian converts to Christianity that the first calls for Arab nationalism were heard.

THE ARAB LITERARY SOCIETIES OF THE LATE NINETEENTH CENTURY

Tensions among Muslims and Christians in what is now Lebanon and Syria had erupted in the 1860s, claiming the lives of thousands of civilians from both sides. This in turn led to European pressures on the Sublime Porte by which more Ottoman Christians came under European protection. Again, just like the Egyptian landowning elite, towards the end of the nineteenth century, Ottoman Christians had the incentive to break away from Ottoman domination, and the necessary European protection to do so. Nonetheless, it was obvious that no such movement, based on Arabism, could work if the ties to Europeans were so close as to make the new nationalists look like colonial agents, or if the majority of the Arab Muslim population was alienated.

It would also be a sweeping generalization to argue that all Christian Syrian Arab nationalists had agendas that corresponded to that of the colonial powers interested in the Levant (mainly France), for not all missionaries were the same. In his study of Arab nationalism, Bassam Tibi differentiates between French missionaries, whom he strictly associates with a colonial agenda, and American and Russian missionaries, who appeared to have no direct territorial interests in the Levant at the time.

It is significant that the early Arab Nationalists did not emerge from the French but from the American protestant missionary schools, whose activities were less directly tied to colonial aims. For its part, the United States had no definite colonial interests in the area at the time, since its activities were concentrated to a far greater extent on Latin America. In addition, since Protestantism situates Christianity firmly within the vernacular, the American missionaries learnt Arabic. The missions also employed Arab scholars on a new evangelical translation of the Bible into Arabic. In addition they encouraged a number of other scholars who were attempting to revitalize the Arabic language, and with their help religious texts were written in Arabic for use in the missionary schools. The American missions naturally worked in Arabic because this brought greater and more obvious successes. The revitalization of Arabic also meant the revitalization of the national culture, and thus the creation of a new national identity, which pushed religious identity, formerly the substance of the Arabs' loyalty to the Ottoman Empire, into the background. The successes achieved by the American missions occasionally forced their competitors to imitate them. (Tibi 1990: 100–101)

I have cited Tibi on this because I want to make two points: I want first to underline the link between the missionaries and the Arab nationalists, and second, to point out this relation between the revival of Arabic culture and the creation of a new national identity. It is part of the misinterpretation of history by nationalist writers to assume that the revival of Arabic has started exclusively at the hands of the missionaries. Scholars like Abdul Rahman Al-Jabarty who chronicled the French invasion of Egypt, and Rifaa'a Rafi' Al-Tahtawi who wrote his classics on issues of tradition and modernity, had formed their literary knowledge of Arabic at Al-Azhar university in Cairo before any contact with Europe; the same could go for renowned poet Mahmoud Sami Al-Baroudi, as well as later Syrian writers such as Abdul Rahman Al-Kawakibi and Mohammad Rashid Rida. All are usually cited by historians of Arabic literature as head figures in the renaissance of Arabic which Tibi mentions. Arabic has been a dominant language in the Ottoman Empire since its inception. An Islamic Empire with Maturidi and Ash'arite Sunnism as its source of legitimacy and the Hanafi school of law as its official source of legislation, Arabic was vital in all legal matters in the Ottoman Empire, whether in the provinces or in Istanbul. It is true that Arabic was gradually being pushed out of the official institutions of the Ottoman Empire in the nineteenth century, but that took place as part of the modernization move towards creating an Ottoman European-style nation-state at the time. Therefore, the revival of Arabic was not always a move towards the establishment of a modern national identity. At times, it was just an attempt by the classical intellectuals of the traditional Islamic state, that is, the scholars, the sheikhs and the Ulama, to defend their social position, and the traditional order of things in the Ottoman Empire.

Moreover, the language that was being promoted by the missionaries was a functional one, one that could be understood by the largest number of Arabs, even those who were unlearned. It was a simplification of the canonical Arabic, a version closer to the vernacular. In many cases, the Arabic used by the revivalists was a product of a literary movement in the opposite direction, that is, a movement towards authenticity, towards older traditions and forms of expression.[4]

That being said, the western-educated Syrian Christians did play a significant role in the revival of Arabic, albeit with a different agenda than that of the above mentioned writers. Towards the end of the nineteenth century and the beginning of the twentieth century, cultural societies with the declared purpose of promoting knowledge of Arabic literature and history were established in various cities in greater Syria.

Significant Maronite Christian intellectuals either started out or joined these societies, such as Burtus Al-Bustani (1819–83), who created the first modern Arabic Encyclopedia, Adib Ishaq (1856–85) who worked closely with Jamaludin Al-Afghani and issued a number of newspapers from Cairo and Paris, and Nasif Al-Yaziji, a prominent writer and scholar (1800–71).

As mentioned above, this generation of Arab intellectuals did not officially push for nationalist or separatist demands. Adib Ishaq was a student of Jamaludin Al-Afghani, the principal advocate of Islamic solidarity. The intersection between Ishaq's 'nationalism' and Al-Afghani's is that they both accepted the concepts of the Umma and the Dawla. Ishaq, who harboured liberal ideas on democracy, accountability and human rights, did not question the legitimacy or the authority of the Ottoman Empire. Rather, he advocated more rational forms of government and more decentralization within the empire. Al-Afghani's call for Islamic solidarity did not contradict such demands. His understanding of the Islamic bond was that it was a tool to resist colonialism and preserve native culture. Once this bond was established, the decentralization of administration, the endorsement of individual liberties, and the thriving of literary production, in Arabic as in any other language of the Empire, was more than

4. This movement for authenticity was not confined to Muslims or the clergy. Faris al-Chidiac (1805–1878), a Lebanese Maronite Christian who converted to Protestantism and helped translate the Bible into Arabic, remarks in his classic work 'Al-Mukhabba fi Ahwal Orobba' (That which is Hidden about Europe) that he was pushed by Dr Lea, the British orientalist who supervised his translation, towards clumsy forms of Arabic expressions in order not to make the translation sound Quranic. Chidiac, who worked for years with the Protestant missionaries, later converted to Islam, to become known as Ahmad Faris Al-Chidiac, moved to Istanbul and worked with the Ottoman Sultan. (On Chidiac's position on the missionaries' Arabic see his writings in Tarabolsi and Al-Azmeh 1995: 99–109.)

welcome. Another example for this nexus of Arabism and Islam could be traced to the fact that Mohammad Rashid Rida, another student of Al-Afghani, and one of the founders of Islamic fundamentalism in the early twentieth century, was also a member of these literary political societies. His demands, as expressed in his paper *Al-Manar* (The Lighthouse), which he published in Cairo around 1910, were strictly reformatory (see Kawtharani 1980, Introduction: 41–3).

In 1847, Nasif Al-Yaziji joined Butrus Al-Bustani in establishing the first literary society in the Arab world, Jam'yat Al-Adaab wa al-Ulum (the literary and scientific society) whose members were exclusively Syrian Christians. He and his family issued the magazine *Al-Jinan* (The Paradises) between 1870 and 1886 and was forced to close down because of Abdulhamid II's harsh censorship. The motto of *Al-Jinan* was '*Hubb ul-Watani min al-Iman*' the translation of which is 'Love of the homeland is an article of faith'.

The motto of the paper is typical of the attempt to reconcile the Islamic affiliation of the Ottoman subjects with the idea of terra patria. This motto is just an expression of the general trend of the Arab nationalist movement at this stage. While some Christian as well as Sunni Muslim merchants from Beirut did have direct colonial links to France, the bulk of the movement attempted to reconcile the newly acquired concept of nationalism, with the native concept of the Umma as the basis of political association. 'Love of the homeland is an article of faith' was thus a political programme. Arab nationalists did not have separatist demands in the sense of creating an Arab state away from the Ottoman Empire. Their alliance with the Young Turks against Abdulhamid II, was a move towards decentralization and recognition of an Arab cultural identity within the Ottoman Empire, but it was not, at least declaredly, a move towards separation.

The developments of the first 15 years of the twentieth century, however, changed that trend. The Turkish officers who were sent to Europe during the Tanzimat period returned with even more enthusiasm towards nation building and modernization. The tyranny of Abdulhamid II triggered them to adopt more violent means. The Young Turks, as they were called, formed the Committee of Union and Progress, and took control in 1908. This move set them face to face with the contradictions in their political doctrine. They wanted to strengthen the vast Ottoman Empire with an ideology that was devised for nation-states; their previous alliance with Arab nationalists on issues like recognizing Arab cultural rights and reducing Abdulhamid's tyranny had to be sacrificed as they moved towards a more militarized central government. In their attempt to turn the empire into a nation-state, they followed the example of nation-states turned empires, that is, colonialism. The only problem, however, was that the world had already been divided among colonial powers. Turning the Ottoman Sultanate from an Islamic Empire into a nation-state, then into a colonial imperial nation-state, could not be achieved in just a few years. In 1911 and 1912 the Ottoman Empire suffered fatal military defeats, losing modern-day Libya and the Balkans. This, in turn, led the ruling elite to be even more irritated with Arab demands for decentralization.

At this point, France, with direct colonial interests in Syria, intervened to host the first Arab nationalist conference in the summer of 1913. While some of the participants in the conference came from the literary societies mentioned above, others represented the local commercial elites in greater Syria with direct links to Europe and to France in particular. As Wajih Kawtharani correctly remarks, the documents of the conference were canonized among Arab nationalists of the twentieth century as the defining documents of the movement (Kawtharani 1980, Introduction: 75). A closer look at such documents is therefore appropriate, to see whether they included elements of representation and replacement similar to those traceable in Egyptian nationalism.

THE FIRST ARAB NATIONALIST CONGRESS 1913

Before the conference was convened in Paris, a Reform Committee in Beirut, still a Syrian city at the time, which consisted of Maronite Christian merchants of the port, sent a letter to the French consul explaining why they had decided to join forces with Muslims on the issues of reform and decentralization. After stating that the Ottoman government's call for the local notables to present it with proposed reform projects was but a trick to avert European pressure for real reform, the statement goes:

The Christians of Beirut nonetheless agreed to cooperate with the Muslims in drafting a reform project for two reasons: 1- to frustrate the maneuver of the Turkish government so that the project is drafted in the manner it wishes 2- to be able to include a proposal calling for European supervision in all branches of the administration. Even in the hypothetical case of implementing such reforms without Europe's support, still the final solution has to take into consideration the aspirations of Syria's Christians, for those are definitely attached to France.

And they can never forget what they owe to Her greatness and civilization, nor can they forget their gratitude for the sympathy France showed in times of difficulty. The greatest wish of Syrian Christians is to declare a French protectorate in Syria [...] given the above, we the undersigned, working on behalf of the Christians of Beirut who had delegated us, present the following list, sorted by preference, of the solutions that we see as the only ones befitting the political situation in Syria: 1- either the French protectorate is declared in Syria, 2- or the province (welaya) of Beirut is granted autonomy under France's protection and supervision, 3- or the province (welaya) of Beirut is annexed to [the already autonomous district of mount] Lebanon on the condition that they both be put under the direct supervision of France. ('Memorandum by the Christian Members of the Beirut Reform Committees to the French Foreign Minister through the Consul in Beirut' in Kawtharani 1980: 51–3)

It is true that not all Arab nationalists had the same aspirations, nor did all Syrian Christians. Nonetheless, France's sponsorship of the first Arab Nationalist Congress did have an impact on the conference's political orientation. The vice-chair of the conference, Choukri Ghanem, who also happened to be the head of the Lebanese Committee in Paris, formed to prepare for the conference, sent a letter on 17 June to the same French Foreign Minister stating that France's sponsorship of the conference would definitely help win the hearts and minds of the Muslims of the Orient, which in turn would help France have easier control over its Muslim subjects in Algeria and North Africa (Kawtharani 1980: Introduction: 55).

The above position was adopted by the whole conference, as its chair, a Muslim notable from the Syrian city of Homs, Abdulhamid al-Zahrawi, insisted in an interview with the French paper *Le Temps* that Arab nationalist demands presented in Paris only concerned Ottoman Arabs and had nothing to do whatsoever with Arabs outside the empire (see Tibi 1990: 111).

The message that was being delivered by Arab nationalists to France was that their movement was destined to benefit its Near Eastern policies. In a sense, they were introducing themselves as middle men between France and their people. In the process, however, their 'people' were being redefined. Despite basing their movement on European concepts of nationhood, which would have definitely included the Arab Muslims under French colonial rule, and would have called for their liberation as well, they excluded those Arabs in order to make their endeavour worthwhile for France. The process of redefinition did not stop there: the societies participating in the congress also excluded Egyptian and Sudanese Arabs from their definition, although Egypt and Sudan were still legally part of the Ottoman Empire. This of course was a sign of the Arab nationalists' sensitivity and consideration to France's relations with Britain; it was also because one of the main societies participating in the conference was the Ottoman decentralization party which was based in British-occupied Cairo with the consent of the British. A real Arab nationalist congress would have been dangerous to French-occupied Algeria or British occupied Egypt (see ibid.)

Moreover, even for the Asian Arabs whom the members of the conference wished to liberate, liberty meant the introduction of French colonial supervision. It is worth noting that supervision, not direct occupation, was the demand. For those Arabs definitely wished to have a share of power. In a sense, they wished that France delegate such power to them, supervision was a guarantee that they would use that power in France's interest in return for France's recognition and protection.

When one of the participants presented a question to a Christian Syrian nationalist, who was talking about Syria's autonomy, asking whether the speaker could deny that France had colonial interests in the lands of Arabs including Syria, Zahrawi, as chair of the conference, intervened, stating that the conference should only discuss the domestic policies of the Ottoman Empire and that no discussion of the foreign policies of states was allowed. This was far from being a personal position by Zahrawi. After his intervention, another Muslim member of the conference, one Khalil Zainiyya, whom the French Consul in Beirut had described as a faithful informer to the French Republic, presented a motion to forbid any discussion of foreign policy throughout the conference. The motion was unanimously accepted ('The Speech of Nudra Bek Mutran' in Kawtharani, *Documents of the First Arab Congress 1913*, 64, also in Kawtharani 1980, Introduction: 69–70).

This position played a role in choosing the very persons who led the movement as representatives of Arab nationalism. In a report on Zahrawi and another Arab nationalist participating in the congress, the French Consul in Cairo stated that the political credentials of the said notables were 'satisfactory' as far as the interests of France were concerned, and that therefore they should be allowed to steer the conference (Kawtharani, 1980: 62).

This paradox of representation, where native middle men are happy to redefine themselves and their constituencies to fit the colonial design, naturally resulted in a fatal confusion in theory, discourse and language. The following quotation from the speech of one of the participants at the conference shows the amount of confusion about the issue of the Umma and the nation:

The Arab nation does not desire secession from the Ottoman Empire...but merely changes in the existing political system. It should be replaced by one in which all nationalities in the Empire have equal rights. In such a system the primary source of legislation becomes the nation, in which the nationalities are proportionately represented. (Tibi 1990: 111; for the full text of Ammun's speech see 'Reform on the Basis of Decentralization, the Speech of Alexander Bek Ammun, the Delegate of the Decentralization Party' in Kawtharani, 1980: 98–106).

The confusion is obvious where the word 'nation' or 'Umma' is used simultaneously to refer to the Arabs and the people of the Ottoman Empire. Ammun's position was that of the new Ottoman intellectual looking to substitute the Islamic bond on which the Ottoman Empire was founded with one of secular Ottoman nationalism. However, the difficulty lay in the fact that nothing other than Islam brought the various peoples of the Asian Ottoman Empire together. His vague understanding of the meaning of nation, and confusing it with that of the Umma is indicative of the confusion of the whole political movement. Another participant demonstrated the same confusion regarding the terms 'nation', 'community' and 'Umma': Abdel Ghani Al-Arisi, talked about the criteria of being a nation:

Are the Arabs a community (Jama'a)? Communities only deserves this name, in the opinion of political philosophers, if – according to the Germans – they have a common language and a common race; if – according to the Italians – they have a common history and common customs; if – according to the French – they consist of a single political will. If we look at the Arabs from any of these perspectives, we shall see that they have all the features mentioned, so that in the view of all political thinkers, without exception, they can claim to be a community (Jama'a). a people (Sha'b), and a nation (Umma) ('The Speech of Abdul Ghani Efendi Al-Arisi' in Kawtharani, Documents of the First Arab Congress, 42–3; also quoted in Tibi 1990: 112)

As is obvious from the above quotation, Arisi lists what would be the definitions of the term 'nation' as definitions of the term 'Jama'a' which in Arabic only means 'group' or 'community' and then uses the words 'people' ('sha'b') and 'Umma' as synonymous with 'Jama'a'. This is of course due to the lack of theoretical work on the definitions of the terms in Arabic at the time (and up until now for that matter). However, it is also worth noting that in listing the criteria by which a certain group of people are to be declared a nation, he does not make any reference to Arabic or Islamic sources. Arabs are to become a nation according to criteria of nationhood set by the French, the Italians or the Germans. This is more than just a form of psychological admiration or intellectual preference of western political theory; the sentence assumes that the theoreticians of the mentioned countries are *the* authority on nationhood; there is an acceptance of the western identity of the idea of the nation to start with. There is also an element of representation here. The immediate audience of Arisi was made of the Arabs attending the conference, yet, by citing the authority of the non-Arabs on the issue of nationhood, he was also addressing the French, the Italians and the Germans in proving to them that, according to their own criteria, Arabs *deserved* to be called a nation.

One could go on citing speeches of many participants in the congress, of which the above two citations are but examples. One can easily see that their logic is strikingly similar to that of Ahmad Lutfi Al-Sayidd, writing around the same time advocating Egyptian nationalism. I shall add only a few important citations here by the chair of the Congress. In his opening speech Zahrawi states:

We didn't come to Europe, the light source of the teachers of humanity in order, to ask her to add yet another region to her vast kingdoms, we are too wise to burden ourselves with such an intrusive mission, and Europe is too wise to need people like us. We came to Europe, and we want many others to come to Europe, so that our minds and spirits could grow as we watch the products of their minds and spirits. We came to Europe to increase our knowledge of her civilization and the ways of her advanced societies. And if we succeeded in increasing Europe's knowledge of us by one grain, it would be a great achievement. ... Europe is not the Ghoul;[5] the Ghoul is misadministration, and corrupt government. Had Europe been the Ghoul it would not have helped our state [the Ottoman State] at all. Those who know how much Europe has helped us for the past one hundred years, regret to have missed the opportunities that came with such assistance, and hope that the [Ottoman] State would benefit from future [European] assistance. ('Our Political Education: the Speech of the Chair of the Conference Mr. Abdulhamid Al-Zahrawi' in Kawtharani 1980: 37–8)

5. The Ghoul in Arabic is a mythical female monster who eats children. With a woman's body, a cat's face, a serpent's tongue, and breasts thrown backwards over her shoulders, she is ironically referred to in vernacular fairy tales as 'Mother Ghoul'.

The issue of representation does not need further comment. The passage that follows is a classic example of the native elite's internalization of the colonial discourse; Zahrawi views his own people as children who have to learn from mature Europe:

If we believe, like many others do, that politics begins and ends in lies, and if we forget that lying to Europe is like children lying to able men who laugh at them, then the end result of this policy will be the same as its beginning [it will end in defeat as it started with defeat] (Zahrawi in Kawtharani 1980: 38–9)

It is clear that in these passages Zahrawi is explaining and legitimizing his attitude towards Europe, that is, he is principally addressing his Arab audience giving them his reasons for adopting this unusual and unpopular position towards the continent whose forces occupied significant portions of their lands stretching from Algeria to Egypt.

Here I shall add one last quotation regarding the reconciliation between the new nationalism advocated by the participants of the conference and the Islamic tendencies among their people. In an interview with *Le Temps*, Zahrawi explained his position on decentralization. He emphasized that full secession from the Ottoman Empire was not in the Arabs' interest, and that they were keen on defending Ottoman unity. His interviewer then asked him whether it was for religious ties that he and his colleagues wanted to keep the relationship with Turkey. Zahrawi stated that religion had always failed to provide the basis for political association, that his aspirations revolved around the production of a new Ottoman community, one which he stops short of calling secular, but leaves that to be inferred from his previous remarks about the political failure of religion. He is then asked 'Is what you say about religious ties commensurate with the opinion of the people?', to which he replies:

I am speaking of the opinion of the enlightened stratum [of the people]. And since this stratum could believe in this opinion [about religion] without finding it contradictory to their religious principles, I don't see why the people could not come to the same conclusion. I know that they [the Ottoman government] are using religious sentiments to oppose reform, but this failed policy of theirs cannot survive. The people will eventually realize their hoaxes. We have had enough of this blind ignorance that has lingered among us for too long, we have to realize the scientific facts immediately; that the world is being run today by a handful of enlightened men who illuminate east and west with their sharp minds, and that these men are not from us. (Zahrawi, 'Mr. Zahrawi's Interview with the Editor of *Le Temps*', in Kawtharani 1980: 20–1)

Seemingly encouraged by this answer, the interviewer takes his question one step further: 'So you are quite far from this hatred that some Muslims show towards Europe and her men?', to which Zahrawi replies:

Those who deny Europe's favours are driven by nothing but blind selfishness. We look at them in sorrow and pity when we cannot remove their illusions. For there is one clear shining truth, we can't even claim any credit for making it known, for it is known by everyone, it is that European civilization saved us from our deep slumber. If our past inclinations had numbed our senses and were the reason that lied behind our idleness, our new inclinations will push us towards progress to regain the position that our fathers had before us in the world of past civilizations (Zahrawi, 'Mr. Zahrawi's interview with the Editor of Le Temps', in Kawtharani 1980)

On the face of it, Zahrawi's words sound elitist or downright arrogant. Not only does he make a sweeping historical generaliza- tion regarding the failure of religion to form political communities, a conclusion that cannot hold even in Europe's experience, but he also refers to hundreds of years of Arab history as being years of slumber and numbness. Nonetheless, on a closer look, one could sense a tone of reconciliation in his words. He emphasizes that the 'enlightened elite' do not find the new way of thinking, 'nationalism', offensive to their religious creeds, and that he hopes that the masses follow suit. Moreover, the aim of that nationalism, as he puts it in his final sentence, is to regain the position 'our fathers had in the world of past civilizations'.

Now the contradictions are clear. His assertion that Islam and nationalism are reconcilable, contradicts his arguments about Islam's role in causing the millennial slumber of Muslims. This contradiction could only be resolved if Islam was redefined. The political part of Islam whose presence Zahrawi acknowledges yet condemns, has to be discarded. Some new Islam, an apolitical one, should be embraced, one that would accept nationalism and that would not hate Europe.

One could trace the same logic in his final sentences regarding the glory of 'our fathers'. Zahrawi is referring to the Arab civilization. Nonetheless, such a civilization could seldom be separated from Islam. The only Arab Empires were Islamic ones, based on, and animated by, interpretations of the Islamic texts. Zahrawi's words were precursors to Arab nationalist thinkers of the mid-twentieth century, who attempted to redefine Islamic history to become some sort of non-Islamic Arab history. This is the tendency I discussed above, of reading nationalism into everything that might have slightly resembled it.

In the arguments made by Zahrawi (the one on the elite and the masses, and the one about history), the contradiction between the new identity quoted from Europe and the native identity is resolved by a redefinition of the latter. Nonetheless, the purpose of this very act of redefinition is to have a new identity legitimized in terms of the old one. Nationalism contradicted the current notions of political identity in Islam, yet in order for it to have any popularity it had to be judged and legitimized by Islam, it had to fit into the system it wanted to substitute. It is clear how problematic such an intellectual process of fitting squares into circles must be. Moreover, despite admitting that nationalism was here to substitute Islam as a political bond, Arab nationalists never stopped saying that its principal function was to restore the lost glory of the Arabs, which was in fact Islamic.

These ideas could easily be traced in the works of the next generation of Arab nationalists such as Sati' Al-Husri and Michael Aflaq, the latter of whom was the main ideologue and founder of the Arab nationalist movement and the Baath Party in Syria and Iraq after World War Two. Before we discuss their work and the development of Arab nationalism during the cold war, there is still another version of pre-World War Two Arab nationalism that merits our attention. While the above discussion has shown the contradictions inherent in the discourse of the early Arab nationalists, the following section will look at the same contradictions in the political movement that resulted in the creation of four Arab nation-states in the Middle East – the Arab Revolt.

THE ARAB REVOLT AND ITS OFFSPRING[6]

According to mainstream Arab historians, and even in history school books in Jordan and pre-1958 Iraq, the Arab Revolt was an act of national rebellion against foreign domination by the Turks. Nonetheless, the argument made by the man who headed the revolt, Sharif Hussein Ibn Ali, the Ottoman governor of Hijaz and the custodian of the Two Holy Shrines of Islam in Mecca and Medina, was that the revolt took place to save Islam. It was thus yet

6. This section heavily draws on my MA thesis 'State Building in Palestine and Jordan: The Impact of the Colonial Powers', The American University in Cairo, 2000.

another attempt to reconcile the idea of the Umma with that of the nation.

Just before World War One, Sharif Hussein Ibn Ali wrote a letter to the Sultan advising him not to go to war in support of Germany. His reasons were the following:

Your Majesty knows how the Balkan war ended, and that the state is now in need of military equipments and preparations which are not yet available. Your Majesty also knows that going to war in alliance with Germany is extremely dangerous, since all the state's weaponry, spare-parts and ammunition are from Germany, and that the Ottoman factories could not guarantee to replace the weapons that would be lost in battle. Moreover, the distant provinces far to the south of the body of the state like Basra, Yemen and Hijaz are surrounded from every direction by well prepared naval enemy forces, the situation will thus be very difficult for these provinces. The state (the Ottoman Empire) might be relying on the courage of the people in these provinces for defense, yet these people are not organized nor armed in a manner that would enable them to match the regular armies of Europe. I, therefore, call upon your majesty by God not to go to this war, and I want your Majesty to know that I see in anyone who supports going to war on the Germans' side either stupidity or high treason. (Sharif Hussein's Letter to Sultan Mohammed Rashad, in King Abdallah I of Jordan, *Mudakkarati* 1989: 103–4)

In the first statement of the Arab Revolt Sharif Hussein explained the reasons for his movement with the following lines:

Anyone with some knowledge of history knows that the Emirs [Princes] of Mecca were the first to recognize the Ottoman State amongst the rulers and princes of Muslims because they wanted to keep Islamic unity and strengthen its ties, since the Ottoman Sultans, may God grant them paradise, held to the creed of God, the Quran, the Sharia and the Sunna of the Prophet...I even fought Arabs with Arabs in 1327 [1909 AD] during the siege of Abha to save the state's honor...until the Committee of Unity and Progress was created and took control of the admin-istration of the State and all other matters by way of force and revolt. They deserted the path of religion, paved the way for heresy and humiliation of the Imams, deprived the great Sultan of his rights of religious and legal control, and made him, the national assembly and the council of deputies, mere executors of the secret decisions taken by their rebellious Committee...This State has been taken over by a committee that has raped the rights of the gracious Ottoman family by force and robbed their kingdom...while we, when seeing their deeds, used to try to interpret them in a manner that would excuse them, until no more excuses could be found, and each time we knew of a crime they [the CUP] had committed against the State or the Arabs, we used to consider it a fault on which they would go back shortly. We also used to say that it was not allowed to resist them in order not to cause a rupture in the State and in order not to deepen the rift between the Arabs and the Turks ... But when we saw that they exposed the independence of the State to elimination, and that they did not respect the dignity of religion, nor the rulings of the Sharia, nor the independence of the Sultan, there was no reason for which we had to bear this injustice and humiliation. (Mahafza 1991, 2: 5–11)

The main argument in the above quotation is that the Ottoman Empire, as a symbol, was the cause for which, rather than the target against which, the Arab Revolt started. It is obvious from the letter Hussein sent to the Sultan before the war that he expected a crippling defeat of the Ottoman Empire. Even if the Empire didn't fall, he was almost sure that the southern provinces would undoubtedly come under foreign occupation (probably under British occupation). In his second statement after the revolt had started, Hussein emphasized the fact that the Ottoman Empire had long coasts and was the only Islamic state with a Caliph. It was thus the policy of the 'gracious Ottoman Sultans' to keep good relations with empires that had great naval powers and ruled over great numbers of Muslims (namely Britain). Hussein's greatest fear was that if the Ottoman Empire was defeated there would be no Islamic state nor a Caliphate able to keep the spiritual and moral authority over the Islamic world. As is obvious from Hussein's first statement, he considered the Caliphate to be one of the necessities of religion; limiting the authorities of the Caliph was, to him, a breach of the Sharia and a danger to Islam. Since defending the present Caliphate was useless in his view (which was militarily correct), he had to find a way to create an alternative that would perfrom the functions of religious and political leadership for Muslims world-wide. Accordingly, Hussein saw it necessary to keep some Islamic state alive, one that would be a valid successor to the Ottoman Empire. Moreover, the idea that Hijaz was under threat of Christian occupation electrified the Hashemite Sharif, not only because his sharifate would vanish, but also because the fall of the holy shrines in Mecca and Medina into non-Muslim hands had never occurred in history and had usually been equated with the end of Islam. His idea was to make a deal with the British, before they won the war, since nothing would motivate them to grant him what he wanted once they did. Hussein understood British interests to be the guaranteeing of a safe passage to India as well as the control over the economic resources of the Middle East. To the Sharif, these interests were reconcilable with his own. Moreover, he expected the public opinion to be receptive of the idea that the Arab Revolt was for the sake of Islam (as is obvious from the first statement quoted above).

As for the rest of the Arab Revolt discourse, the idea of Hussein himself being the head of that Islamic successor state was emphasized. Right from the beginning, he declared that Arabs, more so than the Turks, had the right to assume the Caliphate since the Caliph was but the successor of the Prophet and the Prophet was an Arab. Despite the fact that his claim to the Caliphate did not materialize until 1925 after it was abolished in Turkey, the theme of his Hashemite origin was always present. Even in delaying his bid for the Caliphate, Hussein seemed to be consistent with his Sunni Islamic doctrine. His rebellion was namely against the secular Young Turks who had hijacked the Caliph. Rebelling against an existing Caliph was forbidden; claiming the Caliphate in the life of an existing Caliph was a reason for civil war. It should be remembered that according to the late Sunni interpretations of Islam discussed in Chapter 2, he who claims the Caliphate while a Caliph already reigned is to be fought because he would be splitting the ranks of the Muslims and weakening the Umma. Therefore claiming the Caliphate while a Caliph still nominally reigned in Turkey would have shed doubts on Hussein's initial arguments that his revolt was aimed at saving the Umma in the first place.

Hussein might have been acting with pure Machiavellian motives, but he nonetheless always made sure that his acts could be legitimized within the context of Islamic Sharia.

Moreover, the link between saving Islam and the Arabs' right to the Caliphate made Hussein's discourse acceptable to the conservative tribes in the Hijaz as well as to the modernist nationalists in Syria and Iraq. This was also the window through which the Islamic rhetoric of the Arab Revolt in Hijaz would gradually turn into a nationalistic discourse in Jordan and Iraq under Hussein's sons, Abdallah I and Faisal I.

This logic continued to govern the Arab nationalist kingdoms that emereged from the Arab Revolt, Faisal's Iraq, and Abdallah's Jordan. Yet this King Lear of Arabia stopped one step short of his two sons, who were willing to make more concessions than he was in order to secure their thrones in Jordan and Iraq.

Unlike his sons, Hussein had not been able to make a successful transition from the old Ottoman framework and the new regional order dominated by Britain, Abdallah had made the necessary compromises and had got, in return a throne, more or less secure. Faisal, had made similar compromises and had also got a throne (owing to the structure of Iraq he was able to counter the weight of Britain's imperial interests with local ones, thus creating a greater sense of independence for himself than Abdallah was ever able to do). Hussein however, never gave up trying to Justify and legitimize his initial act of breaking away from the Ottoman Empire. Even after it became politically impossible to create the Arab kingdom he had hoped for, he continually strove to impose his moral hegemony, which was the only way left for him to win the approbation of Arabs and Muslims divided into rival states for the most part dominated by Europe. To this end in part he assumed the Caliphate. To this end also he had supported Arab demands in Palestine, refusing to conclude a treaty with Britain which would imply acceptance of Britain's Jewish national home policy. His refusal in Abdallah's analysis cost him his throne. (Wilson 1987: 88)

The colonial threat and the colonial promise gave the opportunity to Hussein to form this image of the world. Hussein's position in the Hijaz was different from that of his sons in the northern parts of the Arab world. In Hijaz he had his tribal base, he had the legitimacy and symbolism of being the caretaker of the two holy shrines in Mecca and Medina and he had the claim to Islamic moral guidance and saving the Caliphate to which he had attached himself right from the beginning of the Arab Revolt. It was the colonial threat that initiated the whole movement. His fear of the colonial stick of occupying the two shrines, and his hope for the colonial carrot of establishing a vast Arab kingdom, caused him to start his revolt.

However, just as in the case of Egyptian and secular Arab nationalisms, Hussein's nationalist Islam held the seeds of the paradoxes of replacement and representation. While on the native side he tried to keep his actions in line with the Sharia and popular sentiments, on the colonial side he tried to accommodate as much of the colonial agenda as he could. His drive for creating a state, one recognized by Britain and the international community, led him to reformulate his original Islamic discourse in a manner commensurate with colonial interests. He claimed to be the representative of Arabs, then of Muslims, to Britain. He demanded that the colonial power give him a share in power, and in return he had to promise to use that power in the interests of the colonial power which delegated it to him.

The shape of the states that would be the fruits of the Arab Revolt was partly determined by the Hussein-McMahon correspondence. These were the letters in which the promises between the colonizer and the colonized were exchanged: the former promising delegated power, and the latter promising to use it in a manner satisfactory to his master. One could thus easily trace the logics of replacement therein.

The economic ties between both parties started then. The Sharif's continuous demands for economic aid could be viewed as part of the military needs of war. But this aid was also needed to provide for the civilian economic needs of Hussein's province in Hijaz, the local revenues from *Zakat*, Islamic charity money collected by local governments in the Ottoman Empire, and taxes on Hajj, were not sufficient for running the province, especially as it was going to war with the Empire of which it was a part. Hussein, in a kind of a trade-off, guaranteed to Sir Henry McMahon, the British High Commissioner in Egypt, that Britain would have economic rights in the expected Arab kingdom. In his third message to McMahon on 7 November 1915, the Sharif specified the terms of the political and economic relations he intended to have with Britain in the future Arab state, especially in provinces where Britain had vital interests.[7]

In order to preserve your rights, which are mixed with our rights as if they were of one unique essence, we can accept to leave the quarters that are now under British use…as far as their economic resources and facilities are concerned, and [in return] the Arab kingdom would be paid during the period of this use [occupation] the appropriate amount of money to fulfil the needs of any nascent kingdom. ('From Sharif Hussein to Sir Henry McMahon', *The File of Palestine Documents*, Document No. 62, 1969, 1: 177)

His dependence, although much less than the dependence of his sons later on, still affected the way Hussein perceived of the events taking place around him and the way he understood the messages he was receiving from his allies. Getting increasingly dependent as the British closed in on Hijaz, Hussein could not afford to confront the fact that his potential allies were not willing to give him what he demanded, that is, the Arab state. This psychological state of denial seems to have lingered on with later Arab nationalists. In Arab school books, it is generally accepted that Britain promised Sharif Hussein of Mecca an Arab state stretching from Turkey in the north to the Indian

7. The correspondence took place in Arabic. The current quotations are of my translation.

ocean in the south, including Iraq and Syria, in return for siding with them against the Turks. The British rule of Iraq and the French rule of Syria according to the Sykes-Picot Agreement are then seen as profound breaches of the promises made to the Arabs by Britain. Yet it seems clear from the very beginning in McMahon's letters to Sharif Hussein that the northern borders of the promised Arab state were controversial and subject to further discussion. Britain's direct rule of Iraq, 'Welayat Al Mawsil', 'Welayat Baghdad' and 'Welayat Al Basra' was hinted at, and so was French rule of great parts of Syria 'Welayat Beirut' and 'Welayat Halab'. The most the Sharif could get from Sir Henry on the issue of these borders was to postpone the discussion till the war was over. In this context, the preamble of the following letter from McMahon to Hussein seems painfully ironic:

To his Highness of honorable descent, the Progeny of the house of Prophecy, the One of pure heritage and proud lineage, the Great Sharif, Sayyid,[8] Hussein son of Ali, the Prince of Revered Mecca, the place where Islam and Muslims turn for prayer, may God always keep him in greatness and glory...As for the provinces [Welayat] of Aleppo and Beirut, the government of Great Britain has understood all what you have mentioned concerning them and has carefully noted them. But, as the interests of our ally, France, are involved in these two provinces, the issue requires careful consideration, and we shall contact you on that matter at the appropriate time. The Government of Great Britain, as it has informed you before, is ready to give all the guarantees and aid to the Arab Kingdom, but her interests in the province of Baghdad [Welayat Baghdad] need friendly *permanent* administration...the preservation of these interests needs more accurate discussion than what is now possible due to the present situation and the hastiness of these negotiations. ('From Sir Henry McMahon to ash-Sharif Hussein on 14 December 1915', *The File of Palestine Documents*, Document No. 62, 1969, 1: 179, emphasis mine)

8. 'Sayyid' which means Lord, Master, or simply Mr, is the title given to the descendants of Prophet Mohammad through his grandson Hussein son of Ali and Fatima, who is also the third Shiite infallible Imam, martyred by the Umayyads in Karbala. The title is more current among Shiites. Sayyid Mohammad Khatamy, former president of Iran, and Sayyid Hasan Nasrallah, the leader of the Lebanese Hezballah, sometimes have their title confused with their actual names. The lineage of Sharif Hussein of Mecca, however, goes back not to Hussein the martyr of Karbala, but to his older brother Hassan. The descendants of Hassan are usually given the title 'Sharif'. In his somewhat theatrical compilation of the Sharif's praise and pompous titles, McMahon seems to have mixed the usage of these two titles.

At this point Sharif Hussein declared that the Arabs would fight France for the province of Beirut (most of today's Lebanon) after the war was over:

As soon as these wars end we will take up the opportunity to demand from you what we are now leaving to France in Beirut and its coast...the French presence in our neighborhood would be the germ for problems and quarrels that could never allow for stability [in the region]. ('From Sharif Hussein to Sir Henry McMahon 25 of Safar al Khair 1334 Hijri', 1 January 1916, *The File of Palestine Documents*, Document No. 62, 1969, 1: 181)

However, Sir Henry refused to guarantee any British approval and pointed clearly to the fact that British-French relations after the war were expected to improve:

As soon as this war ends, the friendship between England and France will become deeper and stronger, for they will have sacrificed English and French blood, side by side, to defend rights and liberties...and now, since the Arab countries have decided to join us in protecting rights and liberties and to work in the service of this cause, we pray to God that the result of these efforts be an everlasting friendship that would bring happiness and satisfaction to all. ('From McMahon to ash-Sharif Hussein on 24 Rabee' al-Awwal 1334 Hijri', 30 January 1916, *The File of Palestine Documents*, Document No. 62, 1: 183)

No further discussion of the northern and eastern borders of the Arab state followed. Hussein's extreme dependence on the British caused him to understand the ambiguous position of his allies in a way which was compatible with his own ambitions. In order to solve the contradiction between his expectations and those of his allies, Hussein seems to have decided to understand McMahon's words as promising him the kingdom he desired. This is not to say that Britian did not break its promise to Hussein – it certainly did, for he was not even allowed to keep his own Kingdom of Hijaz, let alone having a united Arab state. Also, the creation of a national home for the Jews in Palestine was definitely a breach of the agreement between Hussein and Britain, for nothing is mentioned in the above correspondence to suggest the exclusion of Palestine from the promised Arab state. Nonetheless, even as an imaginary state, this colonially created kingdom captivated Hussein and trapped him in the paradox of replacement. He considered himself the King of the Arabs and a friend of Britain; he then tried to reconcile the contradiction therein, since Britain was definitely not the friend of the people it was about to have under its occupation.

Even in understanding the correspondence with McMahon, Hussein seems to have been blind to the trap he was walking into; he didn't see that he was collaborating with Britain with no guarantee whatsover. Texts might have different interpretations, but the point is that the King of the Arabs chose the interpretation that troubled him the least. However, Hussein declared that, while keeping his alliance with Britain for the reasons mentioned above, he would not make an accommodation with the French. The possibility of confrontation was not totally ruled out due to Hussein's position in Hijaz. It was the colonial threats and promises to Hijaz that led Hussein to collaborate with Britain, but not the colonial creation of Hijaz. Hussein had a base of power that was independent from Britain. The colonial influence, then, only shaped his external environment, rather than shaping his whole political entity.

Hussein's stubbornness was short-lived, however. After the defeat of the Ottoman Empire, Hijaz was transformed from a province to a kingdom. In the process it fell hostage to colonial designs. Hijaz became no better than Transjordan or Iraq, or even mandatory Palestine. After his hope for an Arab kingdom was aborted, the Welayat of Hijaz was deprived both of the Ottoman subsidy and of the self-sustaining status of a large Arab kingdom. Hijaz became totally dependent on Britain, a dependence which had to be formalized by the British Hijazi Treaty. When Hussein refused that treaty, he did not realize that by that time he had lost the edge over his sons. The external influence of the British had spilled over into his internal settings in Hijaz. The British subsidy was cut off, Hussein could not arrange a good defence and Hijaz fell to Ibn Saud in a situation that could be compared to the rise of Islamic movements and institutions in Iraq after the fall of Saddam's regime.

The Wahhabis under Ibn Saud stretched their influence to cover most of the Arab Peninsula right after the war. Britain decided to cooperate with them. And when Hussein became more of a liability than an asset, his former allies allowed his kingdom to fall to the Saudis. Britain, however, could not let an Islamist movement control the northern parts of the peninsula, threatening its imperial routes and its 'national home for the Jews in Palestine' project. Thus Iraq and Jordan were created, and Hussein's sons were granted the thrones.

Having lost his kingdom, the old King Lear of the Arabs sought refuge in the kingdoms of his two sons. However, his claiming the Caliphate threatened to become a focus of some pan-Arab, pan-

Islamic movement, or at least to provide the symbolic basis for the unity of Iraq and Jordan. Therefore he was not allowed to stay in either Jordan or Iraq. He was exiled to Cyprus and was only allowed to return to Jordan on his death in 1931.

The creation of Jordan and Iraq was also typical of the paradox of replacement. Faisal, the second son of Sharif Hussein, and T.E. Lawrence's personal friend, first claimed the throne of Syria after his legion triumphantly entered Damascus. His position in Syria would have been a breach of the British-French agreement to divide the Middle East, usually referred to as the Sykes-Picot Agreement. After a series of failed negotiations, the French troops stationed at the Syrian coast marched east and drove Faisal out of Damascus. The Ottoman province of Aleppo (Welayat Halab), Damascus (Welayat Dimashq), the autonomous province of Mount Lebanon and the coastal province of Beirut, became the modern states of Syria and Lebanon, both under French mandate. To appease Faisal, the British awarded him the throne of Iraq. In return, Faisal had to sign the secret Faisal-Weizmann treaty[9] in which he committed himself to the establishment of a national home for the Jews in Palestine, as well as a series of agreements with the British regarding their interests in Iraq (see *The File of Palestine Documents*, Document No. 85, 1969, 2: 251).

Abdullah, Hussein's eldest son, who was initially given nothing, tried to attack the French in Syria. In order to calm down the situation, the British granted him the land east of Palestine and west of Iraq. In a meeting in Jerusalem, in March 1921, T.E. Lawrence and Winston Churchill promised him that Britain would use its good offices to convince France to appoint him King of Syria under mandate, but only if he could secure the southern borders of the French mandate area against the attacks of Arab rebels. The man whose aim was initially to liberate Syria from French occupation assumed the task of defending that very occupation against native resistance with the pretext that that was the surest way to liberate the land.

The Arab Revolt thus created the kingdoms of Hijaz, Syria, Jordan and Iraq, of which only the last two survived. In terms of discourse as well as in terms of institutions, these political entities embodied the paradox of replacement and its failure. In the interwar period, like the Egyptian kingdom, the kingdoms of Iraq and Jordan continued to play colonial roles, attempting to reconcile colonial agendas with

9. See, for example, Avi Shlaim (1988, 1997 and 2000). Also see Mary Wilson (1987). On the Arab side, see M.H. Haykal (1996 and 1998).

native sentiments. One can expand on a series of events that indicate how these states were but colonial tools that could not contradict the colonial agenda. Such examples might include King Abdullah I of Jordan's attempts to reconcile Britain's 'national home for the Jews in Palestine' policy with his Arab and Islamic discourse, when he proposed in 1937 that such a Jewish national home be established under his sovereignty as a king of both banks of the Jordan. Another example is the 1948 Palestinian episode, when most Arab kings reached an understanding with the British and the Jewish organizations that, despite sending Arab armies to Palestine, the partition of Palestine would be implemented. However, these cases have long been studied by historians on both sides of the Arab-Israeli conflict. What concerns us here is the colonial origin of Arab nationalism, and the theoretical attempts to reconcile it with the concepts of Umma and Dawla. For that reason I shall skip the historical part, and directly discuss Arab nationalism in its cold war version, where it developed into a revolutionary leftist movement. I shall focus on the works of Michael Aflaq, the main ideologue and founder of the Baath Party. The party still rules Syria today, and ruled Iraq for most of the cold war.

THE ARAB NATIONALISM OF THE COLD WAR

In the interwar period, and then in the cold war period, Arab nationalism gained more theoretical sophistication and political momentum. It also gained significant popularity as it found itself in confrontation with the colonial plans of which it was part before World War One. The more Arab nationalists found themselves at odds with Britain and France the more popular they became, and the more need they felt for a well crafted ideological body. The speeches of the attendees of the first Arab Nationalist Conference in Paris were no longer sufficient to define a modern anti-imperialist pan-Arab movement.

It might be worth noting that, just as 'Umma' was mistranslated into 'nation' by Europeans, Arabs have had problems with translating the term 'nationalism' into Arabic.[10] The word currently has two Arabic translations that are sometimes seen as mutually exclusive: '*Qawmiyya*' and '*Wataniyya*'. '*Qawmiyya*' means to belong to a certain group of people, '*qawm*', and is therefore usually associated with

10.   For example, see the quotation from Abdul Ghani Al-Arisi's speech to the First Arab Nationalist Congress (see p. 164).

Arab nationalism; Arabs have the same origin, the same language, and the overwhelming majority of them have the same religion and the same collective memory. *Wataniyya*, on the other hand, means belonging to the homeland, to a certain territory: *'watan'*. It is therefore frequently used in reference to local nationalisms such as Egyptian or Lebanese nationalisms. But it is also used to indicate a positive moral judgment, meaning anti-colonialism. In that sense even communists or Islamists are often referred to as *'wataniyyeen'*. In this last case the term is more suitably translated into 'patriotism', though paradoxically it does not refer as much to belonging to a certain homeland as it does to opposing a foreign invasion. In this usages, the term *Wataniyya* leaves the definition of the homeland and the basis on which the foreignness of the foreigner is decided, unsaid. Also, *Wataniyya* does not hold much content regarding the political identity or the form of government; it only refers to the bond among different groups of people that have little in common other than being against colonial domination.

On the other hand, the term *Qawmiyya*, while still void of any indication of the form of government, is closely associated with political identity. The term must be followed by an adjective that indicates the group of people referred to. *Al-qawmiyya Al-misriyya* is the Egyptian local nationalism, *Al-qawmiyya Al-Arabiyya* is pan-Arab nationalism, and so on. It is also associated with the drive to create a united state that rules over the concerned group of people, making it the closest Arabic term to the European meaning of 'nationalism'. The difference between the two concepts, however, comes from the difference in the historical processes that produced them. In Europe nationalism was the product of humanism, of the belief in the centrality of human beings in determining the forms of government, the social and moral codes, as well as the basis of political solidarity that affected their lives. In the Arab world, *Qawmiyya* was but a translation of the European term 'nationalism', for which Arab nationalists then strove to find roots in the Arabic cultural heritage. Not only did this deprive the Arabic *Qawmiyya*, like a treeless fruit, of the philosophical lineage and moral content of the European 'nationalism', it also led Arab nationalists to see their history as a fruitless tree, since it did not produce a corresponding concept. To remedy that, they tried to attach the European fruit to the Arab tree by reinterpreting their own history in order to find anything that might resemble or even lead to this *Qawmiyya* in the writings of pre-colonial Arab thinkers.

The most prominent pre-colonial Arab thinker in whose ideas they could find something to resemble nationalism was Ibn Khaldoun. His concept of *Assabiyya*, which we shall now discuss, was reinterpreted as a precursor of Arab nationalism. Typically, the attempt to assimilate with the colonial master resulted in deforming both the colonially imported culture and the native one. Unsurprisingly, the colonial hybrid, here the concept of *Qawmiyya*, lacked the consistency of both its parents, European nationalism and Khaldounian *Assabiyya*.

Ibn Khaldoun's *Assabiyya* and the Late Arab Nationalists

Ibn Khaldoun was a fourteenth-century sociologist who presented a theory on the rise and fall of kingdoms. He argued that the nomadic way of life, which depended largely on hunting and on fighting other tribes over scarce resources of water and grazing lands, deprived nomads of all forms of social association except that of kinship and tribalism. Because of their continuous mobility, nomads could not associate on the basis of neighbourhood, Greek-style citizenship, agricultural cooperation, or absolute obedience to an imperial despot.

The nomadic 'mode of production' created its superstructure in an ethic of tribal solidarity that Ibn Khaldoun calls *Assabiyya*.[11] Since raiding was one of the main sources of income, fighting was a mode of production. According to Ibn Khaldoun, this mode of life bettered the tribal people's fighting and organizational skills. The whole population was a military organization bound together not by common interests but by blood and a deeply felt ethic of solidarity with one's kinsmen. These traits eventually allow tribes to overcome settled communities. Once they settle they gradually adopt the more relaxed living style of villages and cities. With urbanization comes a specialized economy, part of which is the specialized military. No longer would the men of the tribe, that is, 100 per cent of the male labour force of society, be available for military service. Rather, a hired army of mercenaries is tasked with protecting the previously nomadic, now settled community. Ibn Khaldoun then uses arguments similar to those of Machiavelli as he counts the disadvantage of

11. The suffix *'iyya'* in Arabic is equivilant to the suffix 'ism' in English. *'Assab'* and *'Osba'* are two words that mean the bond, the bundle or the group of people bound together, like a clan, a family or a gang. It also means, nerve, binding rope, or vein. The word nearly always refers to the bond of blood or kinship. It is therefore closest to the English meaning of nationalism in terms of it being derived from common birth and origin, as in the Latin *'nasci'*.

mercenary armies; in time they become stronger than their own employers, they compete with one another, as they have nothing in common other than being hired by a political elite whose influence keeps on dwindling. In the meantime, other nomadic tribes in the vicinity, who had kept their Bedouin mode of production and therefore their military prowess, continue their attacks on the settled community and history repeats itself. Ibn Khaldoun argues that the rise and fall of Islamic and non-Islamic states up until his time could be explained by the above described model. His theory was celebrated by many modern scholars as one of the first 'secular' theories of socio-political history in Islam since it applies to Muslims and non-Muslims alike and attributes nothing to metaphysics. The argument that a group of people's mode of production creates a superstructure of ethics and norms has been quite attractive to Arab Marxists and nationalist socialists.

Nonetheless, such scholars usually focus on the first half of Ibn Khaldoun's history cycle, where the nomadic economy produces the ethic of tribal solidarity or *Assabiyya*. They overlook that this superstructure is what leads the community to change its mode of production as it allows them to conquer settled empires and city states, and gradually switch into rural and urban life. If one were to apply Marxist terms to Ibn Khaldoun's arguments, one would say that the fourteenth-century Arab thinker argued that infrastructures created and changed superstructures *and vice versa*.

Another point usually overlooked in Ibn Khaldoun's theory is his opinion on religion. Ibn Khaldoun mentions that it is a force alongside *Assabiyya* and that having a common belief system, ideology or charismatic religious leader boosts tribal solidarity and allows nomads to conquer settled cities more easily. This is of course in line with the argument of Arab nationalists, such as Husari and Aflaq, where *Assabiyya*, read in modern times as nationalism, is seen as the point of origin, while religion is only a secondary source of strength in support of it. As such, Ibn Khaldoun's ideas were seen as a precursor to Arab nationalism.[12]

---

12. On Husari's position Tibi says: 'In the discussion of the general theoretical framework of Al-Husri's [Husari's] work, it was concluded that, following Ibn Khaldoun, religion plays only a secondary role in the formation of nations, and that, following the nineteenth-century German romantics, it can only be of real significance if it is a national religion. Hence the gist of Al-Husri's [Husari's] controversy with the Pan-Islamists, on both theoretical and practical levels, is that Pan-Arabism is easier to

However, a closer look at his work reveals otherwise. The above arguments by Ibn Khaldoun concern power politics but not legitimacy. In fact, in the section on religion, he does not stop at stating that religion gives a boost to tribal solidarity as such, but he also argues that it gives legitimacy and therefore some sort of stability to the settled rule that follows the nomadic invasion of fertile lands.[13] He was all too familiar with the difference between the illegitimate and therefore short-lived, upheaval-filled, era of the Umayyads (nearly 90 years) and that of the Abbasids which lasted for six centuries in Baghdad, before it moved to Cairo for another 300 years. In Ibn Khaldoun's time, in fact, the belief was that the Abbasids would still rule till the end of time.[14] In short, while *Assabiyya* worked to bring elites belonging to different tribes to power, religion, and to Ibn

---

put into practice than Pan-Islamism. Al-Husri [Husari] says that the universal religions of Christianity and Islam have been unable to achieve a political unity of peoples speaking different languages, and if this has taken place, it has done so only for brief historical periods within a very limited framework, from this he concludes that irredentist movements cannot be successful if based on religion, but only if based on a common culture, language and historical heritage. He knows that such secular ideas would be bitterly opposed as heretical by the influential Islamic Ulama and he therefore makes tactical allowances in order to avoid open conflict with them, he attempts a definition of Pan-Islamism which does not conflict with the political assumptions of his own theory. He explains that he always uses unity in the sense of the unity of the national state, and he is not opposed to Islamic solidarity and brotherhood as such. He suggests that there should be a strict distinction between Pan-Islamism and Islamic solidarity, and that the first should be given up for the sake of the second, particularly because of the creation of an Islamic national state as postulated by Pan-Islamism is impossible. However he does not seek to force the idea upon the Islamic Ulama' (Tibi 1990: 172–3).

13. Ibn Khaldoun writes in his first section on religion that Arabs cannot establish kingdoms unless they are based on some sort of religious doctrine. He argues that this is because of Bedouin nature which is proud and competitive (Ibn Khaldoun 1: 126), meaning that *Assabiyya* might only bring them together when Arabs are fighting non-Arabs. Otherwise, their nomadic way of life would probably result in their tribes fighting one another over material wealth and political power. According to Ibn Khaldoun, religion is what abates this tendency and allows them to form a supra-tribal political organization which is the Dawla (see also the other two chapters where he elaborates on this idea, Ibn Khaldoun 1996, 1: 132–3).

14. For other historical examples on the role of religion see Ibn Khaldoun (1996, 1: 133).

Khaldoun this meant any interpretation of the Quran, made such change in power more legitimate and therefore stable.[15]

This last part of Ibn Khaldoun's ideas is the one emphasized by the various Islamic groups. They state in their handbooks that nationalism would only be legitimate if it were commensurate with religion. As such it is but a form of *Assabiyya*, one that was promoted by the Prophet, if it were applied in the service of a higher goal, and shunned by him if it were not. One is inclined to think that neither Arab nationalists nor the Islamists really understood the meaning of nationalism as a product of science, and as a source of moral codes. For in a proper nationalist ideology, the nation is the product of nature, and so is that nation's common sense which is then expressed in its collective will, its constitution, laws and codes. For both Arab nationalists and Islamists, nationalism was but *Assabiyya*, an emotional force that could be either good or bad, and that needed some sort of moral guidance.

Arab nationalists tried to find some moral guidance, some theory of social behaviour and government that was Arab yet not Islamic, and they could not find any. The slogan of the Baath Party was 'One Arab Nation, with an Eternal Message'. The party theoreticians Sati' Al-Husari, his disciple Michael Aflaq and others spent a lot of time trying and failing to find any Arab 'message' that was disassociated from Islam.

Therefore, in the final analysis, to Arab nationalists, the moral guidance of the blind power of *Assabiyya* which they called nationalism, had to come from European humanism, no matter how it was disguised in Arabic literature and ideological jargon. To *Assabiyya* they added humanism, which they called modernity, in its liberal or socialist versions. In the first two phases of Arab nationalism, the one before World War One and the one in the interwar period, Arab nationalism was associated with liberalism.

15. In his first section on religion, Ibn Khaldoun writes that Arabs cannot establish kingdoms unless they are based on some sort of religious doctrine. He attributes this to their nomadic ethics of competitiveness, pride and independence (Ibn Khaldoun 1: 126). Their tribal solidarity only brings them together when they are fighting non Arabs. Otherwise, their nomadic way of life would probably result in their tribes fighting one another over material wealth and political power. According to Ibn Khaldoun, religion is what abates this tendency and allows them to form a supra-tribal political organization which is the Dawla (see also the other two chapters where he elaborates on this idea, Ibn Khaldoun 1996, 1: 132–3).

In the cold war period, as Arab nationalists broke away from their liberal colonial masters and leaned more towards the Soviet Union, Arab nationalism became associated with socialism.

It should be remembered that, as mentioned in Chapter 2 of this book, looking at Arab nationalism as a form of *Assabiyya* was true also of the Muslim Brothers and other Islamists. To them, however, the 'eternal message' of the 'one Arab nation' was Islam.

Late Arab Nationalism and the Umma: The Example of the Baath

Unlike Egyptian nationalists, the late Arab nationalists did not opt for a full confrontation with the Islamic sense of identity; sometimes they even portrayed Arab nationalism as being a possible step towards Islamic unity.[16]

Here it might be worthwhile to examine the works of Michael Aflaq. Aflaq was a Christian-born Syrian politician, who worked directly in founding the Baath Party, the party which eventually came to power in Syria and Iraq and determined the destiny of many in the Arab world. His writings therefore best represent the main tenets of the official Arab nationalist movement in the Middle East. In an article written in February 1949, Aflaq wrote about the new party:

It won't be far from truth to say that the party which the Arab Umma calls upon from the depth of her heart, and which befits the ancient Arab glories is the one whose purpose is the Umma, not the Dawla.[17] It is the one that is a miniature Umma, a model for the greater Umma. We all have this feeling, we all feel that our need is not just to fix the state apparatus, rather it's a deep all encompassing coup. (Aflaq 1986: 70)

If one takes a look at the rest of Aflaq's article, it will be clear that he uses the terms 'Umma' and 'Dawla' meaning 'nation' and 'state' respectively. Nonetheless, the relation he explains between the state and the nation is somewhat similar to the relation between the Umma and the Dawla in their medieval Islamic sense. He is speaking of a party, the Baath Party, one that is modelled after modern centralized

16. Sometimes this was by way of convincing Islamists that their opposition to Arab nationalism was inconsistent with their Islamism; more so than a genuine political programme by Arab nationalists. See for example Husari's arguments in Tibi (1990: 173).

17. Aflaq's usage of the terms here is confused as will be shown below. In the first sentence, he apparently he uses the terms 'Umma' and 'Dawla' meaning 'nation' and 'state' respectively. In the second sentence, when he talks of the state being a small Umma, it becomes difficult to say with certainty which of the two meanings he has in mind.

totalitarian parties in Western and Eastern Europe. Nonetheless, he speaks of the field of operation of that party as being the whole 'Arab' Umma/nation. That is to say, the purpose of the party and its point of reference does not lie in the legal and constitutional boundaries of the states in which it operates but rather in a supra-state entity called the Arab Umma. In that sense the party, whether in or out of power, becomes an entity whose allegiance lies outside its immediate field of operations.

Similarly, once the party comes to power, it becomes the duty of the state apparatuses it controls to continue working in the interests of the whole Arab Umma, rather than working exclusively in the interests of their citizens. Moreover, it becomes the duty of such states to eventually dissolve themselves in the overarching Arab state. Until Arab unity is realized, and as far as inter-Arab relations are concerned, neither the territory nor the sovereignty of small Arab states is a priority.

The main difference, however, between the Arab Umma-Dawla system and its Islamic ancestor is the lack of the common text of reference that constitutes the Arab Umma outside Islam. A sense of unity, a sense of togetherness, and a common memory do exist, yet there is no theory of government or ethics that is uniquely Arab and non-Islamic. This brings us back again to the painful search for that 'eternal' message Aflaq and his colleagues were striving to find. The Umma-Dawla system is mainly composed of a number of political entities with a common reference, guide, textual-ideal-Imam, therefore finding that reference, that quasi-'constitution', was crucial.

Aflaq tried to find that common reference in two ways. On the one hand he assumed the existence of an Arab ethic that was independent from Islam; a pattern of behaviour, a bundle of moral values embedded in tradition, or what he called the 'spirit' of the nation. On the other hand, he tried to reconcile himself with the fact that Islam was the main socio-political work of the Arabs, and therefore has to be the embodiment of that 'spirit' of the nation. As such Islam was reinterpreted to become the religion that Arabs brought to humanity; in other words, Aflaq gave Arabs their copyrights on Islam:

Gentlemen, The Islam-movement which is embodied in the life of the Gracious Prophet is not only a historical event to the Arabs, one that is explained in terms of time and place, causes and consequences, rather, and due to its depth and magnitude, it is directly linked to the absolute existence of the Arabs. I mean that it is the true image, and perfect eternal symbol, of the nature of the Arab self, its rich potentials, and authentic orientation. Therefore, it is correct to assume that it can be repeatedly renewed in its spirit, *not in its letters*. For Islam is the vital stimulus that can move the dormant energies of the Arab Umma, so that it can bubble with life, sweeping aside the obstacles and dams of tradition...reconnecting with the deep meanings of the universe, taken by enthusiasm and pride, expressing its enthusiasm and pride in new words and glorious deeds that can then spill over to other nations. (Aflaq 1986: 142–3, emphasis mine)

Flowery language aside, this is not too far from the Umayyad discourse on Arab superiority over other races of Muslims in the early days of Islamic expansion. In fact the Umayyad imperial era has been one of the historical eras repeatedly drawn upon by Arab nationalists as a source of inspiration. It is also not very far from being a call for a traditional Umma-Dawla system, where Islam is being reinterpreted from being just a religion, to an Arab religion, which the Arabs still have to propagate around the world as their message. The only problem with this last understanding of Aflaq's view on Islam is that it would have entailed that the Arab governments themselves adopt legal and constitutional systems derived from some inter-pretation of Islam, making the Quran and the Hadith, rather than socialism or liberalism, their point of reference. To a Christian-born secular Aflaq, that would have been unacceptable. The reinterpreta-tion of the meaning of Islam had to be taken one step further; not only was Islam turned into a 'religion of the Arabs' but it was also stripped of most of its philosophical, legal and juridical content and reduced to a revolutionary spirit. Islam was nothing more than an Arab revolution in the seventh century – a model revolution indeed, but one whose political fruits, in terms of political theory and actual forms of government, were to be ignored (see his articles on religion: 'Our View on Religion' and 'The Issue of Religion in the Arab Baath', in Aflaq 1986: 116–33).

In the final analysis one could say that to Aflaq, and subsequently to the Baathis, the concept of the Arab nation was a hybrid. In a sense, even if Islam was reduced to a glorious revolution of the Arabs in the seventh century, it was still a model revolution, an ideal which the Baath Party and modern Arab nationalists supposedly sought to imitate. It should be remembered the 'Umma' means an entity of people following an ideal image or a guide, and who are defined by such an act of following and pursuing. According to Aflaq, it is this act of pursuing the all encompassing perfect Arab revolution that brings the Arabs together and allows them to express their national identity. As far as this goes, Aflaq's version of Arab nationalism is very much similar to the Islamic political allegiance to the Umma.

On the other hand, Aflaq's Arab nation is different from the Islamic Umma in a number of ways. First of all, attaching Islam to Arabs excludes all non-Arab contributions to the body of writings and political theories that make the religion; and second, by reducing it to a social-national revolution in the seventh century, Aflaq strips Islam, which he calls the 'spirit' of the nation, from any moral, social, political or philosophical content. The eternal message of the Arabs becomes nothing more than their will to revolt, hence his calling the Baath Party 'the party of the coup'. In fact, there is a whole chapter in the first volume of his complete political works including eight articles he wrote between 1949 and 1955 where he associates the Baath with the coup, one of which has the simple title 'The Baath is the Coup' (see Aflaq 1986: 66–101). In his language this means that the Baath, the party whose name in Arabic means 'resurrection', is the physical embodiment of the Arab rebellious spirit, it is the truthful heir to the early Muslims, to the Prophet and the Companions as rebels. The problem, however, is that this revolution, knows what it is fighting against – colonialism, dependent capitalism and fragmentation – but it is not so clear about what it is for in terms of government and society.

Aflaq realizes this, but he cannot remedy it. His only answer is to speak of Arab socialism. It is with this Arab socialism that one could finally find a tangible suggestion as to how Arab communities should be run. But nothing differentiates Arab socialism from everybody else's socialism. Adding the term 'Arab' to socialism is similar to adding it to Islam: it is little more than an attempt to attach an Arab identity to a theory that transcends Arabs, and to an extent contradicts Aflaq's nationalist tendencies.

Nasser

Little change was introduced to Aflaq's ideas from the 1950s up until the end of the twentieth century. His ideas still represent the main tenets of the Baath Party's ideology. Many can argue, though, that neither Aflaq nor the Baath exclusively represent the post-World War Two socialist version of Arab nationalism. The Nasserist regime in Egypt (1952–71) could be cited as the main other representative. Nasser's popularity was unmatched by that of any other Arab nationalist leader. He was also the most influential. Unlike Aflaq's

Baathism, however, Nasserism is more of a historical legacy than a political theory. A quick look at Nasser's legacy is therefore appropriate at this point.

In July 1952, Nasser, still a colonel in the Egyptian army, led the coup/revolution that brought down the monarchy in Egypt. In 1954 he signed a treaty with Britain by which all British troops were to evacuate the country. In 1955, after Britain, France and the United States declared that a balance of power should be maintained in the Middle East by selling more arms to Israel than to any individual Arab country, Nasser broke the western powers' monopoly on the international arms market with a deal to buy Russian arms. Also in 1955, he established the Non-Alignment Movement along with India and Yugoslavia, thus enhancing the third world's bargaining power in international politics. This eventually led the World Bank to withdraw its pledge to finance Nasser's project of building a dam on the Nile. To answer the challenge and secure the funds, Nasser nationalized the Suez Canal, which was up until then owned by the British and the French. Britain, France and Israel invaded Egypt in response. Nasser's decision to fight the new invasion made him the absolute hero of the Arab world. It is noteworthy that Nasser chose to declare his decision from the pulpit of Al-Azhar mosque, the main centre of Islamic resistance against the Napoleonic invasion. His decision translated into a movement of massive popular resistance in the occupied cities around the Suez Canal. This was in sharp contrast with the Wafd's policy in the early 1950s to fight the British Army using the Egyptian police, rather than allowing for a people's war of attrition. The popular resistance in 1956 depended largely on the demographic advantage of the Egyptians over the invading troops. Nasser's popularity rocketed even before the conflict came to an end. It was reported that when the Egyptian radio station was bombed in Cairo, Radio Damascus started broadcasting the Egyptian military declarations, headed by the phrase 'This is Cairo'.

Despite the surge in emotions in 1956, it is undeniable that the shift in the global balance of power was a decisive factor in ending the conflict in Nasser's favour. Neither the Soviet Union nor the United States wanted to see classical colonial powers take control of the Middle East again. Due to pressure from the United States, and a blunt military warning from the Soviet Union that Egypt was a redline, Britain, France and later Israel had to withdraw, leaving Nasser to be crowned as the hero of Arabs, Muslims and many in the third world. In 1958 Syria and Egypt merged into one state and the United Arab Republic was declared. Jordan and Iraq, both under Hashemite thrones, the only remnants of the liberal pro-western version of Arab nationalism, declared a nominal unity under the title of the United Arab Kingdom. Before the year came to an end, though, a violent coup of nationalist and socialist officers brought down the Iraqi Hashemite monarchy, Iraq became a republic and negotiations for it to join the Syro-Egyptian unity were expected to begin.

Many of the officers who led the coup in Iraq were driven towards unity with Egypt and Syria; their organization was named after Nasser's original organization: the Free Officers. The leader of the coup, however, now the ruler of Iraq, Abdul Karim Qassem, was unwilling to give up his authority to Nasser. Alliance with the United States being out of the question, Qassem allied himself with the Iraqi communists. He presented himself to the Soviet Union as a Middle Eastern ally who was willing to go one step further than Nasser.

Here the first signs of Nasser's weakness appeared. Neither the Soviet Union nor the United States wanted to see a new super or even middle power emerge in the Middle East under Nasser. The Soviets chose to ally themselves with the now communist Qassem, and the Americans, while depending on Nasser's nationalism to limit the influence of the communist Iraqi regime, still worked on breaking the unity between Syria and Egypt. in 1961, an American-backed coup took place in Damascus, sending the Egyptian governor of Syria back to Cairo. Turkey, a member of NATO, vowed to protect Syria's 'independence', and Nasser was politically defeated.

In 1963 Israel attempted to redirect the flow of the River Jordan, in response to which Nasser called for an Arab summit. Held in 1964, this summit produced the Palestine Liberation Organization. A decision was taken by the Arab League to organize Palestinian refugees into an internationally recognized political body. Palestinian refugees driven out of their land in 1948 had formed a number of armed groups from the late 1950s onwards and were conducting operations in Israel with the backing of the Egyptians and Syrians. Tension rose as such attacks intensified from the Syrian front and Israel amassed its troops on the Syrian border. Syria, whose separatist regime had been overthrown by the Arab nationalist Baathis in 1963, was now again an ally of Egypt. In a move intended to save Syria, Nasser made a statement to the effect that if Syria was invaded, Egypt would go to war with Israel. He also asked the United Nations peace-keeping force in Sinai, which had been sent there after Israel's withdrawal in 1956, to leave. Finally he closed the Tiran Straits in the

Aqaba bay, blocking Israel's outlet to the Red Sea. On 5 June 1967, Israel launched an attack against Egypt, Syria and Jordan, and in six days it had occupied the Gaza Strip and the Sinai on the western front, East Jerusalem, the West Bank, and the Golan Heights on the eastern front. Nasser's defeat was shocking to all Arabs. Again, as in 1961, it seemed that neither of the two Superpowers wanted to see Nasser win the war. Nasser's victory in 1967 would have rendered his influence in the Middle East unbearable for both Superpowers. The war also revealed the fragility of Arab armies and the states that supported them. Though Palestinian non-state organizations had been established to fight Israel since the 1950s, after the Six Day War they became the weapon of choice of Palestinians and Arabs; the tactics of guerrilla warfare have since become a strategy all over the region.

At the end of the war, Nasser, assuming his responsibility for the defeat, declared his resignation in a televised address. Before he had finished his resignation speech, hundreds of thousands of Egyptians filled the streets of Cairo calling upon him to stay in office, and the demonstrators shouted slogans that called for 'completing the journey' and 'continuing the fight'. We shall return to the significance of these demonstrations in a moment. At this point, it is noteworthy that Nasser's personal image was not harmed by the war as much as his Arab nationalist, and above all statist, project was. Even Nasser himself turned the Egyptian army into guerrilla-type brigades and conducted a war of attrition along the Suez Canal. In 1970 Nasser died. His funeral, attended by 6 million people, was the largest in recorded history.

As mentioned above, Nasserism was not so much a body of theoretical work as it was a political trend in support of Nasser's legacy. Nasserists usually point to his deeds for guidance, rather than his writings, and they do not attempt to conceptualize his actions as part of a grand ideological structure. It is therefore difficult to compare Nasserism to Baathism; the former is a series of deeds while the latter is a series of writings. Moreover, Nasser and the Baathists believed in Arab nationalism, and that the duty of all Arab states was to act as Dawlas whose allegiance lay with the whole Umma of Arabs. Both also believed in the same relation between the Arab Umma as a whole and the Islamic Umma, the former being a subset of the latter. As a president of an internationally recognized state of Egypt though, Nasser could not be as supportive of the Baath's declared plan to conduct a series of coups in Arab countries. Moreover, Nasser, like the Wafd of the 1930s, the Baath of the 1960s and the PLO of the 1990s, fell into the trap of the state. That is, while he adopted an ideology of pan-Arabism, by which he was supposed to dissolve his state into a larger entity, he was obliged by international law and by economic dependency to keep working with the colonially created nation-state he ruled. Even in Nasser's legacy, one could find elements of the paradox of representation and replacement. Nasser's claim to be a representative of the Egyptians, or the Arabs, was derived from his being a president of Egypt. There were a number of incidents in which he could have seen the possibility of retaining his legitimacy without being a president, and without conducting the struggle against imperialism using a colonially created institution. This was the case during the popular resistance in 1956, and in 1967 when hundreds of thousands of Egyptians still believed in him after he resigned. Despite his huge popularity, Nasser was still the son of one of the most statist of the state's institutions, the army. He never seemed to trust non-state forms of power. He totally subscribed to cold war realism in international relations; to him the world of politics was one of states, and the balance of power referred to the balance in conventional economic and military abilities of such states. This strategic choice trapped him in an institution called the state of Egypt that was designed by Britain and confined by an international law whose guardian was the United States, and therefore was destined to frustrate his pan-Arab, anti-colonial intentions. Again, he was less powerful precisely because he was in power. He identified colonial powers, including Britain and Israel, as his enemies, yet he knew that he could never elevate Egypt's military abilities to those of its enemies. The very structure of Egypt was still hostage to the will of the Superpowers. As mentioned above, this became clear in the incidents of 1961 and 1967; when the Superpowers agreed on something, there was nothing Nasser, in his statist chains, could do about it.

Nasser and the Umma

Again, looking at Nasserism, as a legacy, one could find attempts to reconcile Arab nationalism with the sense of the Islamic Umma. As we have seen, Nasser's attachment to the state was a corollary of his cold war realism. In that context, Islamism as an international political programme was not at all feasible. As a political religious force it would have directly collided with the Soviet Union; given Nasser's anti-imperialist programme, the Soviet Union was not an ally to lose. The Soviet Union also ruled over significant numbers of Muslims, and not only would pan-Islamism curb communist influence in the Middle East, it could potentially destabilize the Soviet Union itself. On the other hand the Soviet Union seemed to give Nasser and many Arab modernists some hope in European humanism after all. Socialism seemed to offer a version of modernity that was not colonial or imperialist, and that was sympathetic to the poor peoples of the world.

It should be stressed that there was a circular relation between Nasser's attachment to the modern state as a vehicle of salvation on the one hand, and his belief in the above arguments on the other. Belief in modernity suited his grip on power and his attachment to the state, and vice versa. This situation is not incomparable with the situation of the early Egyptian and Arab nationalists of the inter-war period. Just like Nasser, they were politically recognized by the Superpowers on which they depended, on the condition of their belief in modernity, and their acceptance of the redefinition of their identity. Egyptian nationalists accepted the identity Cromer chose for them; their need for Cromer's support led them to such acceptance. Once they accepted that identity, and once they became part of the institutions that embodied it, their need for Cromer and Cromer's country only became more acute. Thus they fell into the state trap. Like them, Nasser accepted the identity suggested to him by his need for either the Soviet Union or the United States. That identity, of a statist modern Arab nationalist, did not help reduce his dependence on either one of the Superpowers. It remains to be said, however, that Nasser does not seem to have been aware of his dependence as much as his Egyptian nationalist predecessors were. The two Superpowers therefore cruelly reminded him of that in 1961 and 1967.

The above concerns Nasser's relations with the outside world, that is, his acceptance of an imported self definition in return for recognition, his paradox of representation. The other side of the coin is Nasser's relation to his audiences in Egypt and the Arab world. Here Nasser tried to accommodate Arab nationalism with Islam. He established that Egypt should move internationally in three circles; the Arab world, the Islamic world and Africa. The fact that he saw Egypt at the centre of all three circles shows an understanding that the overall interests of Egyptians, Arabs and Muslims were more or less in line. In this he was not far from accepting the concept of the Umma in its Islamic sense, where the state of Egypt should act as a Dawla whose allegiance lies with the whole Arab Nation, and that Arab nation as a whole should act in service of the Islamic Umma.

Like Aflaq, Nasser had to redefine Islam in order to accommodate his political orientation with the local culture. Since this is not a comprehensive study of Nasser's discourse, I shall here provide one example of his redefinition of Islamic history that corresponds to those of Aflaq and other Arab nationalists. Before he officially became the president of Egypt, Nasser, in an address to the first Arab Islamic Conference, gives an account of the history of Islam as U-shaped; it started at a peak of glory with the rule of the Prophet and the establishment of the empires, then began to decline in the late middle ages until it reached its lowest point during the colonial era in the nineteenth century. The decline of Islamic history was reversed with the Arab liberation movements[18] ('The Speech of Colonel Jamal Abdul Nasser at the Arab Islamic Conference in Cairo', 26 August 1953. http://nasser.bibalex.org/Speeches/browser.aspx?SID=64).

By the above discourse Nasser was emphasizing that his movement of the Free Officers in Egypt did not contradict the interests of the rest of the Muslim population. On the other hand, he still made the same mistake of Arab nationalists in reading nationalism where it did not exist. For example, he stated that the Crusades had been colonial wars, and that the 'banner of Arabism rose as the ancestors of Arabs defeated the invaders'. It is true that the Crusades have been repeatedly used in the collective Arab memory as an analogy of the colonial attacks, but it is usually the colonial invasion of the modern era that is described as a new Crusade, not the other way around. Moreover, very few historians or even laymen would agree that the banner that defeated the Crusades was one of Arabism. Nasser further emphasizes the Arab nature of the victory against the Crusaders by stating that Arabs, both Christian and Muslim, stood up to the invaders.[19] This type of argument is not unlike Aflaq's

18. It should be remembered that this is congruent with the image of Islamic history described in Chapters 1 and 2, where the early middle ages, the Umayyad and the Abbasid caliphates, are considered points of reference, while the Mamlouk and Turkish eras of the late middle ages and early modern times are more or less ignored.

19. A famous film about Saladin, the Muslim Sultan of Kurdish origin who liberated Jerusalem, Palestine and Lebanon from the Crusaders in 1087, was made in the 1960s. In the film Saladin's character identifies himself as 'the servant of the Arabs'; no reference is made to Islam, or to Saladin's Kurdish origin. Moreover, one of Saladin's lieutenants is shown to be a Christian by the name of Eissa the Swimmer. This was typical of the Arab nationalist presentation of Islamic history. There was in fact a historical figure by the name of Eissa the Swimmer, yet he was not Christian, nor a lieutenant in Saladin's army. Arab chroniclers of the Crusades report that

arguments about Islam being the spirit of the Arabs. While the people fighting against the Crusaders defined themselves primarily as Muslims, Nasser here makes the argument that they were Arabs in disguise. Similar arguments could be found in many speeches of Nasser throughout his political life.[20]

Nasser, like Egyptian and Arab nationalists, was attempting to find some middle ground between modernity and Islam, some compromise by which he would enjoy the recognition of the international community and legitimacy at home. But as in the case of the other nationalists, his compromise failed. To the Superpowers his modernism was fine, but his pan-Arabism, a remnant of his Umma-oriented inclinations, was too much to bear. For his constituencies at home, anti-imperialism was his main asset. This Umma-oriented strategy, embodied in his support of the Palestinian plight, the Algerian struggle for independence, and even his decision to save Syria in 1967 which was fatal to his political agenda, seemed to increase his popular appeal regardless of the actual outcome of his policy. His modernism was never as much a focus of popular admiration at home. In fact, the most significant opposition he ever encountered in Egypt came from the Muslim Brothers, with whom he had been closely affiliated before 1952. Their main grievance might have been that he kept them out of power, but in their political discourse they argue that the only problem was that he was too modern and not Islamic enough.

While Nasser's statist approach to politics was dealt a fatal blow in 1967, pan-Arabism, which was more reconcilable with the Umma than his modernism, survived, and was taken up by non-state organizations attempting to avoid his mistakes. The failure of the

---

he was a soldier who used to swim under Frankish ships during the siege of Acre to deliver messages to the besieged Muslim garrison in the city. His name, which is the Arabic for 'Jesus', was seemingly the reason why he was depicted as a high-ranking Christian lieutenant in Saladin's army. The Nasserist secular slogan 'religion belongs to God, but the homeland belongs to everyone' is also repeated by Saladin's character and by Eissa's, making them both look like eleventh-century humanists. The film was named after Saladin's official title *Saladin the Victory Bringer*, which in Arabic read *Al-Nasser Saladin*.

20. Professor Huda Abdul Nasser, Jamal's daughter and the professor of political science at Cairo University, has compiled all of her father's speeches, along with a significant number of interviews and reports. The documents were published on the internet by Bibliotheca Alexandrina and the Jamal Abdul Nasser Foundation, the URL is: http://nasser.bibalex.org/.

compromise on Nasser's terms in 1967 is correctly associated with the rise of rejectionist Islamic non-state actors. However, three more Arab nationalist entities had to fail before Islamism could monopolize anti-imperialism in the Middle East. The PLO was defeated in Lebanon, made peace treaties with Israel and failed even at that; Iraq fought an extremely unpopular war with Iran, alienating the majority of its population, then invaded Kuwait, a move that eventually landed American troops in Baghdad. Finally, Syria, whose troops were in Lebanon when Israel invaded it for the second time in 1982, needed the help of Lebanese non-state militias, the most important of which was the Islamic Hezballah, to drive them out.

THE FALL OF ARAB NATIONALISM

It may be useful to link the theoretical material above to more recent developments in the Middle East. It is, however, important to point out that the impression established in 1967 of the failure of the Arab modernist project has only been confirmed since. Aside from the hastily tailored Arab socialism, the arguments of Arab nationalist regimes such as that of Nasser in Egypt and the Baath in Iraq and Syria emphasized Arab non-alignment and independence, as well as the necessity of creating an Arab nation-state that would rule over all Arabs from Morocco to Bahrain. Such calls were challenged by the inability of those regimes to defend their own territories. The first non-state actors started to make their presence felt in the region, the most famous of which was Fateh, an armed Palestinian group that came to lead the PLO and which had been created three years before the Six Day War. The founders of Fateh, including the famous Yasser Arafat (Abu Ammar), Khalil al-Wazir (Abu Jihad) and Salah Khalaf (Abu Iyad), had connections, one way or another, with the Muslim Brothers. Their views became less ideological later as they came to lead the PLO. The operations of the PLO threatened the stability of the regimes in Lebanon and Jordan. In 1969 the PLO's presence in Lebanon was confined to the south of the country, and in 1970 it was violently expelled from Jordan by the Jordanian army. In 1973 Egypt and Syria waged war against Israel to liberate the lands the Israelis had occupied in 1967. The war was militarily indecisive. Both countries gained territorially, but Egypt had to sign an unpopular peace treaty with Israel by which it was neutralized in any future military conflicts between the Arabs and Israel, in return for the Egyptian-occupied Sinai Peninsula. The legitimacy of the Egyptian government was thus bruised, and Egypt's importance as a regional player was drastically reduced. Also, the signing of the treaty and the subsequent freezing of Egypt's membership of the Arab League signalled Egypt's final abandonment of Arab nationalism as a state ideology. Arab nationalism, however, still existed in Syria and Iraq.

The presence of the PLO, an armed organization whose bases were overwhelmingly Muslim, and whose discourse and rhetoric was quite close to Arab nationalism, disturbed the delicate Christian-Muslim sectarian balance in Lebanon. Civil war started there in 1975, thus engaging Syria in another conflict before it could take a breath after the 1973 war. In 1978 the Iranian Islamic Revolution broke out, and the same year, Israel failed in an attempted invasion of Lebanon. Both these events strengthened Islamic movements in the region, and established non-state resistance as a viable alternative to the anti-imperialist state paradigm. In 1981, Anwar al-Sadat, the Egyptian president, was assassinated by Islamic Jihad, an organization closer to revolutionary Iran than to conservative Saudi Arabia. In the same year, another Arab nationalist regime, Iraq, engaged itself in a war with Iran that severely damaged its legitimacy. While Iraq was supported by the United States and other Arab governments in the Gulf, its war against Iran ignored the religious feelings of the majority of its Shiite population. As mentioned above, religious feelings in the world of Islam cannot be separated from political affiliations. With Syria engaged in a war in Lebanon, and Iraq engaged in a war with Iran, the two remaining Arab nationalist regimes were largely gambling with their legitimacy, and were suffering considerable degrees of domestic violence. In 1981 President Hafez Assad of Syria had to use his air force to bomb the Syrian city of Hama in his fight with the Syrian Muslim Brothers. Also in the 1980s Saddam Hussein conducted various attacks against the Islamic Shiite parties in the south of Iraq, such as the Dawa Party, and the Supreme Council of the Islamic Revolution in Iraq.

The 1982 Arab-Israeli war in Lebanon was the first between Israel and an Arab non-state. A number of resistance organizations and civil war factions resisted the Israeli occupation and the PLO was replaced by the Islamic Hezballah which, gradually becoming the strongest organization in the country, drove out the Israelis in 2000 and stood its ground against another Israeli war in 2006. Another form of non-state resistance took place shortly after the PLO left Lebanon in 1982. In 1987 the first Palestinian Intifada broke out in the occupied territories, the Islamic movements of Hamas and the

Palestinian Islamic Jihad were declared in Gaza and the West Bank and conducted operations against Israel.

In 1990 and 1991, another failure of the Arab state system came to the world's attention when the Arab states could not deal with the crisis of Iraq's occupation of Kuwait. The occupation was justified in the Iraqi discourse as an act of unification – Arab unity has long been an objective of Arab states[21] – and the subsequent war with the United States and its allies was justified in terms of a war in the name of Muslims against the American occupation of Arabia. Saudi Arabia, on the other hand, had to fall back on the unfamiliar grounds of national interests. Iraq, a secular Arab state, thus resorted to Islamic discourse, while another religious Arab state, Saudi Arabia, resorted to a discourse that was secular in content if not in form. The war thus further weakened the Arab state. Some of the organizations that were supported by the US, Saudi Arabia and Pakistan to fight against the Soviet Union in Afghanistan, and who had been fighting one another on the eve of the first Iraq war, turned against Saudi Arabia and the United States as a direct result of the war.

Also in 1991, the PLO political leadership, based in Tunisia after being driven out from Lebanon a decade earlier, came under severe pressure. The popular sentiment in the Palestinian Occupied Territories was supportive of Iraq in its first war against the United States, while the leadership in Tunis was financially dependent on Saudi Arabia and other Gulf states, and it was also attempting to be recognized as a representative of the Palestinian people by the United States. Nonetheless, the PLO realized that losing legitimacy in the West Bank and Gaza might lead to the emergence of an alternative leadership, which would in turn frustrate its efforts to be recognized by the United States or financially aided by the Arab Gulf states. The decision was therefore to keep in line with the popular sentiments in Palestine, support Iraq, wait out the war, and try to mend relations with the West and the Gulf later. Thus, after the war ended, the PLO agreed to negotiate with Israel, though indirectly, by allowing Palestinians from the West Bank and Gaza to attend the 1991 Madrid Peace Conference as part of the Jordanian delegation. The PLO also conducted secret negotiations with Israel which resulted in the signing

21. This is an example of the contradictions in the discourse of Arab states resultant from their attempt to reconcile their existence with the doctrine of the Umma and the Dawla; in the constitutions of Arab states under Arab nationalist rule, such as Iraq, the purpose of the Arab state is to achieve Arab unity, thus the purpose of the state is its own dissolution.

of the Declaration of Principles, known as the Oslo Agreement. This was the first of a series of temporary peace treaties between the PLO and Israel which resulted in the establishment of a Palestinian National Authority in parts of the West Bank and Gaza. The peace deal did not mention the right of return of Palestinian refugees, thus alienating 50 per cent of the population of the Palestinian Occupied Territories who, in 1948, were driven from their homes in what is now Israel proper to cities like Ramallah and Gaza. This strengthened Islamic Palestinian organizations such as Hamas and Islamic Jihad, especially among those refugees. As such, yet another Arab nationalist entity, the PLO, suffered a significant loss of legitimacy. The increased activity of Hamas and Islamic Jihad and the continuation of the Israeli occupation and settlement building further frustrated the peace process. By the time final status negotiations started, the Chairman of the PLO and head of the Palestinian Authority, Yasser Arafat, knew he could not compromise his legitimacy any further. He thus rejected a deal that included unacceptable concessions on Jerusalem and the right of return in the summer of 2000. In September the second Palestinian Intifada broke out. Israel destroyed the institutions of the Palestinian Authority and inflicted unprecedented suffering on the Palestinian people. By 2007 the number of Palestinian civilians killed by Israeli armed forces or Jewish settlers in the Occupied Territories was five times the number of the total Israeli casualties since the beginning of the Intifada.[22] The whole Palestinian episode thus further delegitimized the possibility of compromise and played directly into the hands of Islamic resistance movements.

From the 1990s onwards, the whole Middle East seemed to be caught in a war between non-state organizations which were generally Islamic, ranging from non-violent civil society groups, to popular violent resistance movements against military occupation, to terrorist groups with international reach, and the United States. The American invasion of Iraq in 2003 put the United States in direct confrontations with Arab-Islamic non-states. Arab governments seemed to be caught in the middle trying to secure the interests

22. According to the Israeli Information Center for Human Rights in the Occupied Territories, B'tselem, 4058 Palestinians were killed by Israeli security forces from 29 September 2000 to 31 May 2007, while 668 Israelis, including civilians and military personnel, were killed by Palestinians during the same period. These numbers do not include 43 Palestinians who died after medical treatment was delayed due to Israeli-imposed restriction of movement, see http://www.btselem.org/English/Statistics/Casualties.asp.

of the United States because of the way they were structured while trying to retain whatever legitimacy they might still have among their own populations, if only because such legitimacy reduced the costs of securing American interests. Islamic non-territorial organizations seemed to be as much a threat to their existence as the United States army. Hence the story of the Arab nation-states came full circle as they became embodiments of impossible compromises between a foreign Superpower and the native population, just like the Egyptian nation of Napoleon and the Arab mandate governments installed by Britain and France. From the fall of Cairo in 1798 to the fall of Baghdad in 2003, the experience of the self-interested colonially created state in the Middle East had failed. It was clear that such states, constrained by economic dependency, military vulnerability and imperially controlled institutions of international law, could not fulfil their promises to their populations. Such promises were quite clear in their political discourse; to end Zionism in Palestine, to prevent foreign troops from occupying the region, and to achieve social and economic development. Arab states also failed to fulfil their promises to the international community (which mainly means the Superpowers of the day). These promises included the survival and safety of Israel, the flow of oil and the overall stability of the region. As mentioned above, this was an attempted compromise between two definitions of the self, and consequently two definitions of self-interest. The failure of such a compromise can be watched on TV channels as the war is being fought today in Iraq, the West Bank and Gaza, Lebanon, Saudi Arabia, and all around the world from Bali to New York.

6

Conclusion
A Working Compromise?

FIRST, THE COMPROMISE THAT DOES NOT WORK

In 2005, the new Iraqi constitution was voted in by referendum. Some observers in the United States must have seen that the referendum was a step towards building a new democracy in Iraq. Opponents of the United States argued that, under international law, referenda and elections held under occupation were void, like contracts signed at gunpoint. The United States' response was that under the same international law, Iraq was not under occupation when the referendum took place. Legally, the occupation of Iraq had ended when Paul Bremer, America's twenty-first-century version of Lord Cromer of Egypt, handed the powers of his occupation administration to a transitional Iraqi government. It was under the auspices of this government, the United States advocates argued, not under occupation, that the new constitution was drafted and passed, notwithstanding the fact that the United States still had 154,000 troops in the country.

The transitional Iraqi government ruled under a temporary constitution which was not voted in. The Law of Administration for the State of Iraq for the Transitional Period, as it was called, was supposed to guarantee freedom of expression and political association so as to prepare for the process of drafting and passing the permanent constitution and the subsequent elections law. The transitional constitution did in fact include some provisions that guaranteed civil and political rights, yet, like the Egyptian constitutions of 1923 and 1931, it also included articles that rendered the exercise of such rights quite risky. For example, Article 22 of the transitional constitution read:

If, in the course of his work, an official of any government office, whether in the federal government, the regional governments, the governorate and municipal administrations, or the local administrations, deprives an individual or a group of the rights guaranteed by this Law or any other Iraqi laws in force, this individual or group shall have the right to maintain a cause of action against that employee to seek compensation for the damages caused by such deprivation, to vindicate his rights, and to seek any other legal measure. *If the court decides that the official had acted with a sufficient degree of good faith and in the belief that his actions were consistent with the law, then he is not required to pay compensation.* (The Law of Administration for the State of Iraq for the Transitional Period, http://www.cpa-iraq.org/government/TAL.html#, emphasis mine)

The transitional constitution was a typical colonial constitution. That is, it was a document that established the institutions of the state of Iraq in such a manner as to serve the interest of its patron power of occupation. It can be argued that that is to be expected. After all, the transitional constitution was drafted and enacted when Iraq was, even by the legalistic criteria of the United States and the Security Council, under occupation. Therefore, I am not going to examine its articles, but will focus on those of the permanent constitution, the one that was voted in by a significant percentage of the Iraqi population in 2005. Let's start at the top, the preamble of the constitution.[1]

We the sons of Mesopotamia, land of the prophets, resting place of the holy imams, the leaders of civilization and the creators of the alphabet, the cradle of arithmetic: on our land, the first law put in place by mankind was written; in our nation, the most noble era of justice in the politics of nations was laid down; on our soil, the followers of the prophet and the saints prayed, the philosophers and the scientists theorized and the writers and poets created. Recognizing God's right upon us; obeying the call of our nation and our citizens; responding to the call of our religious and national leaders and the insistence of our great religious authorities and our leaders and our reformers, we went by the millions for the first time in our history to the ballot box.

On the face of it there should be nothing particularly problematic about this beginning. A closer look, however, would reveal otherwise. The first paragraph of the preamble mixes symbols from Iraq's pre-Islamic and non-Arab past with Arab and Islamic symbols, thus assuming some continuity between those millennial phases in the history of the land. The land is actually the only common factor between the various symbols mentioned in the paragraph. The

1. All quotations from the Iraqi constitutions are taken from the Associated Press translation, published on the BBC website: http://news.bbc.co.uk/1/shared/bsp/hi/pdfs/24_08_05_constit.pdf. The translation is compared to the official Arabic text of the Iraqi constitution published by the official website of the Iraqi government: http://www.iraqigovernment.org/, accessed on 13 June 2007.

territory of Iraq, in itself a product of a Franco-British treaty, becomes the point of reference, the stem from which symbols as different as Hamourabi and Harun al-Rashid branch out. This fixing of a certain territory and mixing of its past symbols in order to create some sort of a continuous national history is typical of nationalist narratives, and is therefore not particular to Iraq or to colonially created states. What makes the Iraqi constitution typically colonial is therefore not the nationalism expressed in the first sentence of the preamble, but rather the manner by which the drafters attempted to reconcile such nationalism with Islam in the sentence that follows. The phrase 'Recognizing God's right upon us' might not be a sentence that is easily understood in English. In Arabic, the expression 'your right upon me' means 'my duty towards you'. The establishment of the state of Iraq then becomes legitimized as a duty towards God, that is, as God's will. The next phrase, 'obeying the call of our nation' might also be misunderstood. The Arabic word which is here translated into 'nation' is of course 'Umma'. It has been mentioned in the course of the book that that term had a pre-colonial meaning where it referred to the Muslim community guided by some interpretation of the Quran and expecting any government ruling over any portion of them to be accountable to the whole group. As such, the preamble of the Iraqi constitution would mean that the establishment of the new regime in Iraq was sanctioned by God's will and by the will of all Muslims. Nonetheless, it should also be remembered that, since the late nineteenth century, the meaning of the term 'Umma' has been used frequently to mean 'nation' in the European sense. The preamble is therefore left ambiguous on what Umma it refers to, the nation of Iraq, the Arabs or the Muslim Umma. What makes the sentence even more ambiguous is the fact that the reference to the Umma is mentioned in between a reference to God and a reference to 'our citizens'. Had the drafters of the constitutions meant, by Umma, a proper nation of Iraq in the European sense, the phrase about 'our citizens' would be quite redundant. Whether the drafters were redundant or not, the rest of the sentence still suggests an attempt to reconcile the existence of an Iraqi nation with Islam: 'responding to the call of our religious and national leaders and the insistence of our great religious authorities and our leaders and our reformers, we went by the millions for the first time in our history to the ballot box'. Religious figures are mentioned twice here; first as 'religious leaders' and then as 'religious authorities'. Again, to an English reader this might appear tautologous; in Arabic it isn't. While 'religious leaders' is a reference to political leaders of Islamic parties such as the Supreme Council for the Islamic Revolution in Iraq, the Arab phrase here translated as 'religious authorities' refers to a particular position in the politico-academic hierarchy of Shiite jurists, the *'Marji el-Taqlid'*. Literally, *'Marji' el-Taqlid'* means the reference or source to be followed and emulated. After a Shiite jurist reaches the highest academic rank of an Ayatollah, he becomes an authority on religious issues; his interpretations of the Quran have greater value that those of younger scholars. In Twelvist Shiism, there can be more than one such authority at any time, with different interpretations of the Holy Text that result in different rulings. People are free then to choose which 'reference' or 'authority' to 'imitate' or follow. When this constitution was passed the greatest such authority alive in Iraq was Ayatollah Ali Sistani, who had supported the political process under occupation. The point here is that the preamble was legitimizing the political institutions and processes embodied in the constitution, in terms of religious figures and their interpretation of the Quran. This emphasis on it being in line with an interpretation of Islam is so recurrent in the preamble that it is almost apologetic. After all, it is quite difficult to cover the fact that the constitution, no matter how much it says about being in line with Islam, was creating an entity sponsored by the United States and kept in place by more than 100,000 of its troops.

This contradiction does not take long to reveal itself. Still in the preamble, after having stressed their affiliation to the Umma, the American agenda for which the state apparatus was created is set out:

Terrorism and 'takfir' (declaring someone an infidel) did not divert us from moving forward to build a *nation*[2] of law. Sectarianism and racism did not stop us from marching together to strengthen our national unity, set ways to peacefully transfer power, adopt a manner to fairly distribute wealth and give equal opportunity to all. We the people of Iraq, newly arisen from our disasters and looking with confidence to the future through *a democratic, federal, republican* system, are determined – men and women, old and young – to respect the rule of law, reject the policy of aggression, pay attention to women and their rights, the elderly and their cares, the children and their affairs, spread the culture of diversity and *defuse terrorism*. We are the people of Iraq, who in all our forms and groupings undertake to establish our union freely and

2. The phrase mistranslated here as 'nation of law' is *'Dawlat-Al-Qanun'*; the Arabic phrase refers to state apparatus rather than to the whole nation.

by choice, to learn yesterday's lessons for tomorrow, and to *write down this permanent constitution from the high values and ideals of the heavenly messages and the developments of science and human civilization*, and to adhere to this constitution, which shall preserve for Iraq its free union of people, land and sovereignty. [emphasis mine]

There are two remarks to be made about this last part of the preamble: first that the establishment of the 'nation of law', here meaning a state where the rule of law is supreme, is considered synonymous with the establishment of 'a democratic federal republic'. This is a typical case of the colonial master's attempt to recreate the native after his own image. In their imperial heyday, royal Britain went around the world building 'constitutional monarchies' in its colonies, while centralist France went around establishing centralized authorities. One cannot avoid seeing the resemblance when the federal republican United States decides to establish a federal democracy in Iraq, one that should be measured against its patron. Just as the white man calls the people in Africa black, taking his own colour to be the standard human colour, the political systems colonial powers establish in their conquered territories are built after their own model. This is not because such imperial powers are incapable of installing systems that differ from their own, for surely the systems that end up being established in the colonies are different from the systems of such imperial powers. Rather, it is a structural element in the colonial position; it is necessary that colonialism be presented as an educational endeavour whereby the colonized are trained and brought up to resemble the colonizers. To cover the colonial assumption of native inferiority, the philanthropic argument, that that native has the potential of becoming like, and therefore equal to, his patron, has to be asserted.

The second remark to be made is that the main obstacle in reaching the salvation of establishing the 'democratic federal republic' is terrorism and 'takfir' (calling someone an infidel). Of course, as in most usages of the word 'terrorism', it can refer to a wide range of very different organizations, acts, political programmes, and even ethnic groups. In this particular case, the term is assumed to refer to those who violently oppose the American military presence in Iraq and the political process that it oversees. While terrorist acts do frequently occur in Iraq, violent acts against the coalition forces' military personnel are also frequent. From the point of view of international law, as from the point of view of a significant number of Iraqis, those are two different kinds of activity. Any people with a colonial history, and Iraq is a country with a colonial history, knows the tendency of every colonial power to call those who resist military occupation terrorists. They also know that such a name is highly dependent on the outcome of the conflict.

Thus the drafters of the constitutions knew that by mentioning the word terrorism, they were alienating an influential force in Iraq. The word that directly follows 'terrorism', 'takfir' is noteworthy. More specific than terrorism, it refers to Islamists, those who 'would call their enemy an infidel'. While it might look like just another case of political finger pointing, its inclusion in the constitution, betrays the fact that the drafters recognize that their political actions can in fact be seen by some as acts of apostasy. Combined with the apologetic sentences in the first part of the preamble, which repeatedly express that the constitution is in line with Islam, these phrases on 'terrorism' and 'takfir' make the constitution look like it is engaged in a dialogue with an invisible, inaudible other, one that is quite sceptical about the legitimacy of the very existence of the constitution, and the institution it is about to establish. For polemics is the other side of apologies. The final sentence in the preamble only supports the above understanding, where the reconciliatory tone is restored, the writing down of the constitution, the building of the new Iraq will depend on both Islam and modernity, the Umma and the nation-state. In the preamble's language it will depend on 'the high values and ideals of heavenly messages' and 'the development of science and human civilization'.

Despite all the above, a preamble remains a preamble; it can be argued that the contradictions therein are but the product of poor style or political incompetence. A look at the articles of the constitution, however, shows that the contradiction and confusion between two identities, as well as the elements of the paradoxes of representation and replacement, infiltrate the very body of the constitution, and through that, the very structure, function and meaning of the new state of Iraq.

For example, Article 1 properly states that 'The Republic of Iraq is an independent, sovereign nation, and the system of rule in it is a democratic, federal, representative (parliamentary) republic'. Yet, Article 3 states that 'Iraq is a multi-ethnic, multi-religious and multi-sect country. It is part of the Islamic world and its Arab people are part of the Arab nation.' The awkwardness of having a 'sovereign' nation the majority of whose population is part of another nation is clear.

The contradiction is diluted in the Arabic version, as the word 'Dawla' is used instead of 'nation' in Article 1, and the phrase 'member of the Arab league and committed to its charter' is used instead of 'part of the Arab nation' in Article 3. Nonetheless, even in its diluted form, Articles 1 and 3 show the uneasy situation of the drafters: on the one hand they know that a non-Arab Iraq is impossible because of the cultural and demographic make-up of the country, and on the other, they want to avoid the political consequence of admitting that Arab identity of the majority of the population.

Article 2 does with Islam what Articles 1 and 3 do to Arabism. It is an attempt to reconcile Islam with the idea of a sovereign state:

1st – Islam is the official religion of the state and is a basic source of legislation:

(a) No law can be passed that contradicts the undisputed rules of Islam.

(b) No law can be passed that contradicts the principles of democracy.

(c) No law can be passed that contradicts the rights and basic freedoms outlined in this constitution.

2nd – This constitution guarantees the Islamic identity of the majority of the Iraqi people and full religious rights for all individuals and freedom of creed and religious practices.

This article is typical of the paradox of representation, where the local elites adopt a double discourse to appease both colonizer and colonized. It was mentioned above that the nativeness of the native elite is necessary for it to gain colonial recognition. If the native elite did not have any legitimacy among its own people, it would be useless to the colonial power. The same elite, however, should accept the colonial logic, and promise to find a midway solution, by which colonial interests and native sentiments are catered for. In clause (a) of this article, the state of Iraq is presented as an Islamic Dawla. That is, all the regulations and laws passed in the country should be in accordance with Islam. Practically, this means that it should be in accordance with some interpretation of the Islamic Holy Texts. It follows that the judge of that would be all Muslims; since the Holy Text belongs to all Muslims, they are all addressed by any interpretation the advocates of which present as the most correct. Not only would this make the Iraqi legislature subordinate to scholars of Islamic jurisprudence in Iraq, but also to scholars and jurists in Iran, Palestine, Egypt, Morocco or Afghanistan. Such an outcome of course is not intended or welcome by the drafters of the Iraqi constitution, nonetheless, the constitution would have been much more difficult to sell if such a clause were absent.

To balance the scales, clauses (b) and (c) were added to this article, as well as Article 5 which states that 'The law is sovereign; the people are the source of authority and its legitimacy, which they exercise through direct, secret ballot and its constitutional institutions.' Here it is stipulated that no Iraqi legislation could violate the principles of democracy and human rights. The underlying assumption of the overall article is thus that Islam, democracy and human rights are reconcilable, which on the face of it is indisputable. Islam is indeed compatible with democracy; it is also compatible with a wide range of political systems. It has been shown in Chapters 1 and 2 of this book how every interpretation of Islam results in a different political arrangement. That being said, it is off point, for the Iraqi constitution is not a work in moral philosophy. The claim that is made by this article is that the Iraqi ruling elite, through the constitution and the institutions it creates, shall be able to mediate between Islamic political affiliations and the 'democratic federal republic' suggested to them by the occupation forces. It should be remembered that this was the same strategy used by the Egyptian nationalists under the British, the Arab nationalists under the French, and during the cold war. It is the claim to be able to reconcile two different identities which entail two different and, more often than not, contradictory agendas.

In that context, it might not be too difficult to see that the native elite's promise of creating a sovereign democratic Iraq which is also an Islamic Dawla is but a tool by which it can harvest just enough legitimacy to fulfil the other promise it made to the colonial power. This is the paradox of replacement discussed in Chapter 3 of this book. The United States installed the Iraqi government in order to be able to delegate to it some of the powers and responsibilities of occupation. That is, the Iraqi government was created to replace the American occupation administration. The Iraqi government, like a student, has to be trained then tested as to whether it is worth trusting.[3] It thus has to perform the tasks of occupation, and the more it succeeds in keeping law and order and securing American interests, the more powers it is granted and vice versa. Such a process is documented in a series of agreements between the colonizer and

3. See Allenby's argument about 'trusting' the Egyptians in 1919, in Chapter 4.

the colonized. The elites' commitments to performing the tasks of occupation become the conditions and terms of Iraq's independence. They become embedded in the formative documents that establish the Iraqi institutions, foremost of which is the constitution. Therefore, Articles such as 7, 8 and 9, which, in normal circumstances, could have been found in a treaty of cooperation on security matters, are part of Iraq's constitution. For example, the second clause in Article 7 reads:

The state will be committed to fighting terrorism in all its forms and will work to prevent its territory from being a base or corridor or an arena for its (terrorism's) activities.

Article 8 reads:

Iraq will abide by the principles of good neighbourliness and by not intervening in the internal affairs of other countries, it will seek to peacefully resolve conflicts and establish its relations on the basis of shared interests and similar treatment and it will respect its international obligations.

And clause (e) of Article 9 reads

The Iraqi government will respect and implement Iraq's international commitments regarding the non-proliferation, non-development, non-production, and non-use of nuclear, chemical, and biological weapons. Associated equipment, material, technologies and communications systems for use in the development, manufacture, production and use of such weapons will be banned.

The point worth noting here is not Iraq's commitment to fight terrorism and to abide by its international commitments regarding unconventional weapons. Rather, it is the fact that such commitments were set in the constitution. That is, they constitute what Iraq is, not what Iraq does. The very existence of Iraq depends on its fulfilment of such duties. It was mentioned before that the production of security has been the principal purpose behind the colonial establishment of Arab states. It has also been mentioned that the colonial powers require the native elites to have some legitimacy in order to be more efficient in producing security. This in turn pushes the native elites into futile attempts to reconcile their security-producing political entities with native culture and its political institutions and entities. This attempted reconciliation between two irreconcilables expresses itself in the overall symbolism and meaning of the colonially created state in its political discourse and in its individual institutions. This is the difficult reconciliation between the nation-state and the Dawla, the nation and the Umma. It is as difficult a reconciliation as the one attempted by clause 1 (a) of the same Article 9 quoted above, as it promises that the Iraqi army will fulfil Iraq's international commitments without becoming a tool in the oppression of the Iraqi people.

A COMPROMISE THAT WORKS?

It is obvious that the Iraqi compromise, like its nineteenth- and twentieth-century predecessors, does not work. It should also be obvious that, when someone makes an argument that the blonde girls in a certain class did not do well, it does not necessarily mean that the brunettes did any better. This book is not an attempt to advocate any form of political solution for the tense situation in the Middle East. It is true that I have explained the concepts of the Umma and the Dawla on the one hand, and that I have shown the contradictions in the region's nationalisms on the other. But that does not mean that I am making an argument in favour of a political system based on the concepts of the Umma and the Dawla. A good example of why I would not like to do that would be the case of Saudi Arabia. Saudi Arabia started as a typical Islamic Dawla, an alliance between a religious scholar, Mohammad Ibn Abdel Wahhab, and a tribal leader, Ibn Saud, under the overarching sovereignty of the Ottoman Caliph/ Sultan in the late eighteenth century. Political authority was based on Wahhabism, an interpretation of the Quran, which led the Saudi Dawla to present itself as accountable to and responsible for the whole Umma, not only the people under its jurisdiction. We can see this in the very name of the entity: Saudi Arabia. The official name in English reads 'the Kingdom of Saudi Arabia', that is, there is a geographical reference to a certain territory which is known to non-Arabs as Arabia. This English name conforms to the modern concept of the territorial state. The official name in Arabic is 'Al-Mamlaka Al-Arabiyya Al-Saudiyya'; a literal translation of the name would be 'the Arab Saudi kingdom'. Here the political entity is named after a certain group of people, Arabs, and among the Arabs, the sons of Saud. It is thus a name befitting a Dawla, a power arrangement associated with the ruling elite. Nonetheless, today, Saudi Arabia is not faring much better in terms of legitimacy than Egypt, Syria, Jordan, or any other Arab state that was created by a colonial power. In fact, the Umma-bound, Dawla-like discourse of Saudi Arabia may have contributed to its legitimacy problem.

As defenders of what they claim to be the most righteous interpretation of the Holy Texts, the elites in Saudi Arabia legitimized their power as defenders of the true faith world-wide. During the cold war, an alliance with the United States, in all matters except the Arab-Israeli conflict, could be sold domestically as an alliance with a Christian power to fend off the atheist-communist alternative. Such an alliance could easily fit into the dictates of traditional Islamism, where Christians have a higher status than atheists. Saudi Arabia's role as a Dawla responsible for and accountable to all Muslims seemed to be reconcilable with the dictates of international politics. Even with regards to the Arab-Israeli conflict, Saudi Arabia was the principal financial sponsor for the PLO. Despite the United States' hostility to the PLO, its existence seemed permissible, as the alternative would have been uncontrolled violence by Palestinian groups around the region with no political body with which to negotiate. Moreover, the PLO's close financial ties to Saudi Arabia rendered vital American interests in the Gulf immune from Palestinian attacks. But precisely because Saudi Arabia could, more or less, reconcile its image as an Islamic Dawla throughout the cold war with its alliance with the United States, when the cold war ended in the American military expansion in the Gulf, such an alliance severely damaged the legitimacy of Saudi Arabia.

The Islamic regimes in Afghanistan or Sudan did not work either, nor do non-state organizations offer a solution. Such organizations use radical means to achieve reformatory goals. They represent a strike on the production of security and, as mentioned in Chapter 3, no matter how violent a strike is, it is not a revolution. Even if they did have radical suggestions regarding government and international relations, the lifestyles suggested to the Umma by the Taliban and Al-Qaeda are hardly attractive by any moral or practical criterion. The popularity of such organizations in the Middle East stems mostly from the fact that they are being fought by a neo-colonial power, namely, by the United States, ally of Israel and occupier of Iraq. It does not primarily stem from the attractiveness of their experience in governance or their theoretical interpretations of the Islamic texts. Such texts, it has been shown in Chapter 1, have always been subjected to so many interpretations and reinterpretations that it is highly unlikely that one exclusive understanding of them could become final.

What, then, might work? I have no final answer to that. The only thing I am sure of is that colonialism does not work, and therefore less colonial intervention might help. By colonialism, I do not only mean military occupation; I rather mean a pattern of behaviour by which the international community, led by the current Superpower, denies the very basic right of humans to be treated equally. Equality applies to individuals and to cultures alike. If Muslims want to organize themselves as Dawlas, they should certainly have the right to do so. There is no guarantee that such Dawlas will be their salvation, but it is guaranteed that no other form of government imposed on them by force of arms will either. Turkey and Iran are two Muslim countries on whom the colonial pressure was relatively less than it was on Arab states; they were not occupied, nor were they structured through the dictates of gentlemen in London, Paris, New York or Washington. Both countries took two very different routes, yet they enjoy much more legitimacy and stability than most if not all of their Arab neighbours.

The purpose of the long section above on Iraq was to show that, despite the clear failure of previous colonial endeavours to occupy the region by proxy, it is still being attempted by neo-colonial Superpowers such as the United States. More colonialism will not solve a problem that was created by colonialism in the first place.

Yes, some might look at the impressive skylines of cities like Dubai, Manamah, Doha and Kuwait City, and see a working compromise. Here are Arab Muslim states, whose boundaries, political structures, and economies were shaped by colonial powers, but who are enjoying considerable degrees of stability and prosperity. That might be true, but it is also true that such countries have very high revenues and very low population levels. Even if we accepted the smaller Gulf city state model to be a working compromise, it is quite impossible to generalize.[4] Moreover, the stability of these princedoms is under constant threat, as was demonstrated in Kuwait in 1990.

4. For example, according to published CIA estimates, the per capita income in the United Arab Emirates is $49,700; in Egypt, it is $4200. Egypt's population is over 80 million. Thus Egypt's income will have to be increased from the current figure of 328 billion to become 3976 billion, that is, 3.9 trillion. If it is assumed that the United Arab Emirates model can be generalized, and that Egypt can be stabilized by allowing it to receive as much income as the UAE, then Egypt's income has to increase at least tenfold to reach the target level. It should be noted that Germany, France, the United Kingdom and Russia all make less than the targeted $3.9 trillion in GDP per annum. Egypt will have to be turned into a Superpower before

As mentioned in Chapter 3, I am not making a Huntingtonian argument about the 'clash of civilizations'. Traditions and cultures do not, in and by themselves, start and end wars. It is not because of the difference between how Arabs define themselves and how Britain, France and today the United States define themselves that the conflict breaks out. Rather, it is due to the difference between how the Arabs define themselves and how the elegant and powerful gentlemen in elegant and powerful cities beyond the sea define the Arabs, and the attempt to impose that definition of Arabs on the Arabs by the force of missiles, that the conflict breaks out.

PREDICTION AND PRESCRIPTION: QUESTIONS FOR FURTHER RESEARCH

Like a poem's definite meaning to a critic, prediction and prescription seem to be the forbidden-to-reach goal of the scholar. I shall, however, trespass and end this book with one prediction and one prescription regarding the ongoing conflict in the Middle East. Of course both are but questions and hypotheses that are uncertain, and in need of further research.

My prediction is that the current war in the region, between the United States and various Islamic organizations, will have two results that might not now seem pleasant to either of the belligerents. First, it will end America's unipolar control of the world, and second it will change Islam beyond recognition. It will end America's unipolar control, because the region is simply too important to be left for one Superpower to control. One could go back to innumerable cases in history that support this argument, from Rome and Persia to the cold war. Despite the fact that the advocates of the war in Iraq thought of it as part of a project to secure an 'American century' in running the world, the war was a step to reduce rather than increase America's military and political control over events in Iraq, the region and the rest of the world. In fact it might be precisely because the planners of the war intended it to be the opening chapter of an American century that it failed to become one. The move to establish American hegemony in and by itself intimidates other powers in the world.

---

it becomes as peaceful and stable as the United Arab Emirates. By this ratio, each four Arab countries combined will have to make as much money as the United States. Thus it is clear how misleading the calm and quiet of the Arab gulf countries is (see https://www.cia.gov/library/publications/the-world-factbook/index.html).

Moreover, the strategy of Islamic organizations is to attack in different places all around the world with the declared intention of over-stretching the United States. Of course, it is not the economic cost of sending troops around that will cause the United States to lose its world hegemony. Rather, it is the political cost; the unsettling situation that Russia and China find themselves in, when American military bases come closer and closer to their borders in Asia and Eastern Europe, and when American troops control more and more of world energy resources. It was mentioned above that sovereignty and territorial integrity do not matter much to the Islamic organizations fighting the United States; heavy losses in civilian lives do not seem to harm their political standing either. It is precisely because of this that the more territorial advances the United States makes, the more it intimidates its would-be partners, without necessarily making any real advances on fighting terrorism.

On the other hand this war will change Islam beyond recognition, because more and more Muslims feel that they are being challenged by models of economic and political organization that made their enemy quite powerful, and put them in a serious nightmare that threatens the very essence of their existence. The deaths in Iraq and Afghanistan, the inability of Arab governments to protect their own citizens, the traditional defeats of Arab regular armies in any confrontation with Israel, all motivate young and old intellectuals and politicians to search for alternatives. That search will probably result in drastic changes in cultural production and socio-political behaviour. Islam will develop because it has never stopped developing and because, as we mentioned above, it is a paradigm based on metaphors and interpretations. It might not turn into liberalism or socialism, and it probably will not become the docile moderate religion anticipated by the United States, yet trends will emerge that will cater for the security, political, cultural and aesthetic needs of Muslims. Such needs are not currently fulfilled by any of the political actors in the Middle East, yet they are all in search of answers. It was mentioned above that violent Islamic organizations do not consider colonial invasions to be defeats, although many people in the occupied countries do. Thus the current war, like Athenian defeats, will accelerate this search for answers and alternatives among those people who feel the urgency for change and salvation. In this process of cultural development, all is possible and violent, ugly and terrorist versions may emerge as well as brilliant, peaceful and tolerant ones, yet it is quite unlikely that any of them will be willing to accommodate to colonialism and occupation.

As for my prescription, I did mention above that colonialism and neo-colonialism will neither help in pacifying the region, nor in securing the interests of the neo-colonial Superpower. Colonialism is a structurally contradictory, self-defeating process. To be more specific, the invasion of Iraq and the alliance with Israel in the long run will not serve the United States' interests. The experience in Iraq demonstrates how direct military occupation failed in achieving any of the goals of the American campaign. It is thus established that to colonize the region power has to be delegated to local states. These must have some legitimacy in order to make any difference. Israel, and the American military presence, reduces the legitimacy of such Arab elites that their control over their populations becomes quite uncertain.

Israel is quite a problem. Its Jewish citizens have one right more than its non-Jewish citizens; the right of return. If the 4 million Palestinian refugees were to become Jewish, they could return the next morning. Had they been Jewish in 1948, they probably would not have been driven out of their homes. Similarly, another 3.5 million Palestinians living in the West Bank and Gaza have had to live by Israeli military decrees for 40 years, without having the chance to vote for or against any of the laws that control their lives. Again, had they been Jewish, they would have had that right. It has been mentioned in the first two chapters of this book how the legitimacy of governments in the Arab Islamic culture depends on their accountability to the whole Umma. As such, the legitimacy of the Saudi and the Egyptian governments depends highly on their position towards the issue of Palestine. Not only does Israel's behaviour delegitimize and therefore destabilize the states in the region, its religion-based political identity provokes an already active counter-identity among the Muslims. A prescription for that would be to work towards a contractual agreement for a one-state solution with equal rights for Jews, Muslims, Christians and everyone else in the territory between the Mediterranean and River Jordan. If such a state could exist, it could point to the direction in which Islam, Judaism and nationalisms in the region might develop. Despite the utopian tone, the demographic trends among Arab and Jewish citizens of Israel seem to lead to that end, or else to civil war.

In fact, Israel is no exception to the general failure of the colonially created nation-state in the region. It is usually forgotten that Israel,

Egypt, Jordan, Syria and Iraq were all created in the same colonial womb and the fact that they contradict each other is typical of colonial contradictions. Trying to remedy the situation by creating yet another colonially structured state for the Palestinians, one whose main task is to occupy rather than liberate them, would probably have the same results as the previous colonial projects, be they French and British in the nineteenth and twentieth centuries or American in the twenty-first.

As for the American military presence, it has already been mentioned that it propagates a strong sense of defeat in the streets and a sense of victory in the caves. Both feelings are not without consequences, and the consequences are not quite in the United States' interests.

So, for the last time, is there a possible compromise? Yes. But a compromise must ultimately involve concessions from both sides. Any compromise, in which the balance is tilted in favour of one of the two opponents, will be but a truce, a temporary halt of hostilities until the balance of power changes. Classically, the declared national interests of the United States in the Middle East are the flow of oil, the stability of the region, the prevention of any single power to take control of it, the elimination of terrorism, and the existence of Israel. The interests of the Arab Muslim majority of the region are the end of military occupations and embargoes, the end of Zionism, and that the people of the region be left free to choose the type of political entities and forms of government that best reflect their collective cultural identity.

It is not difficult to see how these two apparently opposite sets of interests can be reconciled. On the American side, slight adjustments on the strategic goals mentioned above, would guarantee that they be achieved at much less political and economic costs. Oil will still be flowing to the United States and the rest of the world. Only the companies that extract and market it, the rates by which it is produced and the prices by which it is sold will change, and will be subject to the machinations of the free market.

The people of the region would not like any single power to take control of it, yet they would like to see themselves in control of their own lands. Ultimately the United States must reconcile itself with the political expression of the emotional, cultural and therefore political unity of the region. Terrorism, as mentioned above, is a strike by the producers of security, and strikes are temporary arrangements for bettering the conditions of production. It will therefore be much easier to defeat terrorism once the economic and political conditions mentioned above are met in the region. Finally, the survival of Zionism is different from the survival of the Jewish people in the Middle East. In fact, a one-state solution might guarantee greater security and prosperity to the Jewish population of Israel, than the current militaristic fear-obsessed and civil-war-bound state. In other words, and to use expressions from the political discourse of the United States on freedom and democracy, a more free democratic approach to the region might serve America's interests better. A democratic approach must respect the wishes of the majority of the people of the region, and their rights of self-definition and self-determination.

On the Arab Muslim side, the withdrawal of foreign troops will come sooner or later, but not the withdrawal of the cultural effects of their visit. The 'types of political entities' and 'forms of government' the people of the region are inclined to choose will have to cater for the military, economic, and cultural challenges of the world. An Islamic alternative that comes directly from the thirteenth-century Ashab Al-Hadith school will have to be drastically adjusted to allow for boundless and infinite interpretations of Islam. The modernity imposed on Muslims since Napoleon has not worked, but that does not mean that they should not strive to find their own modernity. In that process, the Golden Age of Islam must look less golden. With colonial imposition gone, Muslims will be free to see the problems in their own culture. After all, it was in that Golden Age that Muslims, like other medieval peoples, practised slavery and discrimination. Once the identity of Muslims is secure from foreign infringement, they will be able to abandon the defensive position that has paralysed their intellectual development for centuries. Enforced change can freeze a culture, and the worst thing one can do to any culture is to prevent it from changing. The Golden Age of Muslims, like the Golden Age of any healthy people, should not be situated in the past, but in the future.

This might allow Muslims to overcome their colonial trauma, their schizophrenic attitude towards the world, simultaneously admiring and condemning New York, London and Paris. The terrorist, violent and ugly inclinations, as well as the under-handed, dependent and imitative inclinations in contemporary Muslim culture, will have to go away. It is natural for an Iraqi to learn about forms of government, philosophy, and ethics from Americans in America, but he shall not learn it from them in Baghdad. There, he will only learn how to get them to leave.

Colonial officers usually portrayed colonialism as a process of education, as a catalyst in developing native cultures, and indeed it is. However, development is made by resistance, not imitation. Neither military occupation nor the installation of colonial native governments has so far worked. A more equal approach to the people of the region, more dignity and less pressure, might just allow for trends in culture and politics to emerge that can produce a working compromise.

References

Abdu, Mohammad. *Muzakkirat Mohammad Abdu* (*The Memoirs of Mohammad Abdu*) ed. Taher Al Tanahi. Cairo: Dar Al Hilal, 1963.

Abdul Majid, Wahid. *Al Ahzab Al Misriyya min Al Dakhil, 1907–1992.* (*Egyptian Parties from Inside 1907–1992*). Cairo: Markaz Al Mahrousa lil Nashr wa Al Tawzi, n.d.

Abdul Malik, Anwar. *Nahdat Misr* (*Egypt's Renaissance*). Cairo: General Egyptian Book Organization, 1983.

Abul Fath, Mahmoud. *Al Mas'ala Al Misriyya wa Al Wafd.* (*The Egyptian Question and the Wafd*). Cairo: no publisher, 1921.

Abul Majd, Sabri. *Sanawat Ma Qabl Al Thawra: Yanayir 1930–23–youlou 1952.* (*The Pre-Revolution Years: January 1930–23 July 1952*) 4 vols. Cairo: General Egyptian Book Organization, 1987–1991.

Abul-Omrein, Khalid. *Hamas: Juzhuruha, Nash'atuha, Fikruha Al-Siyasy* (*Hamas: Roots, Creation and Political Thought*). Cairo: Markaz Al-Hadara Al-Arabiyya, 2000.

Abdullah, Ahmad. *Al Talaba wa Al Siyassa fi Misr* (*The Student Movement and National Politics in Egypt*) trans. Ikram Youssuf. Cairo: Dar Sina lil Nashr, 1991.

Addo, Herb. *Imperialism; The Permanent Stage of Capitalism.* Tokyo: The United Nations University, 1986.

Afghani, Jamaludin Al-. *Al-Athar Al-Kamila.* (Complete Works). Revised by Hadi Khusroshahi, 9 Vols. Cairo, Kuala Lumpur, Jakarta, Los Angeles: Maktabat Al-Shorouq Al-Dawliyya, 2002.

Aflaq, Michael. *Fi Sabil Al-Baath: Al-Kitabat Al-Siyasiyya Al-Kamila.* (*For the Sake of Resurrection, the Complete Political Works*). Baghdad: Dar Al-Hurriyya, 1986.

Ahmad, Aijaz. *In Theory: Classes, Nations, Literatures.* London, New York: Verso, 1994.

Ahmed, Jamal Mohammed. *The Intellectual Orgins of Egyptian Nationalism.* London, New York, Toronto: Oxford University Press, 1960.

Ahmed, Refaat Sayed. *Kor'an wa Seef.* 2nd edition. Cairo: Maktabet Madbuly, 2002.

Alexander, Titus. *Unravelling Global Apartheid: An Overview of World Politics.* Cambridge: Polity Press, 1996.

Al Kayyali, Majed. *At-Tasswiya Wa Qadaya Al Hall An-niha'i* (*The Settlement and the Questions of the Final Solution*). Beirut: Marakaz ad-Dirassat al-Estratejyya wal-Bohouth wat-Tawtheeq, 1998.

Al-Kulaini. Mohammad Ibn Yaqoub (*d.* 329 AH, 941 AD), *Al-Osoul Min Al-Kafi* (*The Original Doctrines from Al-Kafi*). Revised by Ali Akbar Al-Ghafari, 2 Vols. Tehran: Dar Al-Kutub Al-Islamiyya, 1968.

Al-Mufid, Mohammad ibn Mohammad (336–413 AH, 948–1022 AD). *Awa'il al-Maqalat* (*The Initial Doctrines*), Vol. 4 of *Silsilat A'mal AlSshaikh al-Mufid* (*The Complete Works of Shaikh Al-Mufid*), 11 Vols. Beirut: Dar Al-Mufid, 1993.

Alnasrawi, Abbas. *Arab Nationalism, Oil, and the Political Economy of Dependency*. New York: Greenwood Press, 1991.

Al-Qadiyya Al-Misriyya 1882–1954 (The Egyptian Question 1882–1954). Cairo: Al-Matba'a Al-Amiriyya, 1955.

Amer, Ibarhim. *Thawrat Misr Al-Qawmiyya (Egypt's National Revolution)*. Cairo: Dar Al-Nadim, 1957.

Anis, Mohammad. *Dirasat fi Wathayeq Thawrat 1919 (Studies in the Documents of the 1919 Revolution)*. Cairo: Maktabat Al-Anglo Al-Misriyya, 1963.

——. *4 Fibrayir 1942 fi Tareekh Misr Al Siyassi (4 February 1942 in Egypt's Political History)*. Cairo: Maktabat Madbouli, 1982.

——. *Hariq Al Qahira fi 26 Yanayir 1952 (The Burning of Cairo on 26 of January 1952)*. Cairo: Maktabat Madbouli, 1982.

Arab, Mohammad Saber. *Hojoum ala Al Qasr Al Malaki: Hadeth 4 Fibrayir 1942 (An Attack against the Royal Palace: The Event of 4 February 1942)*. Cairo: General Egyptian Book Organization, 2003.

Arnon, Arie, et al. *The Palestinian Economy: Between Imposed Integration and Voluntary Separation*. Lieden: Brill, 1997.

Asfarudin, Asma. *Excellence & Precedence: Medieval Islamic Discourse on Legitimate Leadership*. Leiden, Boston, Koln: Brill, 2002.

Ashcroft, Bill, Gareth Griffiths and Helen Tiffin. *Key Concepts in Post-Colonial Studies*. London, New York: Routledge, 1998.

Awaisi, Abdel Fattah. *The Muslim Brothers and the Palestine Question 1928–1947*. London: I.B. Tauris & Co., 1998.

——. 'Emergence of a Militant Leader: A Study of the Life of Hasan Al Banna 1906–1928'. *Journal of South Asian and Middle Eastern Studies* 22. 1 (1998): 46–63.

Azmeh, Aziz. *Mohammad Ibn Abdel Wahhab*. Beirut: Riad El-Rayyes Books, 2000.

Baer, Gabriel. *A History of Landownership in Modern Egypt, 1800–1950*. London, New York: Oxford University Press, 1962.

Bakr, Abdul Wahhab. *Adwaa' ala Al-Nashat Al-Shoyoui fi Misr 1921–1950 (Light on Communist Activity in Egypt 1921–1950)*. Cairo: Dar Al-Ma'aref, 1983.

Banna, Hasan. *Majmou'at Rasa'il Al-Imam Al-Shahid Hasan Al-Banna. (The Collection of the Treaties of the Martyr Imam Hasan Al Banna)*. Cairo: Dar Al-Shihab, 1992.

——. *Muzakkirat Al-Da'wa wa Al-Da'iya (Memoirs of the Call and the Caller)*. Cairo: Dar Al-Shihab, 1966.

Baqillani, Abu Bakr (*d.* 403 AH, 1013 AD). *Al Tamhid. (The Preamble)*. Revised by Mohamoud Mohammad Khudairi and Mohammad Abdel Hadli Abu Reeda. Cairo: Dar Al-Fekr Al-Arabi, 1947.

Barghouti, Tamim. 'State Building in Palestine and Jordan'. MA Thesis. American University in Cairo, 2000.

Batau, Hanna. *The Old Social Classes and The Revolutionary Movements in Iraq*. Princeton: Princeton University Press, 1978.

Bayyoumi, Zakariyya Suleiman. *Al-Ikhawan Al-Muslimoun wa Al-jam'at Al-Islamiyya fi Al-Siyassa Al-Misriyya 1927–1948 (The Muslim Brothers and Islamic Groups in Egyptian Politics, 1927–1948)*. Cairo: Maktabat Wahba, 1987.

Behbehani, Hashim. *The Soviet Union and Arab Nationalism, 1917–1966*. London, New York: KPI; distributed by Methuen, 1986.

Beinin, Joel. 'Formation of the Egyptian Working Class'. *MERIP Reports* 94 (1981): 14–23.

Beinin, Joel and Zachary Lockman. *Workers on the Nile; Nationalism, Communism, Islam and the Egyptian Working Class, 1882–1954*. Princeton: Princeton University Press, 1987.

Benvenisti, Meron. *The West Bank Data Project: A Survey of Israel's Policies*. Washington DC, London: American Enterprise Institute for Public Policy Research, 1984.

Berque, Jacques. *Egypt: Imperialism and Revolution*. Trans. Jean Stewart. London, Faber and Faber, 1972.

Binder, Leonard. *In a Moment of Enthusiasm*. London: University of Chicago Press, 1978.

Bishri, Tareq. *Dirasat Fi Al-Dimoqratiyya Al Misriyya*. (*Studies in Egyptian Democracy*). Cairo: Dar Al Shorouq, 1987.

——. *Bayn Al-Jami'a Al-Diniyya wa Al-Jami'a Al-Wataniyya Fi Al-Fikr Al-Siyassi* (*Between the Religious Bond and the Patriotic Bond in Political Thought*). Cairo: Dar Al-Shorouq, 1998.

——. *Al-Haraka Al-Siyassiyya Fi Misr 1945–1953* (*The Political Movement in Egypt 1945–1953*). 2nd edition Cairo: Dar Al Shorouq, 2002.

Botman, Selma. *Egypt from Independence to Revolution, 1919–1952*. Syracuse, New York: Syracuse University Press, 1991.

Brown, Carl. *Religion and the State: The Muslim Approach to Politics*. New York: Columbia University Press, 2000.

Brown, Nathan. *Peasant Politics in Modern Egypt: The Struggle against the State*. New Haven, London: Yale University Press, 1990.

——. 'Peasants and Notables in Egyptian Politics'. *Journal of Middle Eastern Studies* 26. 2 (1990): 145–60.

Chaturvedi, Vinayak. ed. *Mapping Subaltern Studies and the Postcolonial*. London: Verso, 2000.

Choueiri, Youssef. *Arab Nationalism, a History: Nation and State in the Arab World* Oxford, Malden: Blackwell Publishers, 2000.

Clements, Frank. *The Emergence of Arab Nationalism, from the Nineteenth Century to 1921*. London: Diploma Press, 1976.

Cobban, Helena. *The Palestinian Liberation Organization: People, Power and Politics*. New York: Cambridge University Press, 1984.

Communist History Documentation Committee. *Men Tareekh Al-Haraka Al-Shoyouiyya fi Misr: Shahat wa Ru'a* (*From the History of the Communist Movement Egypt: Testimonies and Visions*). Cairo: Arab Research Centre for Arab and African Studies and Documentation, 2003.

Cromer, Evelyn Baring, Earl of. *Modern Egypt*. London: Macmillan and Co., 1908 (1962).

Cuno, Kenneth M. *The Pasha's Peasants: Land, Society and Economy, in Lower Egypt, 1740–1858*. Cambridge: Cambridge University Press, 1992.

Dann, Vriel. *King Hussein and the Challenge of Arab Radicalism*. New York: Oxford University Press in cooperation with Moshe Dayan Center for Middle Eastern and African Studies, Tel Aviv University, 1989.

Dawisha, A.I. *Arab Nationalism in the Twentieth Century: From Triumph to Despair.* Princeton: Princeton University Press, 2003.

Dearden, Ann. *Jordan.* London: R. Hale, 1958.

Delong-Bas, Natana. *Wahhabi Islam: From Revival to Global Jihad.* London, New York: I.B. Tauris, 2004.

Desouki, Asem. *Kibar Mullak Al-Aradi Al-Zira'iyya wa Dawruhum fi Al-Mujtama' Al-Misri 1914–1952 (Large Landowners and their Role in Egyptian Society 1914–1952).* Cairo: Dar Al-Thaqafa Al-Jadida, 1975.

——. *Thawrat 1919 fi Al-Aqalim (The 1919 Revolution in the Provinces),* Cairo: Dar Al-Kitab Al-Jame'i, 1981.

——. *Nahw Fahm Tareekh Misr Al-Iqtisadi Al-Ijtima'i (Towards Understanding Egypt's Socio-economic History).* Cairo: Dar Al-Kitab Al-Jame'i, 1981.

Diwan Al-Khawarij (The Poetry Book of the Kharijites). Revised by Nayed Maarouf. Beirut: Dar Al-Masira, 1983.

Doumato, Eleanor Abdella and Starrett, Gregory. Eds. *Teaching Islam: Textbooks and Religion in the Middle East.* Boulder: Lynne Rienner Publishers, 2007.

Fahmy, Khaled. *All the Pasha's Men: Mehmed Ali, his Army and the making of Modern Egypt.* Cambridge, New York, Melbourne: Cambridge University Press, 1997.

Fanon, Frantz. *The Wretched of the Earth.* New York: Grove Press, 1961.

——. *Black Skin, White Masks.* Trans. Lam Marckmann. New York: Grove Press, 1967.

Farah, Tawfic. ed. *Pan-Arabism and Arab nationalism: The Continuing Debate.* Boulder: Westview Press, 1987.

Farid, Mohammad. *Awraq Mohammad Farid: Muzakkirati Ba'd Al-Hijra 1904–1919 (Mohammad Farid Papers: My Memoirs After Emigration 1904–1919).* Cairo: General Egyptian Book Organization, 1978.

The File of Palestine Documents (Arabic), 2 Vols. Cairo: Wezarat al-Irshad al-Qawmi (Ministry of National Guidance), 1969.

Freedman, Robert O. ed. *The Middle East and the Peace Process: The Impact of The Oslo Accords.* Gainesville: University Press of Florida, 1995. (Papers presented at the conference held on 5 November 1995 at Baltimore Hebrew College.)

Frisch, Hillel. *Countdown to Statehood: Palestinian State Formation in the West Bank and Gaza.* Albany: State University of New York Press, 1998.

Fukuyama, Francis. *The End of History and the Last Man.* London: Penguin Books, 1992.

Fuller, Graham E. *The Future of Political Islam.* New York: Palgrave Macmillan, 2003.

Gandhi, Leela. *Postcolonial Theory: A Critical Introduction.* New York: Columbia University Press, 1998.

Gershoni, Israel and James Jankowski. *Egypt, Islam and the Arabs: The Search of Egyptian Nationhood, 1900–1930.* New York, Oxford: Oxford University Press, 1986.

——. *Redefining the Egyptian Nation, 1930–1945.* Cambridge: Cambridge University Press, 1995.

Ghurbal, Mohammad Shafiq. *Tarikh Al-Mufawadat Al-Misriyya Al-Baritaniyya 1882–1936 (The History of the Egyptian British Negotiations).* Cairo: Maktabat Al-Nahda Al-Misriyya, 1952.

Glubb, John Bogot. *A Soldier with the Arabs*. London: Hodder and Stoughton, 1957.

Gordon, Joel. *Nasser's Blessed Movement; Egypt's Free Officers and the July Revolution*. New York, Oxford: Oxford University Press, 1992.

——. 'The False Hopes of the 1950: The Wafd's Last Hurrah and the Demise of Egypt's Old Order'. *International Journal of Middle East Studies* 21. 2 (1989): 193–214.

Greenfeld, Liah. *Nationalism, Five Roads to Modernity*. Cambridge, London: Harvard University Press, 1992.

Guibernau, Montserrat. *Nationalisms: The Nation-State and Nationalism in the Twentieth Century*. Cambridge: Polity Press, 1996.

Guillame, Alfred. Trans. *Ibn Ishaq. The Life of Muhammad*. London: Oxford University Press, 1972.

Hadidy, Alaa Al-Din. 'Mustafa Al-Nahhas and Political Leadership'. *Contemporary Egypt: Through Egyptian Eyes: Essays in Honour of P. J. Vatikiotis*, ed. Charles Tripp. London: Routledge, 1993: 72–88.

Haikal, Mohammad Hussein. *Muzakkirat fil Siyassa Al Misriyya: min Sanat 1912 ila Sanat 1937 (Notes on Egyptian Politics: From 1912 to 1937)*. Cairo: Maktabat Al-Nahda Al-Misriyya, 1951.

——. *Muzakkirat fil Siyassa Al Misriyya: min 29 Youlya Sanat 1937 ila 26 youlya Sanat 1952 (Notes on Egyptian Politics: From 29 July 1937 to 26 July 1952)*. Cairo: Matba'at Misr, 1953.

Hammouda, Hussain. *Asrar Harakat Al-Dubbat Al-Ahrar wa Al-Ikhwan Al-Muslemoun (The Secrets of the Free Officers Movement and the Muslim Brothers)*. Cairo: Al Zahraa' lil I'lam Al Arabi, 1989.

Hamroush, Ahmad. *Thawrat Youlyou: Kharif Abdul Nasser, Ghroub Youlyou, Al-Shahadat (The July Revolution: Abdul Nasser's Autumn, the Sunset of July, the Testimonies)*. Cairo: General Egyptian Book Organization, 1992.

Harris, Christina. *Nationalism and Revolution in Egypt: The Role of the Muslim Brotherhood*. The Hague, London, Paris: Mouton & Co. 1964.

Hashish, Mohammad Farid. *Hizb Al-Wafd 1936–1952 (The Wafd Party 1936–1952)*, 2 Vols. Cairo: General Egyptian Book Organization, 1999.

Hayakal, Mohammad Hassanein. *Al-Mufawadat As-Sirrya bain Al-Arab wa Isra'eel (The Secret Negotiations Between the Arabs and Israel)*. Cairo: Dar al Shurouq, 1996.

——. *Al-Oroush wa Al-Juyoush (The Thrones and the Armies)*. Cairo: Dar al Shurouq, 1998.

Heller, Mark. *A Palestinian State: The Implication for Israel*. Cambridge, Ma.: Harvard University Press, 1983.

Hilal, Jameel. *Al-Nizam Al-Siyassi Al-Falasteeni ba'da Oslo (The Palestinian Political System After Oslo)*. Beirut: Mu'assassat ad-Dirassat al Falastinyya, 1998.

Holt, P.M. ed. *Political and Social Change in Modern Egypt: Historical Studies from the Ottoman Conquest to the United Arab Republic*. (Conference on the Modern History of Egypt (1965: University of London).) London, New York etc.: Oxford University Press, 1968.

Hopwood, Derek. ed. *Arab Nation, Arab Nationalism*. New York: St. Martin's Press, 2000.

Huntington, Samuel P. *The Clash of Civilizations and the Remaking of World Order*. New York: Touchstone, 1997.

Hussein, Mahmoud. *Class Conflict in Egypt 1945–1970*. Trans. Michel and Susanne Chirman, Alfred Ehrenfeld and Kathy Brown. New York, London: Monthly Review Press, 1973.

Ibn Abdel Wahhab, Mohammad (1703–1791 AD), *Kashf Al-Shubuhat (The Clarification of Ambiguities)*. Revised by Mohammad Rashid Rida. Cairo: Dar al Manar, 1927.

——. *Kitab Al-Tawheed (The Book of Monotheism)*. Revised by Mohammad Rashid Rida. Cairo: Dar al Manar, 1927.

Ibn Abd Rabbu, Ahmad ibn Mohammad (d. 328 AH, 940 AD). *Al-Iqd Al-Farid (The Rare Necklace)*. 3rd edition, 9 Vols. Revised by Mufid Mohammad Qumaiha. Beirut: Dar al-Kutub al-Ilmiyya, 1987.

Ibn Al-Athir, Ali Ibn Mohammad (1160–1233). *Al-Kamil Fi Al-Tarikh (The Complete History)*, 10 Vols. Beirut: Dar Sadir, Dar Beirut, 1965.

Ibn Hisham Abdel Malik (d. 833 AD). *Al-Sirah Al-Nabawiyya (The Life of the Prophet)*. 1st edition. Revised by Jamal Thabit, Muhammad Mahmūd and Sayyid Ibrahim. Cairo: Dar al-Hadith, 1996.

Ibn Khaldoun, Abdel Rahman Ibn Mohammad. *Tarikh Ibn Khaldoun (The History of Ibn Khaldoun)*, 7 Vols. Beirut: Mu'assassat Al-'Alami lil-Matbu'at, 1971.

Ibn Manzhour, Mohammad Ibn Makram (630–711 AH, 1232–1312 AD). *Lisan Al-Arab (The Tongue of the Arabs)*, 6 Vols. Beirut: Dar Sadir, n.d.

Ibn Taymiyya, Ahmad Ibn Abdel Halim (1263–1328 AD). *Al-Muntaqa (The Selection)*, selected by Abu Abdallah Al Dahabi (1274–1348 AD). Al-Riyad: Dar Alam al-Kutub, 1996.

——. *As-Siayyassa al-Shar'iyya, fi Salah al-Rai wa al-Ra'iyya (The Legal Policy for the Good of the Ruler and the Ruled)*. Revised by Mohammad Ibrahim Al Banna and Mohammad Ashour. Cairo: Dar Al-Sha'b, 1971.

Idris, Mohammad Al-Said. *Hizb Al-Wafd wa Al-Tabqa Al-Amila Al-Misriyya (The Wafd Party and the Egyptian Working Class 1924–1952)*. Cairo: Dar Al-Thaqafa Al-Jadeeda, 1989.

The International Encyclopedia of Social Sciences. 10 Vols. New York: The Macmillan Company & The Free Press, 1968.

Imara, Mohammad. *Al-Mu'tazala wa Osoul Al-Hukm*. Beirut: Al-Mu'assasa Al-Arabeyya lel Derasat wa Al-Nashr, 1977.

Jabarti, Abdul Rahman. *Ajayeb Al-Athar fil Tarijim wa Al-Akhbar*. Ed. Abdul Aziz Jamaludin, 5 vols. Cairo: Maktabat Madbouli, 1997.

Jankowski, James. *Egypt's Young Rebels: 'Young Egypt': 1933–1952*. Stanford: Hoover Institution Press, 1975.

——. *Nasser's Egypt, Arab Nationalism, and the United Arab Republic*. Boulder: Lynne Rienner Publishers, 2002.

——. 'The Egyptian Wafd and Arab Nationalism, 1918–1944'. *National and International Politics in the Middle East: Essays in Honour of Elie Kedourie*. Ed. Edward Ingram. London: Frank Cass, 1986: 164–86.

Kamel, Najwa. *Al-Sahafa Al-Wafdiyya wa Al-Qadaya Al-Wataniyya 1919–1936 (Wafdist Journalism and the National Questions 1919–1936)*, 2 Vols. Cairo: Al-Hay'a Al-Misriyya Al-Amma lil Kitab, 1996.

Kawtharani, Wajih. *Watha'iq al-Mu'tamar al-Arabi al-Awwal 1913* (*Documents of the First Arab Congress 1913*) with a separately paginated introduction. Beirut: Dar Al-Hadathat, 1980.

Keay, John. *Sowing the Wind: The Mismanagement of the Middle East 1900–1960*. London: John Murray Publishers, 1988.

Kedourie, Elie. *Nationalism*. 3rd edition. London: Hutchinson & Co. Ltd, 1966.

Khalidi, Rashid, et al. eds. *The Origins of Arab Nationalism*. New York: Columbia University Press, c. 1991.

Khamsoun Am ala Thawrat 1919 (*50 Years since the 1919 Revolution*). Cairo: Al-Ahram lil Nashr wa Al-Tawzi's, 1969.

Khomeini, Ruhollah. *Al-Hukumat ul-Islamiyya* (*The Islamic Government*), 1979.

Khoury, Philip. *Urban Notables and Arab Nationalism: The Politics of Damascus, 1860–1920*. Cambridge, New York: Cambridge University Press, 1983.

Killearn, Lord Miles Lampson. *The Killearn Diaries 1934–1946*. Ed. Trefor E. Evans. London: Sidgwick & Jackson, 1972.

Kimmerling, Baruch and Migdal, Joel S. *Palestinians: The Making of a People*. New York: Free Press, 1993.

King Abdallah I of Jordan. *My Memoirs Completed*. Washington: American Council of Learned Societies, 1954.

——. *Mudhakkarati* (*My Memoirs*). Amman: Al Ahlyya lin-Nashr wat-Twazee', 1989.

Lasheen, Abdel Khaleq. *Saad Zaghloul wa Dawruh fi al-Haya al-Siyassiyya al-Missriyyahatta Sanat 1914* (*Saad Zaghloul and his Role in Egyptian Political Life till 1914*), Vol. 1. Cairo: Dar Al Ma'arif, 1971.

——. *Saad Zaghloul wa Dawruh fi al-Haya al-Siyassiyya al-Missriyya* (*Saad Zaghloul and his Role in Egyptian Political Life*), Vol. 2. Beirut: Dar al-Awda, 1975.

Lesch, David. *The Middle East and the United States*. 2nd edition. Boulder: Westview Press, 1999.

Likacs, Yehuda. *Israel, Jordan, and The Peace Process*. Syracuse: Syracuse University Press, 1997.

Little, Tom. *Modern Egypt*. New York, Washington: Frederick A. Praeger, Publishers, 1967.

Lloyd, George Ambrose, Lord. *Egypt since Cromer*. London: Macmillan and Co. Ltd, 1934.

Luciani, Giacomo. ed. *The Arab State*. New York: Routledge, 1990.

Lutfi Al-Sayyid, Ahmad. *Qissat Hayati* (*My Life Story*). Cairo: General Egyptian Book Organization, 1998.

Mahafza, Ali. *Al-Fikr as-siyassi fi al-Urdun* (*Political Thought in Jordan*). Amman: Marakz al-Kutub al-Urduni, 1991.

Mamdani, Mahmood. *Citizen and Subject: Contemporary Africa and the Legacy of Late Colonialism*. Princeton: Princeton University Press, 1996.

Mandaville, Peter. *Transnational Muslim Politics: Reimagining the Umma*. London, New York: Routledge, 2001.

Marlowe, John. *Arab Nationalism and British Imperialism: A Study in Power Politics*. London: Cresset Press, 1961.

Marsot, Afaf Lutfi. *A Short History of Modern Egypt*. Cambridge, New York: Cambridge University Press, 1985.

Mawardi, Ali ibn Muhammad, (974?–1058 AD). *Al-Ahkam Al-Sultaniyya wa-Al-Wilayat Al-Ddiniyya (The Provisions for Sultans and Religious Governance)*. Revised by Ahmad Ibn Mubarak Al-Baghdadi. 1st edition, Riyadh: Dar ibn Qutaiba, 1989.

Milani, Mohsen, M. *The Making of Iran's Islamic Revolution From Monarchy to Islamic Republic*. 2nd edition. Boulder, San Francisco, London: Westview Press, 1994.

Mises, Ludwig Von. *Nation, State and Economy*. New York: New York University Press, 1983.

Mitchell, Richard P. *The Society of the Muslim Brothers*. London: Oxford University Press, 1969.

Mitchell, Timothy. *Colonizing Egypt*. New York: Cambridge University Press, 1988.

Moussalli, Ahmad S. *Radical Islamic Fundamentalism: The Ideological and Political Discourse of Sayyid Qutb*. Beirut: American University of Beirut, 1992.

Murden, Simon W. *Islam, The Middle East, and The New Global Hegemony*. Boulder, London: Lynne Rienner Publishers, Inc., 2002.

Moore-Gilbert, Bart. *Postcolonial Theory: Contexts, Practices, Politics*. London, New York: Verso, 1997.

Mubarrad, Abul Abbas Mohammad ibn Yazid (*d.* 285 AH, 898 AD). *Al-Kamil fi Al-Lugha wa Al-Adab (The Perfect in Language and Literature)*. 2nd edition, 2 Vols. Revised by Taghareed Baidoon and Naim Zarzour. Beirut: Dar Al-Kutub Al-Ilmiyya, 1989.

Mufti, Malik. *Sovereign Creations: Pan Arabism and Political Order in Syria and Iraq*. Ithaca, London: Cornell University Press, 1996.

Musa, Sulaiman and Madi, Muneeb. *Tareekh Al-Urdun fi Al-Qarn Al-'Ishreen (Jordan's History in the Twentieth Century)*. Amman: Makatabat al Muhtaseb, 1988.

Naseef, Majdi. *Hariq Al-Qahira fi Al-Wathayeq Al-Sirriyya Al-Baritaniyya (The Burning of Cairo in British Secret Documents)*. Cairo: Dar Al Hilal, 1996.

Nasif, Erian. *Al-Fallahoun fi Al-Haraka Al-Shoyouiyya Al-Misriyya Hatta Am 1965 (Peasants in the Egyptian Communist Movement until 1965)*. Cairo: Arab Research Centre for Arab and African Studies and Documentation, 2002.

Nevo, Joseph and Ilan Peppe. *Jordan in the Middle East: The Making of a Pivotal State 1948–1988*. Essex: Frank Cass & Co., 1994.

Obaidat, Maisoun Mansour. *At-Tatawwor As-Siyassi Li-Sharq Al-Urdun fi 'Ahd Al-Imara (Transjordan's Political Development During the Time of the Emirate)*. Amman: Manshourat Lajnat Tareekh Biald as-Sham bil-Jame'a al-Urdunyya, 1993.

Ouda, Mohammad. *Kaif Saqatat Al-Malakiyya fi Misr? (How did the Monarchy Fall in Egypt?)*. Cairo: General Egyptian Book Organization, 2002.

Owen, Roger. *Cotton and the Egyptian Economy, 1820–1914: A Study in Trade and Development*. Oxford: Clarendon Press, 1969.

Owen, Roger. ed. *Studies in the Economic and Social History of Palestine in the Nineteenth and the Twentieth Century*. Carbondale: Southern Illinois University Press, 1982.

——. 'Large Landowners, Agricultural Progress and the State in Egypt, 1800–1970: An Overview with Many Questions'. In *Food, State and Peasants: Analysis of the Agrarian Question in the Middle East.* Ed. Alan Richards. London: Westview Press, 1986: 69–94.

——. *State, Power and Politics in the Making of the Modern Middle East.* London, New York: Routledge, 1992.

——. 'Egypt and Europe: From French Expedition to British Occupation'. In *Modern Middle East: A Reader.* Ed. Albert Hourani. London: I.B. Tauris & Co. Ltd, Publishers, 1993: 111–24.

Owen, Roger and Sevket Pamuk. *A History of Middle East Economies in the Twentieth Century.* Cambridge, Ma.: Harvard University Press, 1999.

The Oxford English Dictionary. 2nd edition. Prepared by J.A. Simpson and E.S.C. Weiner. Oxford: Clarendon Press, 1989.

Peleg, Ilan. ed. *The Middle East Peace Process: Interdisciplinary Perspective.* New York: State University of New York Press, 1998.

Provence, Michael. *The Great Syrian Revolt and the Rise of Arab Nationalism.* 1st edition. Austin: University of Texas Press, c. 2005.

The Quran. Trans. M.A.S. Abdel Haleem. Oxford: Oxford University Press, 2004.

Qurany, Bahgat. 'Wafeda, Mutagharreba wa Lakennaha Wujedat Letabqa, Tanaqudat Ad-Dawla Al-Arabyya Al-Qutryya' (Alien, Westrnized but Born to Stay, The Contradictions of the Arab State). *Al Mustaqbal al Arabi.* 105 (November 1987).

Qurany, Bahgat and Dessouki, Ali E. et al. *The Foreign Policies of Arab States.* Boulder, Oxford: Westview Press, 1991.

Rafei, Abdel Rahman. *Asr Ismail (The Age of Ismail),* 2 Vols. Cairo: Matba'at Al-Nahda, 1932.

——. *Mustafa Kamel, Baeth al-Haraka al-Wataniyya (Mustafa Kamel, The Resurrector of the Nationalist [Patriotic] Movement).* Cairo, Mtaba'at al-Sahrq, 1939.

——. *Mohammad Farid, Ramz Al-Ikhlas wa Al-Tadhiyya: Tareekh Mis al-Qawmimen 1908 ila 1919 (Mohammad Farid, the Symbol of Faith and Sacrifice: Egypt's National History from 1908 to 1919).* Cairo: Maktabat wa Matba'at Mustafa Al-Babi al-Halabi, 1941.

——. *Tarikh Al-Qawmiyya wa Tatawwur Nizam Al-Hukm fi Misr: Asr Mohammad Ali (The History of the Nationalist Movement and the Evolution of the Governing System in Egypt: The Age of Mohammad Ali).* Cairo: Maktabat Al-Nahda Al-Misriyya, 1951.

——. *Tharwat 1919: Tarikh Misr Al-Qawmi min Sanat 1914 ila Sanat 1921 (The 1919 Revolution: Egypt's National History from 1914 to 1921).* 2nd edition. Cairo: Maktabat Al-Nahda Al-Misriyya, 1955.

——. *Fi A'qab Al-Thawra Al-Misriyya (In the Aftermath of the Egyptian Revolution).* Part one, 4th edition. Cairo: Dar Al-Ma'aref, 1987.

——. *Muqaddimat Thawrat 23 Youlou 1952 (Preludes to the 23 July 1952 Revolution).* 3rd edition. Cairo: Dar Al-Ma'aref, 1987.

——. *Fi A'qab Al-Thawra Al-Misriyya (In the Aftermath of the Egyptian Revolution).* Part two, 3rd edition. Cairo: Dar Al-Ma'aref, 1988.

——. *Fi A'qab Al-Thawra Al-Misriyya (In the Aftermath of the Egyptian Revolution).* Part three, 2nd edition. Cairo: Dar Al-Ma'aref, 1989.

Ramadan, Abdul Azim. *Tatawwur al-Haraka al-Wataniyya fi Misr, men Sanat 1918 ila Sanat 1936 (The Development of the Nationalist [Patriotic] Movement in Egypt, 1918–1936)*, Vol. 1. Cairo. Al-Mu'assassa Al-Misriyya Al-'Amma li Al-Dirassat wa Al-Nashr, Dar Al-Kateb Al-Arabi li Al-Dirassat wa Al-Nashr, 1968.

——. *Al-Ikhwan Al-Muslimoun wa Al-Tanzim Al Sirri (The Muslim Brothers and the Secret Organization)*. Cairo: Rose El Youssef, 1982.

——. *Tatawwur Al-Haraka Al-Wataniyya fi Misr:1937–1939 (The Evolution of the Nationalist Movement in Egypt: 1937–1939)*, Vol. 2. Cairo: General Egyptian Book Organization, 1998.

——. *Tatawwur Al-Haraka Al-Wataniyya fi Misr: 1939–1945 (The Evolution of the Nationalist Movement in Egypt: 1939–1945)*, Vol. 3, 2nd edn. Cairo: General Egyptian Book Organization, 1999.

Rasafi, Maarouf. *Diwan Al-Rasafi*. Ed. Mustafa Ali. Baghdad: The Iraqi Ministry of Infromation, 1975.

Richardson, John P. *The West Bank: A Portrait*. Washington DC: Middle East Institute, 1984.

Richmond, J.C.B. *Egypt 1798–1952: Her Advance Towards a Modern Identity*. NewYork: Columbia University Press. 1977.

Rida, Mohammad Rashid. *Tarikh Al-Ustadh Al-Imam Al-Shaikh Mohammad Abdu*. 3 Vols. Cairo: Matba'at Al-Manar, 1931–1948.

Rogan, Eugene L. and Traig Tell. eds. *Village, Steppe and State, the Social Origin of Modern Jordan*. London, New York: British Academic Press, 1994.

Rubenberg, Cheryl. *The Palestine Liberation Organization, its Institutional Infrastructure*. Belmont, Ma.: Institute of Arab Studies Inc., 1983.

Safir, Uri. *The Process*. New York: Random House, 1998.

Safran Nadav. *Egypt in Search of Political Community: An Analysis of the Political Evolution of Egypt 1804–1952*. 2nd edition. Cambridge, London: Harvard University Press, 1981.

Sahliyeh, Emile. *In Search of Leadership: West Bank Politics Since 1967*. Washington DC: The Bookings Institute, 1988.

Said, Edward. *Orientalism*. New York: Vintage Books, 1978.

——. *Culture and Imperialism*. New York: Alfred A. Knopf, 1993.

Said, Rif'at. *Tariskh Al-Munazzamat Al-Yasariyya Al-Misriyya 1940–1950 (The History of Egyptian Leftist Organizations 1940–1950)*. Cairo: Dar Al-Thaqafa Al Jadida, 1975.

Salibi, Kamal Sulaiman. *The Modern History of Jordan*. New York: St. Martin's Press, 1993.

Salim, Mohammd Kamel. *Azmat Al-Wafd Al-Kubra: Saad wa Adli (The Wafd's Greatest Crisis: Saad and Adli)*. Cairo: Mu'assassat Akhbar Al-Yawm, 1976.

Saunders, Bonnie F. *The United States and Arab Nationalism: the Syrian Case, 1953–1960*. Westport: Praeger, 1996.

Sayegh, Anis. *13 Ayloul (13 September)*. Beirut: Beesan lin-Nashr wat-tawzee', 1994.

——. *Filastin wa Al-Qawmiyah Al-Arabiyah (Palestine and Arab Nationalism)*. Beirut: PLO Research Center, 1970.

Sayyed, Ahmad Hamed. *Al-Wafd wa Al-Qadiyya Al-Falastiniyya (The Wafd and the Palestinian Question)*. Lajnat Al-Fikr wa Al-Thaqafa be Hizb Al-Wafd, 2001.

Shafiq, Ahmad. *Hawliyyat Misr Al-Siyassiyya: Tamhid, Al-Juz' Al-Awwal (Egypt's Political Annals: Introduction, Part One)*. Cairo: Matba'at Shafiq Basha, 1926.

——. *Hawliyyat Misr Al-Siyassiyya: Tamhid, Al-Juz' Al-Thani (Egypt's Political Annals: Introduction, Part Two)*. Cairo: Matba'at Shafiq Basha, 1927.

——. *Hawliyyat Misr Al-Siyassiyya: Tamhid, Al-Juz' Al-Thaleth (Egypt's Political Annals: Introduction, Part Three)*. Cairo: Matba'at Shafiq Basha, 1928.

——. *Hawliyyat Misr Al-Siyassiyya: Al-Hawliyya Al-Oula 1924 (Egypt's Political Annals: The First Annal 1924)*. Cairo: Matba'at Shafiq Basha, 1928.

——. *Hawliyyat Misr Al-Siyassiyya: Al-Hawliyya Al-Thaniya 1925 (Egypt's Political Annals: The Second Annal 1925)*. Cairo: Matba'at Hawliyyat Misr Al-Siyassiyya, 1928.

——. *Hawliyyat Misr Al-Siyassiyya: Al-Hawliyya Al-Thaletha 1926 (Egypt's Political Annals: The Third Annal 1926)*. Cairo: Matba'at Hawliyyat Misr Al-Siyassiyya, 1929.

——. *Hawliyyat Misr Al-Siyassiyya: Al-Hawliyya Al-Rabi'a 1927 (Egypt's Political Annals: The Fourth Annal 1927)*. Cairo: Matba'at HawliyyatMisr Al-Siyassiyya, 1928.

——. *Hawliyyat Misr Al-Siyassiyya: Al-Hawliyya Al-Khamisa 1928 (Egypt's Political Annals: The Fifth Annal 1928)*. Cairo: Matba'at Hawliyyat Misr Al-Siyassiyya, 1930.

——. *Hawliyyat Misr Al-Siyassiyya: Al-Hawliyya Al-Sadisa 1929 (Egypt's Political Annals: The Sixth Annal 1929)*. Cairo: Matba'at Hawliyyat Misr Al-Siyassiyya, 1931.

——. *Hawliyyat Misr Al-Siyassiyya: Al-Hawliyya Al-Sabi'a 1930 (Egypt's Political Annals: The Seventh Annal 1930)*. Cairo: Al-Matba'a Al-Hindiyya, 1931.

Shahrustani, Abul Fath Mohammad Ibn Abdul Karim (*d.* 548 AH, 1153 AD). *Al-Milal wa Al-Nihal (Religions and Creeds)*. Revised by Ahmad Fahmy Mohammad. Beirut: Dar Al-Kutub Al-Ilmiyya, n.d.

Shalabi, Ali. *Misr Al-Fatah wa Dawruha fi Al-Haya Al-Siyassiyya Al-Misriyya 1933–1941 (Young Egypt and its Role in Egyptian Political Life 1933–1941)*. Cairo: Dar Al-Kitab Al-Jame'i, 1982.

Shalaq, Ahamd Zakariyya. *Hizb Al-Umma Wa Dawruh fi Al-Siyassa Al-Misriyya. (The Al Umma Party and its Role in Egyptian Politics)*. Cairo: Dar Al-Ma'aref, 1979.

——. *Hizb Al-Ahrar Al-Dustouriyyin 1922–1953 (The Constitutional Liberal Party 1922–1953)*. Cairo: Dar Al Ma'aref, 1982.

Sharaf El Din, Nabil. *Bin Laden Taliban, Al-Afghan Al-Arab wa Al-Umameyyah al-Osouleyya*. Cairo: Maktabet Madbuly: 2002.

Sharqawi, Jamal. *Asrar Hariq Al-Qahira fi Al-Wathayeq Al-Sirriyya Al-Baritaniyya (The Secrets of the Burning of Cairo in Secret British Documents)*. Cairo: Dar Shuhdi lil Nashr, n.d.

Shlaim, Avi. *Collusion Across the Jordan: King Abdullah, The Zionist Movement and the Partition of Palestine*. New York: Columbia University Press, 1988.

——. *The Politics of Partition: King Abdullah, the Zionists and Palestine*. Oxford: Oxford University Press, 1997.

——. *The Iron Wall: Israel and the Arab World*. New York: Norton & Company, 2000.

Shwadran, Benjamin. *Jordan: A State of Tension*. New York: Council for Middle Eastern Affairs Press, 1959.

—— ed. *The Formation of National States in Western Europe*. Princeton: Princeton University Press, 1975.

Sluglette, Marion Farouk and Peter Sluglette. *Iraq Since 1958: From Revolution to Dictatorship*. London: KPI Limited, 1987.

Sobhi, Ahmed. *Nazareyet Al Imamah (The Imamate Theory)*. Cairo: Dar Al-Maaref, 1964.

Storrs, Ronald. *Orientations*. London: Ivor Nicholson & Watson Limited, 1937.

Symons, M. Travers. *Britain and Egypt: The Rise of Egyptian Nationalism*. London: C. Palmer, 1925.

Tabari, Mohammad ibn Jarir (224–310 AH, 838–922 AD). *Tareekh Al-Umam wa Al-Mulouk (The History of Nations and Kings)*. 2nd edition, 6 Vols. Revised by Nawaf Al-Jarrah. Beirut: Dar Sader, 2005.

Tahtawi, Rifa'a, Rafi'. *Manahij Al-Albab Al-Misriyya fi Mabahij Al-Adab Al-Asriyya (The Guide of Egyptian Hearts to the Joys of Contemporary Arts)*. 2nd edition. Cairo: Matba'at Sharikat Al-Ragha'ib, 1912.

——. *Takhlis Al Ibriz fi Talkhis Bariz (The Extraction of Gold in Summarizing Paris)*. Cairo: General Egyptian Book Organization, 1993.

Tarabolsi, Fawwaz and Aziz Al-Azmeh. eds. *The Unknown Works of Ahmad Faris Al-Chidiac*. London, Beirut, Cyprus: Riad El-Rayyes Books Ltd, 1995.

Tibi, Bassam, *Arab Nationalism: A Critical Inquiry*. Ed. and trans. Marion Farouk-Sluglett and Peter Sluglett. 2nd edition. London: Macmillan, 1990.

Tousson, Omar. *Muzakkira Bima Sadar Anna Munzu Fajr Al-Haraka Al-Wataniyya Al-Misriyya (A Memorandum regarding what we have done since the Dawn of the Egyptian National Movement)*. Cairo: Matba'at Al-Adl, 1942.

Vatikiotis, P. J. *The Modern History of Egypt*. New York, Washington: Frederick A. Praeger, 1969.

——. *The History of Egypt*. 3rd edition. Baltimore: Johns Hopkins University Press, 1985.

——. *The History of Modern Egypt: From Muhammad Ali to Mubarak*. Baltimore: Johns Hopkins University Press, 1991.

Turner, Ralph H. 'Role: Sociological Aspects'. *International Encyclopedia of the Social Sciences*. Ed. David Sills, Vol. 13. New York: Macmillan Co. & Free Press, 1968.

Watt, W. Montgomery. *Islam and the Integration of Society*. London: Routledge and Kegan Paul, 1961.

Wendell, Charles. *The Evolution of the Egyptian National Image: From its Origins to Ahmad Lutfi al-Sayyid*. Berkeley, Los Angeles, London: University of California Press, 1972.

Williams, Patrick and Laura Chrisman. eds. *Colonial Discourse and Post-Colonial Theory*. New York, London, Toronto, Sydney, Tokyo, Singapore: Harvester, 1993.

Wilson, Keith M. *Imperialism and Nationalism in the Middle East: The Anglo-Egyptian experience, 1882–1982*. London: Mansell Publishers, 1983.

Wilson, Mary C. *King Abdullah, Britain and the Making of Jordan*. New York: Cambridge University Press, 1987.

Woddis, Jack. *New Theories of Revolution: A Commentary on the Views of Frantz Fanon, Regis Debray and Herbert Marcuse.* New York: International Publishers, 1972.

Wood, Michael. 'The Use of the Pharaonic Past in Modern Egyptian Nationalism'. *Journal of the American Research Centre in Egypt* 35 (1998): 179–96.

Youssef, Amine Bey. *Independent Egypt.* London: John Murray, 1940.

Zaghloul, Saad. *Muzzakirat Saad Zaghloul.* Ed. Abdul Azim Ramadan, 9 Vols. Cairo: Marakaz Wathyeq wa Tarikh Misr Al-Hadith, General Egyptian Book Organization, 1987–1998.

ONLINE REFERENCES

'Dostour Jumhuriyyat Al-Iraq' (*The Constitution of the Republic of Iraq*). http://www.iraqigovernment.org/ (accessed 9 June 2007)

'Full Transcript of Bin Laden's Speech', Al-Jazeera.net, archives, 2 November 2004. http://english.aljazeera.net/news/archive/archive?ArchiveId=7403 (accessed 21 February 2007)

'Intifada Fatalities'. B'tselem, The Israeli Information Center for Human Rights in the Occupied Territories. http://www.btselem.org/English/Statistics/Casualties.asp (accessed 10 June 2007)

Text of the Draft Iraqi Constitution. http://news.bbc.co.uk/1/shared/bsp/hi/pdfs/24_08_05_constit.pdf (accessed 9 June 2007)

The CIA World Fact Book. https://www.cia.gov/library/publications/the-world-factbook/index.html (accessed 12 June 2007)

'The Law of Administration for the State of Iraq for the Transitional Period', http://www.cpa-iraq.org/government/TAL.html (accessed 11 June 2007)

'The Speech of Colonel Jamal Abdul Nasser Arab Islamic Conference in Cairo' 26 August, 1953. http://nasser.bibalex.org/Speeches/browser.aspx?SID=64 (accessed 9 June 2007)

Index

Compiled by Sue Carlton